All We Need To Know

Hugh Crago's *Entranced by Story* (2014) was described by reviewers as 'brilliant' and 'visionary'. He has taught literature, lifespan human development and counselling at several universities, and since 2000 has lived in the Blue Mountains, near Sydney, where he continues to write.

Also by Hugh Crago

Prelude to Literacy: A Preschool Child's Encounter with Picture and Story (Southern Illinois University Press, 1983) (with Maureen Crago)

A Circle Unbroken: The Hidden Emotional Patterns that Shape Our Lives (Allen & Unwin, 1999)

Couple, Family and Group Work: First Steps in Interpersonal Intervention (Open University Press, 2006)

A Safe Place for Change: Skills and Capacities for Counselling and Therapy (IP Communications, 2012) (with Penny Gardner)

Entranced by Story: Brain, Tale and Teller, from Infancy to Old Age (Routledge, 2014)

The Stages of Life: Personalities and Patterns in Human Emotional Development (Routledge, 2017)

Wind Age, Wolf Age (poems) (Ginninderra Press, 2017)

The Relational Arts: A Case for Counselling and Psychotherapy (privately published, 2018)

Hugh Crago

All We Need To Know

A Family In Time

Acknowledgements

This book has been so long in the making that by now it is almost impossible to list all of those who have supported me along the way. But their encouragement helped me to persist through the years when no publication seemed possible. Much more recently, I trusted five people to tell me the truth about what I had written. Were they shocked? Was it too confronting? Maureen Crago read every successive version of this book, despite her discomfort with 'so much self-display' on my part. Linda Johnston read drafts of most chapters of this most recent version. Carmel Gold, Maria Quinn and Jewel Jones provided heartfelt and authentic responses to the whole. Stephen Matthews of Ginninderra Press agreed to publish it, to my surprise and delight, and has proved a meticulous and thoughtful editor of the old school – now a dying breed, I fear.

Cover photographs

Front: the Cragos as my mother Gwen would have seen them in 1943 (Note the two 'camps' – Cherie, Beth and Gwyn with their father; Ian, Ted and Dick with their mother. Albert has his head characteristically tilted to one side, the pose that so often betrays uncertainty.)
Back: Hugh, c. 1968; city girls – Eva Sanders and Gwen Sanders, 1940s; 'Soldierly' – Victor Sanders, c. 1917; 'Cousin Henry'; Louisa Lawson.

All We Need To Know: A Family In Time
ISBN 978 1 76041 722 2
Copyright © Hugh Crago 2019

First published 2019 by
GINNINDERRA PRESS
PO Box 3461 Port Adelaide 5015
www.ginninderrapress.com.au

Contents

Preface		7
1	Difference and Dissent	15
	Genogram 1	16
2	Love Found and Lost	29
	Genogram 2	32
3	How Fear Came	45
4	Just a Little Wedding	63
5	Authenticity and Innovation	87
6	Loyalty and Betrayal	106
7	Sanity and Madness	121
	Genogram 3	126
8	Injustice and Entitlement	148
9	Faith and Doubt	171
10	Forgiving and Forgetting	194
Personal Reflections		216
Theoretical Considerations		227
	Genogram 4	230
Notes		247
Sources		252

Preface

Sometime in my middle thirties I conceived the idea of writing an emotional history of my father's family over three generations – my grandfather's, my father's and my own. I intended to go beyond the facts of births, deaths, marriages, careers and offspring, as chronicled in the vast majority of family histories, and to focus instead on relationships, feelings and values. As a recently trained family therapist, I was fired with the idea that any family, however ordinary, could be interesting to read about if only its personalities and its interactions were presented honestly. I planned to confine myself to those still living (who could tell me about their own experiences) and to those whom living relatives had known first-hand, even if I had not. The way they told their stories about one another would say as much, I thought, as the stories themselves.

Through the good offices of my mentor and friend Brian Stagoll, I was offered a publishing contract with McPhee-Gribble – then Australia's leading independent publishing house. My book was to be called *A Family In Time*. I gathered a lot of material – photographs, family trees, documents like school reports and references; detailed notes of visits made to relatives; letters written to me in response to my questions; 'family and friends' Christmas letters – and, over a decade, I produced a very long typescript that was really three books rolled into one. A frank autobiography came first, because I felt that if I was to present the unvarnished truth of my relatives' lives, I had better do the same with my own. Then came a series of narrative chapters devoted to each of my grandparents, my parents and their siblings (I knew hardly anything at that time about my mother's extended family). In the final section, I wrote about the big themes I could see in the century of family lives I had studied: how the family had coped with social and ideological change, the patterns that typified their relationships, their religious faith (or lack of it) and so on.

My publishers sent my 250,000 words to a freelance copy editor, who recommended that the book be cut by two-thirds. Like most authors, I was loath to jettison what I had worked so hard to produce. Then McPhee-Gribble was bought by Penguin Australia, and I lost my sympathetic editors, Hilary McPhee and Sophie Cunningham. Their successor clearly had little interest in reading about 'more and more Cragos' (as he witheringly put it) and eventually I withdrew the book. For another ten years, on and off, I tried and failed to find an alternative publisher.

But there was more. Very confident initially that telling the whole truth was the only way to go, I had failed to reckon with the sensitivities of my relatives. When I showed them the chapters that were most relevant to them, a few recoiled in dismay, angrily telling me I had 'completely misunderstood' their father, mother, or in-laws, even though what I had written was closely based on what I had been told – sometimes by the very person who was now so upset. Other relatives said nothing at all. I am pretty sure they thought it was dreadful stuff but did not want to hurt my feelings by saying so. The only ones who praised the book were one or two cousins so distantly related that they could read it without taking the bad bits personally. And so I tried again. I produced a second version of the manuscript, and then a third, rewriting, rearranging and cutting. But, as Brian Stagoll reminded me later, times had changed in the publishing world, and the window of opportunity for a long book about an ordinary family had closed.

By the time I began the version you are about to read, both of my parents, and all their surviving siblings, had died. My first cousins were now elderly (as I was myself). I had seen my children reach the halfway point in their lives. My wife Maureen, seven and a half years older than I, was in the grip of a non-life-threatening but incurable autoimmune condition that was causing her chronic discomfort and declining physical capacities. Occasional bouts of illness were sharp reminders that my own life was finite.

In September 2016, I started on a completely new approach to the book, with a new organising vision. Time had winnowed out the important from the less important, and the new version would be much shorter. It would also offer a new understanding of what our family had struggled with – a genetic heritage that we (like many other families) had passed on without really realising what we were doing. I called the new version *All We Need to Know*, mindful of the ways that almost all families transmit a version of their past that subtly constrains the understanding of their descendants. Social historian Janet McCalman put it this way in *Journeyings*: 'As they [grow] up… [children take] both the remembered and the hidden past with them.' Rereading *Journeyings* more than twenty years after it first appeared was a moving experience for me, as I encountered, in the words of many of McCalman's interviewees, attitudes, values and even turns of phrase very similar to those of my own relatives.

All We Need to Know preserves the original title in the form of a subtitle. The book is still about one family – the Cragos, with side glances at the principal family lines that have flowed into theirs – my paternal grandmother's (Stears, Alburys), my maternal grandmother's (Kirkhams) and my maternal grandfather's (Sanders). Their genes and family cultures have collectively produced me, so it is hardly surprising that my life-course and personality have echoed theirs. *All We Need To Know* focuses on those echoes, sometimes faint, sometimes loud and startlingly literal, and tries to understand how such repetitions occur.

Families mostly seek to protect their offspring from full knowledge of their heritage. I am far from alone in growing up knowing little about my extended family on either side. Most people are incurious about their ancestry, perfectly content with 'all they need to know', but others are restless and dissatisfied until they have found out more. I am one of the latter. This book is about a quest for family knowledge but, inevitably, it is also about a quest for self-knowledge. The two go together.

When we hear the word 'lifetime', most of us think of an individual's path from birth to death, a journey with turning points and landmarks. Family time is not like that. Family time is cyclic, patterned and repetitive – time as experienced by the limbic system, the old brain that still operates within our vastly larger and more sophisticated cerebral cortex (the human brain), and which roughly corresponds with Freud's 'unconscious'. For the old brain, linear time does not exist, and memories can also be predictions. T.S. Eliot said it best in 'Burnt Norton', the first part of *Four Quartets*, published ten years before my own birth in 1946:

> Time past and time present are both, perhaps, present in time future
> And time future contained in time past…*

As an undergraduate student of literature in the mid-1960s, I whispered these lines over and over to myself, aware that they sounded significant, but unable as yet to link them with anything in my personal experience. For me, art has often come first, and life has lagged a long way behind. Fifty years later, Eliot's words jump into sharply focused, highly personal meaning.

Ten years of learning classical piano in childhood and adolescence have left their imprint on this book, too. I wanted to counterpoint my own life with those of relatives in earlier generations. Initially, I thought of J.S. Bach's famous Forty-eight Preludes and Fugues – otherwise known as *The Well-Tempered Clavier*. In *All We Need To Know*, I selected scenes from my own life to take the place of Bach's preludes – free-form introductions to the closely woven patterns of the fugues that follow them. Some of my personal preludes report just a single event, others cover a year (or several years) which constituted a life-changing period for me. I have headed these preludes 'In My Time'. Following each prelude comes a section called 'In Family Time'. In these sections, I describe events in the lives of relatives which parallel and anticipate events and feelings in my own. 'Family Time' sections are my equivalent of Bach's fugues. The fugue is the artistic form that best mirrors the repetitive yet ever-changing patterns of families over several generations: a wheel that 'may turn and still be forever still', as Eliot expressed it in *Murder in the Cathedral*.

Bach's preludes are more overtly emotional than their accompanying fugues, and this is also the case in the book you are about to read: my own feelings are the only ones that I can ever write about with complete authority. The feelings of others in my extended family must often be inferred, though I have done my best not to go beyond the evidence. What I have said about myself is often embarrassing, and parts of it cause me shame. Yet it needed to be said, because without those disclosures, it would no longer be clear how closely my personality has followed the genetic template I share with the generations that preceded me.

From time to time, I have included inserts dealing with completely unrelated individuals (usually well-known) whose histories and personalities bear some degree of similarity to my own and those of my relatives. I include them to contextualise what may seem to some readers unusual or extreme – other people, at other times in history, have displayed very similar traits and very similar behaviours. Our family is both extraordinary and yet ordinary too. In particular, a number of the inserts recount episodes in the life of John Wesley, who founded the Methodist Church in the eighteenth century. I was born a Methodist and, despite giving up my Christian faith as a young adult, have found Methodism a powerful influence lifelong. The importance of Methodism for my father's family culture is a key theme in *All We Need To Know*, and a century and a half after Wesley's death, the strengths and weaknesses of his personality were still in evidence in many of those who grew up with his version of Christianity.

My study of one family's collective emotional life from the late nineteenth century to the late twentieth can have only limited usefulness unless it illustrates phenomena that can be found in many families, across many centuries. In the final section of each chapter, titled 'What We Need to Know', I write about these phenomena. Many have been described in the past, especially by pioneer family therapists in the 1960s and 1970s, but few of those writers have been prepared to use their own families as material for analysis. Nor did the early family theorists, on the whole, recognise the genetic element in the repeating patterns they saw. They were quite sure that family pain (as Virginia Satir called it) could be healed if only family members were persuaded (or even manipulated) into altering the ways they behaved towards one another in the present. It took me years to realise that this was a comforting oversimplification.

The analytical material in the 'What We Need To Know' sections is taken up and elaborated in the concluding part of this book, which I've called 'Theoretical Reflections'. Anyone who has asked Why? and How? on the way through *All We Need To Know* might benefit from reading it, though it may be of greater interest to professional and academic readers. It explores the whole complex question of 'nature vs nurture' – and the spaces in between the two – and explains in a step-by-step way my hypothesis that family gene pools replicate themselves through partner choice and then through the parenting of the next generation.

All We Need To Know is not a conventional family history. It does not trace my family's history back as far as written records exist. It is not comprehensive. The life story of an individual family member is not to be found in any one chapter, but is typically spread across several, and even then it contains only some aspects of the whole person. (I have included partial family trees for the earlier chapters and fuller ones later.) Last of all, *All We Need To Know* is as emotionally accurate as I can make it. Most family histories suppress details that might cause offence or distress to others within the family. I have not, but I trust it will be clear that I have no wish to judge my relatives, past or present – just to present the evidence as accurately as I can.

Some years ago I realised (much later than I ought to have) that I must respect the privacy of my own generation of the extended family (my siblings and cousins) and of the next – my own children and their cousins. Inevitably, this has left me as almost the only representative of my own generation (something I return to towards the end of this book). That is one way in which my presentation of the family is potentially misleading. It is not the only way.

I have written mostly about unresolved conflicts, times of distress and painful self-realisations, so it is important to add now that contentment, rewarding work and loving relationships have also been part of my life and the lives of many of my relatives – they simply receive less attention here. Had one of my more emotionally stable relatives written the story of the same three generations, she or he would probably have paid more attention to the happy and fulfilling experiences, and much less to the painful side. Their narrative would inevitably have its own bias, albeit one different from mine. Yet to argue this back and forth would be to miss a more important issue: confident, emotionally stable individuals are much less likely to feel impelled to tell their family's story. (Nor, I should add, do confident, emotionally stable individuals generally seek to become therapists!) It is, overwhelmingly, the sensitive and self-doubting individual who wants to find out the truth (about self, about others) and who seeks to achieve some kind of control over distressing experiences by writing about them. *All We Need To Know* has been written by one of those individuals, and it reflects my own genetically shaped empathy for sadness, suffering and conflict.

In 'Personal Reflections', I attempt to engage with some of the questions readers may be left with as they finish the book. How have my realisations about my family affected me as a parent? How has my knowledge influenced my professional work as a therapist with other individuals struggling with themselves and their families? Can a problematic genetic legacy be mitigated by the right kind of upbringing? I hope this section will answer these questions, at least in some measure.

Finally, I have been asked by my siblings to include this statement: the views and judgements of family members and family values presented in this book are entirely my own and in no way represent the views of my brother and sister, nor are they in any way endorsed by them.

Hugh Crago
Blackheath, 2018

''Tis mystery all – let earth adore
Let angel minds enquire no more!'
(Charles Wesley, 1738)

'Beauty is truth; Truth, beauty:
Tis all ye know, and all ye need to know'
(John Keats, 1819)

'Don't know much, but I know I love you
And that may be all there is to know'
(Barry Mann, Cynthia Weill and Tom Snow, 1980)

1

Difference and Dissent

In My Time

'Some very lonely monkey' (Normanhurst, Sydney, 1953)

It was my first day at school, and I was six years old. My parents (both former teachers) would have told me that school was something to look forward to, something exciting and interesting. I can't remember being nervous, although I probably was. What I can remember is what happened in the playground at recess. I found groups of boys scattered around, engaged in games of some sort, and after watching them for a while, I presented myself to one of these gangs (that was the word they used). I was sure that I could contribute. My mind was richly stocked with things that I had read about, things that demanded to be made real by being turned into play.

To my dismay, I found that the boys didn't want me to be part of their gang. And nor did the boys in the next gang I tried. I realised that my exciting ideas were not going to be listened to. I learned that I was different somehow, in a way I did not understand or (at that time) think about.

A year or so later, I thought that if I had been called John (there were several Johns in my class), I would have got on better, but of course that wasn't it. The difference I was confronted with was a difference that went far beyond my individual existence – although of course I did not know that then – and I just felt it.

'Little Red Monkey' was the first popular song that I can remember hearing on the radio, and it was new that year – 1953. I did not like

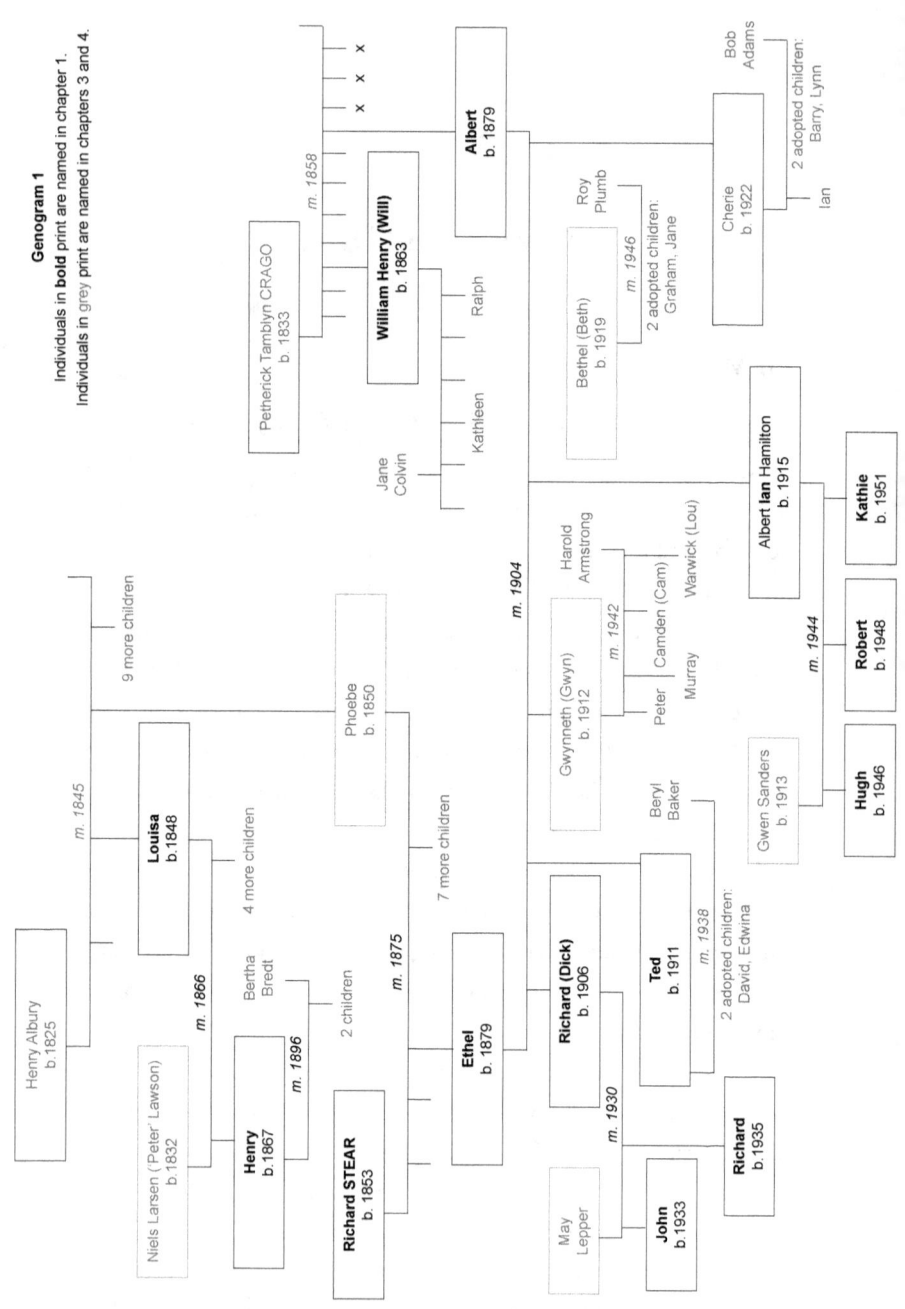

the song, which was in a minor key (like the beginning of 'Teddy Bear's Picnic') and seemed somehow menacing (it was actually the theme tune for a BBC spy series aimed at adults). When I read the lyrics now, I recognise that most of them are about not being accepted or listened to – even by one's own family. 'Little red monkey on his own / Some very lonely monkey is he.' Those words about loneliness would have matched my feelings on my first day at school. No wonder I did not like 'Little Red Monkey'!

Despite my aversion, I never forgot the tune, and would hum or chant to myself the refrain, 'Little red monkey, monkey, monkey…' over and over again. Why would I do this with a song I so disliked? The words irritated me, and yet I could not forget them.

In Family Time

1929

My father Ian's first reported experience of feeling different came much later than mine – when he was fourteen, and sent away from his home in the country town of Yass to attend Fort Street Boys' High School in Sydney. His mother had arranged for Ian to board with one of her sisters, though he was happier when he moved to live with an aunt on his father's side. He was sent to Fort Street because he was a bright boy, perhaps destined for university, and Yass District School didn't take children beyond Intermediate Certificate level. The decision to send Ian into exile (as he clearly felt it) must have been a vote of confidence in his maturity and his intelligence, at least as far as his mother was concerned. Ian was worth educating further, he was grown up enough to cope with living away from home. But my father did not remember it that way. He remembered only what was bad about it. He was eight years older than me when he started at Fort Street, but he failed the same test I was to fail at six. He did not realise that newcomers must earn credibility before they can expect to be welcomed into the tribe. His parents had not prepared him for that and, in his turn, he did not prepare me for it either. The Fort Street boys had all been together since they started high school. He was the new boy and they let him know it. Moreover, he came from the country, a distant and alien place to most of his classmates, and no doubt he was awkward and unsophisticated, a church-oriented goody-goody, although he did not talk about that part to me.

1915–1929

The fourth in a family of six children, Ian had grown up in Yass, where his father Albert, and his uncle Will, were joint owners of a flour mill. Ian, like his two brothers and three sisters, had been raised with strict Methodist principles: church every Sunday, no bad language, no drinking, no smoking and no gambling. Irish Catholics were deeply suspect. Alcohol was the demon drink, and Ian's father belonged to a temperance league, where they sang songs like

> We are coming, we are coming,
> Our brave little band
> By the right side of Temperance
> We do take our stand

'Our brave little band' – the words of the song admit the singers' minority status from the very start, almost as if they will never succeed in convincing others of their position, but have to keep trying anyway. It was a position many of my father's family would have found familiar and even comfortable. You did your best, you did what was right, but you didn't expect too much in return. It wasn't fair, but you had to put up with that.

Methodists believed it was not good to accumulate too much wealth. If you did make more money than you needed, you were expected to give much of it away. Hard work and harmless amusements were acceptable. Education was acceptable. Music was acceptable, partly because it played an important part in church services, and Methodism had created many rousing hymns of its own.

Women were not to set store by their appearance. Make-up and dresses that showed too much flesh were shameful, and attracted the wrong kind of attention. Innocent boys might unwittingly be caught in the toils of a seductive young woman, and find themselves tricked into marriage. The theme was one of extreme caution. Ian's brother Dick, nearly ten years his senior, had joined the Boy Scouts when it was brand-new, and the Scout motto 'Be prepared' fitted admirably for the attitude in which he and his younger siblings were raised. My father's immediate family were cautious people who doubted themselves and doubted others. They were wary of stepping out of line or taking risks. They kept their heads below the parapet. They did not, most of them, ask questions or openly dispute what they had been told by their parents, their ministers of religion, or other authority figures. What they knew was all they needed to know.

1942

John Tamblyn Crago, my Uncle Dick's elder son, was also sent away to school in Sydney, at a younger age than Ian, and to the more total environment of a prestigious boarding school – Knox Grammar. John found the whole experience traumatic. He told his children much later that the first thing he could remember at Knox was 'having a rifle shoved into my hands' – participation in the Cadet Corps was compulsory for all students, as in most of the GPS schools at the time, and besides, Australia was at war. John felt deeply uncomfortable about the idea of killing, even in defence of one's country. For him, this incident epitomised his feeling of being in a completely alien environment, among kids he had nothing in common with – 'the sons of rich Presbyterians, with their narrow little ways'. He was probably depressed for much of his time at Knox, and he could not bring himself to take his academic studies seriously. He eventually failed the Leaving Certificate, and had to repeat it (imposing upon him an extra year at the school he hated). His career as an under-achiever had begun. He would not have been the first or the last intelligent, talented young person to be regarded as a feckless, lazy failure.

c. 1885

My father's father, Albert Crago, was born in 1879. He was the youngest surviving child in a family of eight, several siblings having died in infancy and one in adolescence. Albert was not given to talking to anyone about his private feelings, and even his most loyal supporters among his children agreed that he was very shy. School must have been an unpleasant experience for him: the only school-related story anyone could remember him telling concerned a sadistic teacher (Mr Boyle?) known to the pupils as Old Boylie. Even as a grown man with six children of his own, Albert remained fearful of new experiences, and would panic if confronted by anything unexpected or out of routine – such as an unscheduled visit from a relative he did not like. As circuit steward (Methodists had circuits rather than parishes) it was Albert's duty to make the weekly announcements to the Yass congregation each Sunday, and he dreaded those few minutes in which he had to stand up in front of everyone's gaze. It is easy to imagine how he'd have felt when called on by his schoolteacher to stand up, to read aloud or answer a question.

As an adult, Albert would express his panic in loud shouting which his children hated, and referred to as 'Dad roaring'. Only his second son Ted (my father's next-oldest brother) understood that Dad's roar was 'just his way of expressing himself'. But sensitive children are frightened by adult anger, even when it is not directed at them. My father Ian disliked and distrusted his dad – never realising that Albert Crago was anxious, awkward, and unconfident, ill-equipped to be the sort of warm, encouraging father Ian needed. Ian himself was on the shy and anxious side, but he never acknowledged the resemblance. He simply wouldn't talk about his father. Dad's older brother Dick dealt with his anger and distaste in exactly the same way, saying nothing to his sons John and Richard about their grandfather. Both Ian and Dick idolised their 'wonderful' mother instead.

1883

Like my father, cousin Henry (actually Ian's grandmother's cousin) felt his difference most powerfully when, at sixteen, he moved to Sydney from the country, and worked alongside city boys. He was pale, adenoidal and already going deaf, preoccupied with his own thoughts. He sounded 'Pommy' to the other boys. He scorned his workmates, who were only interested in sports – and in return they laughed at him. Yet when he grew up, 'Let's have a beer' became his ticket of acceptance into male comradeship. Alcohol made him garrulous and grandiose, transforming his difference into a conviction of his own talent, his own worth. Henry had not been raised a teetotaller like my father and grandfather. His nominally Wesleyan mother did not drink, but the family did not consider alcohol 'the demon drink' as the Cragos did. So joining others at the pub was an avenue for Henry to join the mainstream, as it could never have been for my father or grandfather. It also left him an alcoholic.

1709

Rev. Samuel Wesley, Rector of Epworth, was not loved by his parishioners. They had caused him malicious damage on previous occasions, and one night in 1709, when his son John was six years old, the rectory was found to be on fire. Rev. Wesley managed to rescue his other children, but by the time he thought of 'Jacky' (as the family called John) in the upstairs nursery, the fire had so far taken hold that it impossible for him to climb the stairs. Little Jacky had climbed on a chest and called out for help, and was rescued by one of the crowd outside, standing on the shoulders of another.

Susanna Wesley, John's beloved mother – then, and perhaps always, the most important person in his life – saw his rescue as miraculous. 'Is not this a brand plucked out of the burning?' she exclaimed, meaning that God had saved her son because he was intended to do great work on God's behalf.

Her words (contrasted with the fact that John's father had not remembered where he was in time to rescue him) would inspire John with a sense of mission. He felt different and special, and this was no doubt compounded by the fact that the Wesley children were not permitted to play with the village children, and were taught at home by Susanna herself, a formidably educated woman who was almost certainly intellectually superior to her husband. 'Wonderful' mothers and despised fathers were not unique to the Albert Crago family!

What We Need To Know

What's in a name?

Like many Australian subjects of Queen Victoria, my great-grandparents chose names for their children that emphasised their loyalty to the Crown. Albert, the youngest of his parents' large family, was probably[1] named for Prince Albert, Victoria's consort, who was initially disliked and distrusted in England because of his German origins, but who was an outstandingly successful shaper of the constitutional monarchy, and eventually commanded love and respect. In a Victorian updating of an older ballad, it is Prince Albert who rescues and pardons a deserter, 'For he'll make a good soldier for his Queen and Country!' Whether or not young Albert Crago ever heard that ballad, he would surely have identified, not with the prince in his 'carriage and six' but with the hapless working man who deserts twice and is about to be hanged when saved by the prince's clemency. It is the same pattern that Albert encountered in church every Sunday, the pattern of sinful Man redeemed by the infinite grace of Christ. As a youngest son, and a deeply unconfident one at that, Albert Crago would never identify with the great and powerful, however good.

Born in 1915, Albert's third son Ian had started life as an Albert too, presumably after his father. His other two names (Ian Hamilton) were suggested by his mother's father, Richard Stear, who was much preoccupied with the recently launched Allied invasion of the Gallipoli peninsula in Turkey – Ian Hamilton was the British general in overall command of that operation. Ian himself later described how annoying it was 'to have your father's name shoved in front of the name you're going to be called by', a curious turn of phrase that spoke eloquently of his dislike of his father. To him, Ian was his real name, and he hated people calling him Albert. Mr Williams, the headmaster at Fort Street School in 1930, was one of those who made that (understandable) mistake, and Ian could never forgive him for it. Ian had felt loved and protected by his mother Ethel – very much as Albert had probably felt loved and protected by his (when she died, Albert's son Ted recalled, 'it was the only time I ever saw Dad with tears in his eyes') – and the name she had chosen to call him identified him as hers. In his adult career as District Inspector of Schools, Ian styled himself 'I.H. Crago' and would grumble every time he picked up one of the many letters he received addressed to 'Mr Inspector A.I.H. Crago'.

Difference and anxiety

My grandfather, my father, my cousin John, my great-grandmother's cousin Henry and I myself – all of us were sensitive children, lacking the social confidence that enables a thicker-skinned child to shrug off the minor reverses and slights that life will inevitably deal out. It suits today's teachers and psychologists to see resilience as a teachable skill, but I think some of us are born with it, while others are not. Yes, it is possible to learn better coping skills than we started life with, but for most of us they remain grafts, never fully accepted by their genetic host. Temperamental anxiety is very hard to unlearn. Suddenly confronted with the fact that others do not like them, and avoid them, anxious children will feel their difference, as I felt mine at six, and then, typically, attribute it to some visible or obvious cause (in my case, I was too tall, and I had an unusual name, Hugh, that other boys found hard to pronounce). As adults, anxious children may seek an explanation for their difference in externally imposed things like the religious beliefs in which they have been raised. These self-chosen explanations may be partly accurate, and they may offer some comfort. But whatever the explanation, the sense of being different will remain.

Some of the customs and attitudes displayed by my father's family were commonplace at the time. But most of the more extreme ones stemmed directly from Methodism, the dissenting Protestant denomination to which both Ian's parents belonged. Dissenting means that a particular religious sect had refused to accept the full credo of the Church of England, and so (at the time of their origin) were regarded by the majority of believers as beyond the pale. An Anglican clergyman, John Wesley, had founded the Wesleyan (later Methodist) movement in the eighteenth century. Wesley was the greatest British evangelist of his day, a kind of Billy Graham or Martin Luther King. Hundreds flocked to the outdoor meetings where Wesley preached that people were saved, not by doing good or scrupulously performing rituals, but 'by Faith alone'. At the meetings, some in the crowd would fall writhing to the ground, weeping or speaking ecstatically in unknown tongues (actions of which Wesley himself deeply disapproved). Wesley died in 1791, and in his lifetime Methodist chapels had sprung up across England and the American colonies, and, in due course, in the Australian colonies too.

Unlike the celebrated modern evangelists with whom we are familiar, Wesley was not a big personality, not obviously charismatic or flamboyant. He was a small man, and extremely restrained in how he expressed himself. It was said that he seldom smiled and never laughed – though it is unlikely that he would ever have become 'the best-loved man in England' if that were the literal truth. He rose early for prayer, self-examination and Bible study. He took his vocation extremely seriously, reading improving literature even as he rode his horse slowly along country roads to his next appointment. He drank and ate sparingly, and dressed soberly.

Wesley was a cautious man. For a long time, he personally supervised and vetted every one of his centres of worship and their non-ordained local preachers. It was as if he could not fully trust anyone to do it as well as he did himself. For many years, he avoided any open break with the Anglican church, of which he himself was an ordained minister, searching his heart for what he believed God wanted him to do. Eventually, and late in his career, he permitted an open split – dissent.

Once his followers were recognised as no longer Anglicans, doors were immediately closed to them. Methodist men could not become officers in the army or the navy. They could not stand for parliament. They could pursue business interests, or set up educational institutions, and many of them did so. But (as had happened to Quakers, Baptists and Congregationalists before them) the centres of power, status and influence were denied them. They were permanent outsiders.

Yet Wesley, their founding father, had impressed upon them that they must obey the laws of the land, and meekly accept whatever discrimination or unfairness they might encounter. A heavenly reward would compensate them. They should not try to understand too much, apart from what had been revealed to them in Christ's life, and in the Old Testament. That was all they needed to know. John Wesley's younger brother Charles – more openly emotional and artistic than John – wrote in what I consider his most inspiring hymn,

> 'Tis mystery all, let Earth adore!
> Let angel minds enquire no more!

In other words, 'Whatever happens is God's will. The angels accept it unquestioningly,' and that's what we humans must do also. What we know is all we need to know.

Methodism may have emphasised the necessity to obey the laws of the land, to render unto Caesar the things that are Caesar's, yet its founder was, in his own way, a rebel and a radical. He had explicitly challenged the might of the established Church, and his followers dissented not only in their beliefs, but in their customs. Their conduct was an implicit challenge to the mainstream of British society at the time – and subsequently well into the twentieth century. Methodist women dressed quietly and soberly, so as not to attract undue attention. Their men would not enter the doors of a public house, let alone take a drink with the rest of the villagers, or the local community. At a time when the pub was the social centre of the village and (increasingly) of each working-class neighbourhood in Britain's mushrooming industrial cities, refusal to enter its doors automatically ensured that Methodists would be seen as unfriendly loners, as smugly righteous. And perhaps some Methodists did feel smug and self-righteous. But they would all, most certainly, have felt different: Their very way of life constituted a criticism of the majority. When the family itself preserves and transmits the sense of being different, individuals' sense of difference is powerfully reinforced. And a sense of difference leads, almost inevitably, to a sense of isolation.

Difference and isolation

Later memories have a way of crowding out or even obliterating earlier ones on the same theme. By the time most children reach school age, their earliest memories (from the first two years of life) have largely disappeared. No doubt I had experienced being different earlier than six – but at six, a child has more of an observing consciousness than it does at three or four. Might I have felt on my own long before I set foot in the school and was rejected by the other boys? I had not been neglected or abused – if anything, I was overprotected, and made much of by my parents. Yet even at three, so I was told many years later, I had insisted on listening to the ABC program *Kindergarten of the Air* by myself. 'Nobody else is allowed in the room – it is entirely his show!' my father had written to his mother, amused (rather than concerned) at a first-born who was already choosing a world of his own rather than a world that included his parents ('where is his mama, papa, sister, brother?). Would I have needed to dwell in imagination rather than in reality if I had felt that my parents intuitively understood me? Perhaps not.

And although they certainly loved me, I do not think they recognised themselves in me, or were consciously aware of the ways that they might have felt similarly as young children. So, when I went to school, I was primed to feel misunderstood, alone in my intense inner life, a misfit in the great world of cheerfully ordinary people who got on with living instead of imagining alternatives to it.

'Some very lonely monkey is he.'

Lonely, cute, fidgety

Yes, I felt on my own – even though ostensibly surrounded by a loving father and mother, and by two younger siblings. But in a much more literal way I was like the monkey who is described as 'acting so fidgety'.

Sometime in my second year of life (my parents told me later) I had begun to pace the floor. They thought my behaviour was cute, but now I recognise my pacing as a sign of either hyperactivity or anxiety. More likely, in my case, it was the latter. If I could not keep still, it was because I was too anxious to keep still, and needed to keep moving in order to control that anxiety. I continued into middle age to pace up and down when rehearsing a speech, or when fired up with anger or excitement. I barely noticed it in myself, though I hated seeing others do it.

My Uncle Dick, eldest of Albert Crago's three sons, had expressed his anxiety in a similar way. As a child of six, he had arrived alone at Yass railway station with his luggage, announcing that he wanted to go to Bowning. Bowning was only one train stop away, but it was a serious journey for a little boy. It turned out that Dick intended to go and live with his mother's father, Richard Stear (the same grandparent whose given name he shared, and by whom he was treated with special affection). Dick's intention clearly reflected his fear and dislike of his own father.

Even though this particular journey was forestalled by the stationmaster, Dick remained a traveller throughout his life, and the link between 'keeping on the move' and the anxiety that drove it was manifest. His siblings and his own sons all recognised Dick's compulsive need to keep on the move and to get there first, before anyone else. As a teenager he would urge his mother to hurry up when the family was going somewhere. As a middle-aged man on a return voyage from Europe, he was alarmed when the liner had to heave to in the Red Sea for nearly an hour while waiting for its pilot. In his meticulously detailed diary, he wrote, 'While the ship is cutting through the water it is alive and you feel safe, but when it stops you feel dead and helpless.'

I was not as restless as Dick, but I remained fidgety well into adulthood, and am fidgety still. Earlier in my life I would have denied that I was a particularly anxious person. But now I know I am.

In the song, the Little Red Monkey is placed in a zoo, where his clever tricks delight visitors. I often wonder if, as early as six, I had already realised that apparent precocity (like using big words) could win me praise and attention. Certainly my restless pacing earned me the comment (from a visitor), 'That boy will be a professor!' I didn't become a professor during my academic career, but I did confuse wisdom with cleverness for a long time. All in all, there was a good deal more in common between me and that monkey than I could ever have known when I heard the song.

2

Love Found and Lost

In My Time

Lost domain (Artarmon, Sydney, 1957)

Both my grandfathers were dead, I knew that. And I knew I had a grandmother who lived a long way away in the country. She was Grandma Crago. We had visited her once, when I was around six, but I didn't remember much about it. My mother did not talk about her. My father would occasionally tell us that his mother was a wonderful woman. If she was so wonderful, why did we never see her? I could have asked myself these questions but, like so many children, I simply accepted that what I knew was all I needed to know.

The one grandparent I saw regularly – the only grandparent I had, effectively – was my mother's mother, Eva Sanders. She ought to have been Grandma Sanders but my parents never referred to her that way, and we children learned to call her Evie. In 1955, when I was nine years old, we had moved from Sydney to Ballina, a small seaside town five hundred miles to the north, and a new life began, very different from our previous life on Sydney's North Shore, where Evie had lived only a few suburbs away. We had visited her then, I know, but when we first made the long journey back from Ballina to Sydney, at Christmas 1955, it was as if I saw her, and the place she lived in, for the first time. Thereafter, we stayed with her every summer holidays for the next eight years. Her flat in Artarmon became another world to me, utterly different from the world in which I then lived most of the time – the seaside world of Ballina, with its soft, salt-laden air, its heavy downfalls of rain, its heat, and its subtropical growth and ripeness. That was my present. Evie's flat was the past: a world that had stopped, like a clock, before I was born.

Almost everything in Evie's apartment told me about that past – framed photographs of long-dead relatives, steel engravings of literary and historical scenes, books about the two world wars that had dominated the first half of the twentieth century, bundles of old letters with foreign stamps, quaint-looking gramophones that were never played, fine linen that had been stored so long in cupboards that the tablecloths had rust-coloured marks where they had been folded. But the past about which these things spoke was not a past that anyone mentioned, at least not in a way that meant anything to me. The flat and its furnishings had been unchanged for the years we had been coming there on our once-a-year visits. I simply assumed that the building Evie lived in was very old, and that my mother's mother had always lived there. Occasionally, my mother would take us to visit a relative – most often Auntie Ruby or Auntie Annie. I wasn't told, or (more likely) didn't remember, that Ruby was Ruby Sanders, older sister of my long-dead grandfather, while Annie was Evie's much older sister, born a Kirkham. To me, they were just two old ladies living alone in terrace houses with lots of books and furniture.

Years later, I learned that most of Evie's possessions came from the large terrace house in Cleveland Street, Chippendale, where Evie herself had grown up, close to the centre of Sydney. She had moved to the flat, then newly built, in the late 1930s or early 1940s, less than ten years before I was born. The move had been instigated by my mother, who was then a young adult and wanted to live closer to her own friends. But as far as I was concerned, the Artarmon flat and its contents seemed frozen in time, like Sleeping Beauty's castle. To me, it was a place of mystery, presided over by people I had never met: handsome women with big, dark eyes and wide, floppy hats, good-looking, uniformed men with stars on their epaulettes, and who left behind old bullets in the bottoms of wardrobe drawers. By the age of eleven, in the year before I started high school, I was starting to wonder about these people, and although my questions mostly received brief and evasive answers, I was beginning to piece together bits of the story that had been enacted 'before you were born'.

It was my mother's father who had died before I was born. His name had been Victor Sanders, and he had been in the First World War, fighting against the Germans in France. For years I assumed this meant he had been killed in combat. Evie was a widow. She had lived in this flat with my mother, but she also had a son, much younger, who had the same name as me. When I first learned who Hughie (as my mother and grandmother both called him) was, I was too young to know the two great wars of the twentieth century apart. I thought Hughie too must have died in the First World War. Later I realised that he had actually fought in the Second, against the Japanese, the conflict which had ended in 1945, the year before my own birth. My parents referred to the 1939–1945 conflict as 'The War' – neither of them really remembered the earlier one, which had ended when my mother was five, and my father only three. But, it seemed, my uncle Hughie had not been killed in the second war. Instead he had got married to someone called Nancy, and now lived overseas in a variety of exotic places like Aden, Eritrea, Cyprus and Singapore. He moved around a lot because he was an officer in the British army. He had not lived in Australia since The War. That was all I needed to know.

One day, early in 1957, in the middle of our holiday stay at Evie's, Uncle Hughie turned up at her front door. We must have been told of his imminent arrival by plane from Singapore, but to me, he might as well have come by flying carpet from the Land of Green Ginger. Hughie was was tall and well-built. He smoked and drank beer. Neither of my parents smoked, and my father never touched alcohol, so Hughie's smoking and drinking seemed enticingly alien and dangerously glamorous. Hughie also had ears that stuck out, like mine, and legs that were too long to fit under Evie's round kitchen table. He talked with breezy confidence, in a British accent, although I knew he had grown up in Sydney. It was hard

Genogram 2

Individuals in **bold** print are named in chapter 2. Individuals in grey print are named in chapters 3 and 4.

to think of him as my mother's brother – I compared him to me, rather than to her. Uncle Hughie stayed just three days, and then vanished again as mysteriously as he had come.

I was in my last year of primary school. Although I did not realise it, this was the first time Hughie had seen his mother or his sister for thirteen years. Whatever Evie might have felt about the brief reappearance of her son after so long an absence, she said nothing about it, and it would not have occurred to me to wonder. His relationship to Evie was not real to me. It was no more substantial than Evie herself – a quiet, grey ghost who pattered about her cramped domain with a feather duster, or sat in her bedroom listening to the news on the radio. 'Good old Ike!' she exclaimed when Eisenhower was re-elected president of the United States: 'He got us out of trouble in the war, and he'll get us out of trouble now!' It was the only time I can recall her expressing enthusiasm about anything.

In the years that followed 1957, years in which my body slowly edged into adolescence while I continued to feel much like the child I had been, Evie's flat (which we continued to visit every summer) took on layer after layer of significance for me. Throughout every school year in Ballina, and then Grafton, a full day's travel to the north, I longed to be there again. But what I longed for was more than just the flat and the objects it contained. I longed for a life of adventure, risk and glamour. Glamour in its original sense meant under a spell. Glamour transformed the everyday and unexceptionable into the beautiful, the mysterious, the powerful. I craved that glamour, even though I could not have told you why. There was something I needed to know.

In Family Time

I did not read *Le Grand Meaulnes* as a child, or even as an adolescent. I did attempt to read Dickens's *Great Expectations*, at the core of which is a very similar theme of a young man clinging to a romantic vision of his first love. But when I finally read French novelist Alain-Fournier's novel, as a middle-aged man, I immediately recognised my own sense of longing for something I could never possess, a pattern that I was already very familiar with, from my mother's family: the pattern of 'love found and then lost'.

1908–1930

When my grandmother Eva Kirkham married a junior reporter named Victor Sanders in 1908, it looked like a love match between two handsome young people. They were certainly in love, but cracks were already appearing. Eva, the second-youngest in a family of ten, was twenty-eight. Her family was comfortably off, and Eva, unmarried, still lived at home. Victor's family belonged to the professional middle class. One of his uncles was a barrister. Another managed a newspaper, the *Sydney Star*, and had offered the sixteen-year-old Victor a place on his staff after the unexpected death of Victor's father, who had been a solicitor and a senior Mason. Victor had allowed the Kirkhams to believe that he was close to the same age as his intended bride, but the marriage certificate revealed him to be nearly seven years younger. Victor had a relaxed attitude to the truth: Eva's family didn't know what they didn't know, so why bother to make things harder for himself by telling them? Eva had been brought up with a horror of lying, and she was shocked by her new husband's conduct.

Eva was 'a looker' (as they said then), and no doubt her looks had a lot to do with Victor's attraction to her, but she was cripplingly shy, and shrank from parties, flirting and socialising. Victor and his family regarded having a beer or a whisky as an integral part of daily life, and he could not understand her refusal to drink, or her (to him) censorious attitude to 'having a bit of fun'. She disappointed him, and he disappointed her. He wanted her to wear low-cut dresses to show off her figure, but they made her feel 'like a piece of meat'. A nominal Anglican, Eva did not believe in God at all, yet she might as well have been raised a Methodist, for her attitudes seemed just as puritanical.

With her little girl Gwen, who was born in 1913, Eva was an anxious mother who often felt at her wit's end. When the child wailed piteously, Eva would give her whatever she wanted, just to stop her crying. And when Gwen was only two, Victor enlisted in the Australian army and went off to fight on the other side of the world, leaving his wife to cope alone. For him, it was a great adventure. He wrote Eva letters from the troop ship that sounded like something from *The Boy's Own Paper*. Eva was afraid of what might happen to him, felt overwhelmed, and returned to live with her mother and two of her sisters. In a sense, she had never fully left her family, and in times of stress she would always return to them.

Soldiering suited Lieutenant Sanders: he looked the part, and when he gave orders, he sounded stern and authoritative. He was at Gallipoli, in the final stage before the ANZACs were evacuated; on the Western Front, he fought at Bapaume. Promotions happen quickly in wartime; Victor was promoted from second to first lieutenant, and then to the acting rank of captain at a training camp back in England. By 1919, still awaiting demobilisation, and a world away from his disappointing but loyal wife, Victor had fallen for someone else – perhaps the original of the beautiful nurse whose big, sad eyes he would later describe in a story. Yet out of some mixture of duty and fear – fear of the very happiness he longed for, like Augustin Meaulnes in Alain Fournier's novel? – he returned to his wife and daughter in Sydney. He was thirty-three. Their son Hugh (little Gwen was now seven) was conceived then. He did not tell Eva about his affair, but she found out anyway, opening a letter from the other woman that made the whole thing clear. Eva was shocked and furious, and told him to leave. The two lived separately for a time, but he pleaded to return, and she took him back. 'You know, I loved him', she told her niece Jess much later. She may still have loved him, but he had betrayed her and she could not forgive that. She yelled at him sometimes, Gwen remembered, but 'Dad never yelled at her'.

Victor always had dreams and plans. Taking advantage of the government's soldier-settler scheme, he put up his hand for a small property at Kunama, near Batlow, but he found farming tedious, strenuous and lonely. He soon turned to driving a truck instead. Eva could not stand country life either, and simply moved back to Sydney, leaving Victor to settle up and follow her later. Victor wrote a short story and then a novel based partly on his own life abroad, but it never found a publisher (if, indeed, he ever offered it for publication). Pre-war, he had been a journalist, but writing fiction was not as easy as he had imagined, and perhaps he found it confronting to write about experiences so personal and painful as the episode in which he had abandoned his new love, and returned to the wife he had betrayed.

He needed to earn money to support his young family, and he had the gift of the gab. So he took a job as a commercial traveller, selling first boot polish and then whisky. The latter naturally meant having a drink with potential buyers, and one evening in 1930, Victor was doing just that, perhaps at the grand Hydro Majestic hotel in Medlow Bath, perhaps at the newly rebuilt Gardner's Inn in Blackheath. Instead of taking the train back to Sydney as he usually did, he impulsively accepted a lift with a fellow travelling salesman. When their car rounded a bend between Medlow and Katoomba, it collided headlong with a lorry. Victor was critically injured and died a few hours later.

Back home, Eva was in the kitchen cooking tripe (Vic's favourite meal) when a policeman came to the door with the news. She was beside herself, and 'just couldn't face' going to identify the body. She sent her daughter Gwen, then sixteen years old. Gwen never spoke of what that was like for her, but in later life, she dreaded funerals, and would not go to them. Even when Eva died in 1966, Gwen walked up and down outside the crematorium chapel, a bundle of nerves, until her mother's funeral was all over. She could not bring herself to tell me (by then away at university) that my grandmother was no longer living. When I asked her about it years later, she burst into tears and ran from the room.

In 1930, when Victor died aged only forty-four, Hughie was just nine years old (Victor's own father had died at one day short of forty-four, when Victor was sixteen). Hughie was already starting to display the same restless, adventurous spirit as his father, and was soon truanting from school, heading off for a day spent fishing and smoking with his mates. Eva felt powerless to control him. Unlike her late husband, she didn't have a good 'word of command'. Fortunately, Hughie had early formed an ambition to take up soldiering – like his dad. Eva was proud that her son wanted to serve his country. As the 1930s drew to a close, and it became clear that another war was coming, Hughie joined up in 1938, falsifying his age in order to do so. Of course, it was common in wartime for boys to add a year or two to their age in order to enlist,[1] but Hughie's behaviour was also reminiscent of Victor's at the time of his wedding to Eva. Later, there would be even closer parallels between father and son.

Though he joined as a private, Hughie soon stood out from his peers, and was selected for special operations behind Japanese lines. He completed officer training, and was subsequently promoted to first lieutenant. It was while Hughie was posted to Burma in the closing stages of the war that he met a Scots nurse in Rangoon, and wrote home to his mother and sister to say that he and Nancy intended to get married. They duly were – far from Hughie's family – and at around the same time, Hughie had decided that he had better prospects in the British forces than in the Australian army. The photograph he sent home to his mother showed a good-looking, boyish man with three stars on his shoulders – the rank of captain, which his father had temporarily held during the earlier war. And that was the last his mother and sister would see of him for thirteen years. Hughie's three boys grew up on the other side of the world, and Eva never met her grandchildren, or their mother. Gwen had married in 1944, and by 1948, she and her husband also had two sons, with a daughter following two years later. Eva busied herself cooking, washing and cleaning to help Gwen, who, she felt, was often sick and could not cope with all these chores on top of looking after small children. But for Eva, the important part of her life was over.

She had lost her husband, first when he went off to war, and later when he had been unfaithful while in England. Then she had lost him for the final time in the car accident – no doubt caused by 'the drink'. Eva gave Victor's wartime letters and other memorabilia to the new National War Museum in Canberra, but she got rid of his unpublished novel, *The Story of His Life and Mine*. She didn't want to know what it said, and she didn't want anyone else to know either. Gwen remembered the novel's name, but had never read it. She had felt quite separate from her parents' marital conflicts and, if anything, had felt sympathy for her father.

Eva had followed Hughie's military career with pride, but when he chose to marry a woman she had never met, and then to live out the rest of his life as an Englishman, Hughie had died to her as effectively as if he, too, had been killed in an accident – or been killed by a Japanese bullet in 1945. She lived on, alone, with the furniture that she and Victor had bought, and her share of heirlooms from the old Kirkham family home in Cleveland Street. When Gwen and her husband came to stay with her in Artarmon each summer holidays, they occupied the big bed she had once shared with Victor. She herself slept in the little second bedroom. The children ran excitedly around the flat playing wild games and rocking endlessly on her rocking chair, which made a loud creaking. She found it irritating sometimes, but never complained about it. They were 'evil' little creatures (Eva used the word as an endearment), and they seemed to be enjoying themselves.

She and Gwen had always clashed – Gwen was so stubborn, Eva thought, always wanting her own way – but what was the point of complaining? She had put up with Victor's drinking, with his irresponsibility, with his silly dreams, even with 'that woman' over in England. And now he was dead. Religion offered no consolation, and you just had to get on with living, until eventually, it was time for you to die. 'A proud, lonely woman' was how Eva's son-in-law Ian described her, years after her death.

Eva had destroyed Victor's novel, but she failed to find a short story he had written earlier than the longer typescript. I found it many years later, in a box of old books and documents that Eva had kept. The story occupies a foolscap page of single-spaced typing, pasted carefully onto one page of a largely empty army-issue ledger book in which for a short time Victor had recorded the army pays he had sent home 'to Mrs Sanders'.

Victor's story was called 'A Last Request', and its hero is a British officer, Captain Hugh Gordon, who comes across a dying German officer in no-man's-land. The German shows him a photograph of a beautiful nurse who is English, and whom he now will not see again. He begs Captain Gordon to contact her and give her his final message. Gordon, however, recognises the nurse as the same woman he himself had been in love with before the outbreak of hostilities trapped her in Cologne. He is elated at finding that she is still living, and the pair are reunited.

'My Hugh,' she murmured, 'my darling! You will never leave me again? Oh I have waited for you so long, and it has been so lonely. Tell me my love that you will never go away again?' 'No my beloved,' he answered, 'never shall I leave you again. Through death have I found you, and through death only shall I leave you.'

The story is dated 24 March 1919, and seems to have been written in camp at Weymouth, while Victor was awaiting transport back to Sydney and his wife. Victor returned to Eva, and despite their short separation when she found out about his lover, it was indeed 'through death only' that he finally left her, some ten years later.

But after Victor's death, his only son Hugh would grow up to become a soldier himself, and rise to the rank of captain. He would meet and marry a nurse and become an officer in the British army, never to return to Australia, except for two brief visits. Did Hughie read the story as a child, and somehow feel compelled to follow its prescription for his own life? Or did know nothing of his father's story, yet still, inexplicably, follow the story in literal detail? Stranger things have happened in families. And stories – public, literary ones like *Le Grand Meaulnes* or private, never-published ones like Victor's *A Last Request* – can powerfully influence us in childhood, setting up templates or patterns for the implicit stories of our future lives.

What We Need To Know

Silence

What families don't talk about is often more significant than what they do talk about. To be sure, some family members may be reticent by temperament – slow to reveal what they think and feel, brief and laconic in what they say about others. Many people have little curiosity about anybody in the family beyond themselves and their immediate relatives. Silence does not always indicate that something significant is being hidden – but often, it does. I grew to adulthood knowing just one grandparent (Eva), and that one only minimally, because she never talked about herself or her past. I grew to adulthood with few stories about the families whose genes I had inherited. My mother said little about her relatives generally, and hardly anything about her father until I began asking for details as an adult. My father said nothing about his father, and from the time when I started school, we rarely saw his mother or most of his brothers and sisters. He might have talked about them more had not my mother disliked him doing so. He 'took the path of least resistance, I suppose' (as he put it much later).

There are two possible responses to such a climate of silence in a family. One response is simply to accept the silence as normal and appropriate, and (when one grows up) to be as incurious as one's parents had seemed to be. 'All these relatives,' growled my father once, 'you don't know 'em and you've got nothing in common with 'em.' Later, I thought that if he had known them, he might have found that he did have things in common with them, but had never given himself the chance to realise it.

The other response – mine – is to develop an obsession with finding out, with filling the gaps in the story. Who were these people, these relatives I had never met? Why did nobody talk about them? Had they done dreadful things? Were they like me, or completely different? These were the sorts of questions I dwelt on, especially once I reached my early thirties. I knew that there was more I needed to know. Family silence can preserve secrets across generations – but it can also ensure that those secrets are eventually revealed, at least, for those who care enough to want to know them.

Wrong, but romantic

As an adult, I had been able to reacquaint myself with most of my father's brothers and sisters, with several of their offspring – my cousins – and with one or two relatives further removed. I did not get to know more than a handful of them well, but at least I had some sense of who they were. The great majority were hard-working, responsible, law-abiding and, in their own way, caring. Most of them were people of faith – 'simply and sincerely religious' (as Veronica Wedgwood put it in *The King's Peace*).[2] They tried to be good. For the most part, they kept their pain and their disappointments to themselves. But their lives seemed to me, at the time, to be rather uninteresting. None of my father's siblings had had a combat role in either of the two great wars of the twentieth century, although two of his cousins had. There were no heroes among them, and few individuals who achieved reputations outside of their own communities – though one of my father's cousins, Kathleen Crago, had been a long-serving and fondly remembered headmistress of Ravenswood, Sydney's Methodist girls' school. My father's family had not generated scandals or messy divorces (like Eva's older sister Edie, whose husband had done 'terrible things' to her and then deserted her, changing his location and even his name in order to avoid paying any child support). Private tensions – and there were plenty – were kept strictly private.

So on one side I had a handful of relatives whose lives seemed dramatic and interesting, but about whom I knew very little, and on the other side, I had relatives about whom I knew rather more, but whose lives seemed worthy, but rather dull. It was like Sellars and Yeatman's witty characterisation in *1066 and All That* of the difference between the Cavaliers (wrong, but romantic) and the Roundheads (right, but repulsive) in the English Civil War. I found my Sanders relatives romantic in comparison with my Crago relatives (who were usually right and, at least to people like my mother, repulsive), but that said more about me than it did about them. Of course it also reflected the fact that my mother had maintained contact with only a handful of her own relatives, and could tell me little about them beyond the generation to which her own parents had belonged. By the time I started asking, not only her father and mother, but her father's older sibling, Ruby, and her mother's older brothers and sisters were all dead, and although I had many cousins among Evie's family, the Kirkhams, I had met hardly any of them.

Most interestingly of all, I can see now that where my mother had favoured her own family and kept a distance from her husband's (as in fact her mother Eva had done in her own marriage), I was now reversing her bias, 'filling in' the Crago side, but somehow avoiding pursuing my Sanders and Kirkham relatives with equal interest. What I did realise, though, was that I belonged to one of the two personality types that repeated across the generations of both sides of my extended family – the impulsive, enthusiastic, irresponsible, self-preoccupied personality (which might express itself in soldiering, in artistic pursuits, or simply in an unsettled pattern of life – like the wanderer, Augustin Meaulnes, or Charlie Kirkham, my grandmother Eva's youngest brother, who refused to go to war, never married and struggled lifelong with his drinking).

The other personality type, exemplified by many members of my father's family (but also by some members of my mother's, including Evie herself) was almost the exact opposite. This second type was cautious, restrained, responsible and practical – like John Wesley. Some of them – on my father's side – were actually followers of Wesley, but some of the Kirkhams – like Evie's older brother Ern – also displayed such traits, although only a few of the Kirkhams were Methodists. Such individuals may have 'lacked glamour' but they lived law-abiding, hard-working lives. They were dependable and stayed faithful, even when they had 'a lot to put up with' from their spouses. They felt strongly, but they usually kept their feelings to themselves, rarely bursting out in tears or rage.

When I myself married, I would marry a woman of this type, whose emotional restraint often reminded me of my father's. (Indeed, she told me, her own mother had told she 'had no romance in her soul', and sometimes I had to agree.) I did not see myself then as a dashing, feckless Cavalier – though others, including my wife's father, saw it earlier than I did ('You're just a Peter Pan'). I did not see her then as a dedicated soldier of Cromwell's New Model Army, but she was. The family pattern had repeated itself, without our awareness, and the old story contained in the musty, forgotten ledger had told itself over again.

La Belle Alliance

One of the large steel engravings that Evie had inherited from her parents, and which I revisited every summer in her lounge room at Artarmon, showed the battlefield of Waterloo, where Napoleon had just been defeated by the Duke of Wellington. The picture itself had long gone to the tip, but when I searched online among nineteenth-century prints depicting Waterloo, I immediately recognised it: the original (1868) had been by the artist Daniel Maclise, and it was called *Wellington and Blücher Meeting after the Battle of Waterloo*. Marshal Blücher had commanded the Prussians, who arrived only in the final stages of the battle, and whose appearance helped to turn the tide in favour of the allies. After the defeat of the emperor's last army, Blücher had proposed that the battlefield be named for a nearby village called La Belle Alliance – thus commemorating the fact that a coalition had achieved the victory. However, Wellington had already decided to call the battle by the name of a different nearby village (Waterloo) and, as he mostly did, the Iron Duke got his way. It was, after all, Wellington's troops who had stood their ground all day and repulsed Marshal Ney's cavalry again and again before the Prussians arrived on the field and Napoleon fled. 'A damned close-run thing!', the Duke famously remarked after the battle, his laconic words clearly identifying him as a Roundhead outlasting Prince Rupert's gallant cavalry charges.

Just as with great powers and their generals, so with families. There are *belles alliances* and coalitions, some open, others hidden, and the winners get to tell the story of the war from their own point of view. My mother's loud expressions of anger or distress reduced my father to silence and compliance; her allegiance to her family outweighed his loyalty to his. What I learned earliest, and most powerfully, about my father's family – that they were narrow-minded, boring country people with whom we had nothing in common – was what I absorbed from her. Consciously, I admired and tried to emulate my father, but I succeeded only partially. At my genetic core, I was like my mother – and like her father, and like her brother Hughie. I, too, would in years to come express my anger and my fear loudly. My histrionics would prove to be as futile and self-indulgent as Ney's frontal attacks at Waterloo: 'Soldiers, now you will see how a Marshal of France faces his death!' (Only Ney didn't die at Waterloo; he was hanged as a traitor.)

During my growing up years, my mother won the battle, but later, she lost the war. Once I was adult myself, her silence ensured that I would be driven to rediscover the very people she had kept me away from. I would try to rewrite the family's history from the viewpoint of the losing side, restore the balance, show how neither side was free of narrowness, selfishness and destructive bitterness, that neither side had a monopoly on faith, loyalty and idealism.

Families set up patterns, and as children we fall into them without conscious awareness of what it is we are doing. This is the 'lost domain' as Alain Fournier memorably called it in *Le Grand Meaulnes* – the mysterious country of family time, the realm of hidden meanings and repeating patterns, the country of love found and lost, the country of shame and fear.

3

How Fear Came

In My Time

How fear came (Grafton, 1959–1963)

I would have been eleven or twelve when I first read the stories collected in Rudyard Kipling's *Jungle Books*. Though they were (and are) considered children's classics (which is no doubt why Uncle Hughie on his brief visit to our family in 1957 had bought the book for both myself and my brother), they are really adult stories which happen to feature a child protagonist – Mowgli, the human child brought up by wolves – and talking animals (the beasts of the jungle). All the stories, to varying degrees, reflect a very adult consciousness of life's brevity, of danger and death. *The Second Jungle Book* is noticeably darker and more pessimistic than its predecessor. I can remember little of my first reaction to its opening tale, 'How Fear Came', except that I did not like it and avoided rereading it. But what stuck in my mind from the story was its stark, unspecific title. I read that story when I was on the threshold of high school and adolescence, and though I did not know it in my final year of primary school, fear was about to come to me, too.

In February 1958, my childhood came abruptly to an end. My father had been transferred from Ballina to Grafton, a larger town further south, and I was to start at a new school where I knew nobody at all. I stood in the playground on my first day at Grafton High – by far the biggest school I had ever known, with its nine hundred pupils and tall brick buildings – and re-experienced the aloneness I had felt on that long-ago first day at infants' school. But this time there was no question of rushing up to other boys with confident, excited ideas about how to improve their games. For the games had changed to activities about which I knew nothing. The knots of boys that gathered and jostled one another in the playground were sniggering about sex; more specifically, about the underbelly of sex – a world of prostitutes, venereal disease and 'poofters'. Half the time, I had no idea of what my classmates were actually talking about, except that I knew it was somehow bad. I had been raised without exposure to what were then coyly referred to as four-letter words; my parents never said anything worse than 'Damn!' (or, in Mum's case, 'Damn, damn, damn!') and although I was already reading adult novels, I had never seen those words written down: the 1960s relaxation of censorship laws was still to come. When an older boy asked in a soft, wheedling voice, 'Are you gonna be a poofter when you grow up, mate?' I froze with horror. I didn't know what he meant, but I was sure it was something terrible. I had to pretend I understood the jokes, and pretend to laugh (although I don't think I often managed that). When I couldn't answer my classmates' questions ('Hey, mate, have you ever...'), they laughed at me. I was shamed. I felt small and inadequate, a figure of fun to others.

At Ballina Primary School I had been called Hugh by both teachers and classmates. Now, suddenly, I was Crago. To me, Crago meant my father – 'Mr A.I.H. Crago, District Inspector of Schools'; that was how his name appeared on the official letters that arrived constantly in our mailbox. The naked surname hit me like a blow. Even worse was 'long streak of shit', which was how the other boys reacted to my being tall and thin. Like the tiger in Kipling's story, I experienced such names as shameful. To be sure, they were crude, but the shame came from me. I could not hear the words without feeling somehow dirtied.

In 'How Fear Came', fear came first, and shame followed it. And I too was afraid – scared of being made a public spectacle in the change rooms at the swimming pool because my body was still that of a thin, hairless little boy. Scared of being seized from behind and ducked under water in the pool itself. Scared that I could not swim properly, and might never learn, when what everyone else did was to churn effortlessly up and down the fifty-metre pool with clean, powerful strokes. Scared of being made to dive off the high tower when I was terrified of heights; scared of being kicked in the knees from behind during marching practice, so that I stumbled and fell out of step; scared of having my large ears grabbed and rubbed savagely into the hard, wet ground (this minor bullying happened several times). Most of all, I was scared of some nameless thing that might happen to me behind the boys' ablutions block (as the toilets were grandly termed), although it never did happen, and it took me most of the next five years to work out exactly what I would have been subjected to if it had. My main aim every recess and lunchtime was to avoid being seen, and to avoid those areas of the school grounds where the predators might lurk.

Now the words of Kipling's story took on a significance they had not had when I had first read them. For the better part of my first three years at high school, I had to nerve myself to endure the automatic teasing from my classmates every time I entered the room, which of course I reacted to visibly, thereby (of course) encouraging them to continue. For them, it was simply harmless ragging, part of the cut and thrust of the classroom which every kid was expected to grin and bear. It never occurred to me to tell either of my parents about my humiliation and fear. When I complained of being teased, my parents responded (as so many did then) by reciting 'Sticks and stones may break your bones/but names will never hurt you', and when a teacher once asked me in the playground if I was being 'molested', I confidently said, 'Oh, no, sir.' I knew, without any threats ever being uttered, that to rat on my mates was completely impossible. And besides, I was not being molested, only given a hard time. Whatever being molested meant, it had not happened to me. I was super-sensitive, though it took me some time to realise it. And as happens all the time, my strong reaction to being teased or propositioned simply encouraged more from the others. I was an easy target.

Fear coloured my attitude to sex, too. By contrast with my classmates' excitement and delight at the thought of future sexual encounters, I began to associate sex with decay and death. The playground preoccupation with whores and venereal diseases somehow crept into me like the evil greenish mist that had signalled Plague in the Biblical epic *The Ten Commandments*, and the whole thing was crystallised in 'The Ballad of Eskimo Nell', which I heard for the first time in that playground:

> When a man grows old, and his balls grow cold,
> And the tip of his prick turns blue,
> And the hole in the middle refuses to piddle,
> I'd say he was *fucked*, wouldn't you?

This, I decided, must be what happens to you if you have sex with a whore (another word I didn't know the meaning of) like Eskimo Nell, or perhaps with any woman at all. I did not realise it then, but in the song itself, Eskimo Nell uses up men, exhausts them and humiliates them. The ballad is not a celebration of male sexual prowess, but a celebration of the inexhaustible female – the dark, fearful side of men's endless fixation on women's bodies and the pleasure to be had from them. Unexpectedly, I found the same idea in Mary Renault's serious historical novel about ancient Greece, *The King Must Die*. In an early episode, set in Eleusis, the Queen (the Mother Goddess in mortal form) selects a new lover each year, and at the end of the twelve months of feasting, hunting and lovemaking, each year-king in turn is sacrificed to ensure that the corn will continue to grow. Near the end of the same novel, after Theseus escapes from Crete with Ariadne, another goddess-on-earth, he narrowly escapes having his penis ripped off by Ariadne's drunk and frenzied Maenads, who literally tear to pieces any man they encounter while the divine spirit is in them. (I did not fully understand this passage at the time I first read the book; I just knew that something awful had happened, and that 'something' connected sex with death.)

My years at high school were over by 1964, and effectively pre-dated the sexual revolution that was about to occur. My parents had provided books about growing up – books that were enlightened for their time, but carefully unspecific about key details of sexual intercourse. Sex was never talked about in our family home. My parents' sexual relationship was completely invisible and so, to me, unthinkable. Had they kissed or held hands in our presence, I would almost certainly have been embarrassed, but at least I would have understood that they were not. Although my mother was generally more broad-minded about moral issues, she occasionally displayed panic at the uttering of a word with sexual connotations, as when she misheard a dentist's instructions to one of us kids to 'masticate' (chew our food well) as 'masturbate'. Her reaction (I later realised) echoed the values of her own mother, remembered from childhood, rather than her own more worldly values as a young adult. Is it surprising that I associated sex mostly with forbidden things, shameful things, frightening things?

I was a voracious reader, and my reading of adult novels simply reinforced my misunderstandings and fears. In Nicholas Monserrat's novel about the Battle of the Atlantic, a young officer arrives home on leave to find his wife in bed with another man. So acute is the officer's shame that when his ship is torpedoed on its next voyage, he feels relief as he drowns in the freezing water. Another officer's lover becomes pregnant, but then she too drowns, this time in a boating accident. *The Cruel Sea* confirmed my worst fears. Sex led to death. A shadow hung over the adulthood I was fast approaching. When novelists described wedding nights, they described the virgin heroine's shock, the sudden pain, and the sense of being used by the man in his animal pursuit of pleasure. Whether it was Katherine Swynford in Plantagenet England (Anya Seton's *Katherine*) or aspiring movie star Marjorie in Herman Wouk's *Marjorie Morningstar*, the women I read about were alarmed and disillusioned by their first sexual experiences. I found that message because I expected to find it. Fear is the constant companion of fearful people, whether they really have much to fear or not. I can see now how little real cause I had for fear at high school, but that is not how it felt at the time.

Of course there were positive experiences too, both real and fictional – though they did not cancel out my apprehension. I read other novels, novels which offered me accounts of women who enjoyed sex and looked forward to it. Once I reached puberty myself, I understood that sexual feelings could be exciting – although I would never have dreamed of talking about them to anyone else. Even before this, while I still felt very much a little boy, I fell in love with a new girl in my class. Her name was Vicki, and she only stayed in Grafton for two (or was it three?) years before her family moved to Sydney. She was attractive and confident: already at fourteen she was drawing the attention of much older boys. I couldn't compete with them and didn't try. Love from afar suited me very well. I was, after all, a shy person, though I did not think of myself that way.

By my final two years of high school (1962 and 1963), the crueller boys of whom I'd lived in fear had left, and my classmates had finally decided that I was OK – eccentric and 'a brain', but acceptable. I had friends who I had some things (mostly academic) in common with, and one or two of the girls clearly liked me, in a motherly, protective sort of way. The humiliations of compulsory rugby and compulsory swimming were a thing of the past. I would have said that I was once again content and happy, as I had almost always felt in primary school. Fear – and the rage that warded it off – had retreated further into the jungle, but it had not gone away.

As a younger child, inspired by my father's books on popular archaeology, I had built tiny cities and temples in our backyard, then left them to be overgrown by weeds and ravaged by rain so that I could 'excavate' them months later. But as an adolescent my games took on a darker aspect. Fuelled by voracious and repetitive reading, I built citadels and fleets but now I destroyed them with gunfire. Compulsively, I enacted scenarios of 'world empire or downfall' – Assyria, Rome, the Incas, the Aztecs, Napoleon, the Kaiser, Nazi Germany, Soviet Russia. There were no computer games then, not even the complex military board games of the 1970s, but like computer games now, my self-created scenarios lasted through days of high excitement, finishing in triumph and exhaustion. Since I controlled the entire game, I could always make sure that my side won. It was, I now see, a warped substitute for sex.

In Family Time

Sex and fear

As Rudyard Kipling well knew, shame and fear go hand in hand. If you are a fearful person, you are made to feel shame because of your fear. And once you have learned shame, you fear more of it.

La Belle Alliance

My father's family contained three obvious fearful persons – my grandfather, Albert, and his two younger daughters, Beth and Cherie. Yet even the more confident ones had their share of anxiety. Albert's first son, Dick, opinionated and determined, was, lifelong, an anxious person, as we saw in the first chapter of this book.

Albert's oldest daughter, Gwyn, as opinionated as her brother, and even more forthright in expressing her views, betrayed her anxiety in talk that rolled forward like a juggernaut, filling the space and drowning out others' attempts to participate in the conversation. She had been brought up to believe her family were good, hard-working people without much money. As a married woman, Gwyn remained uneasy in the presence of 'class people', and her awkwardness and lack of social graces embarrassed her husband Harold, who was part of that very class Gwyn disliked. Gwyn had absorbed her attitude to social status from her father Albert, who disliked and resented his older brother Will's 'la-di-da' attitudes (as Albert saw them).

The only one of Albert and Ethel's children who appeared relatively free of anxiety and resentment was Ted, the second son. And Ted was the only one who did not fear their father's panicky roaring. Perhaps with the exception of Cherie, the youngest, Ted was also the only one who seemed to feel equally bonded with both his father and his mother. Dick, Gwyn, Ian and Beth all took sides – the boys with their mother, Ethel, the girls with their father, Albert. When children take sides like this, it happens unconsciously, and its effects can be pervasive and last a lifetime. Even as adults, they may not question these alliances.

1930

My father, Ian, born after Gwyn, but before Beth, had clearly started life with a share of the family's sensitivity and fearfulness. As a child and adolescent, he hated and feared his father's outbursts of panicky roaring, but had been consoled and sheltered by his mother's obvious devotion to him, his knowledge that he (like Dick before him) was her special son. His baptism of fire (like mine) did not come until adolescence, and interestingly enough, the year it occurred (1930, when he started at Fort Street) coincided with the major trauma in my mother's early life – the death of her father, Victor, in the car accident. Gwen, my mother, lost her dad, while Ian only lost his innocence and sense of being special, but how much fear and shame we feel depends on our level of sensitivity and anxiety as much as on the magnitude of the trauma. Neither my father nor I suffered sexual or serious physical abuse as children, neither of us was exposed to parental violence or drunkenness, yet we reacted as if we had.

As a fifteen-year-old new boy at Fort Street Boys' High, Ian was horrified at the 'foul language' his classmates used, language that Ian had probably never heard. He did not name the words (adhering strictly to the rules with which he had been brought up) but we can easily guess what they were. He was disgusted, and stubbornly refused to talk that way just to fit in. He never complained of being bullied, but he was certainly teased and treated as a pariah. He never mentioned having any friends at school. His dislike of his classmates extended to almost every aspect of Fort Street (which was a selective school for brighter boys from non-affluent backgrounds, although not in the same league as the private boarding schools where rich kids with la-di-da parents were sent). Ian's later accounts of his Fort Street years – uttered in the mature certainty of his professional competence – focused on the stupidity and educational inadequacy of the teaching he had endured there.

My father despised nearly all his teachers. When Ian applied to join the school choir, even though he knew he had an excellent voice he was not admitted on his first attempt. He deeply resented that. He must have enjoyed some of his classes, and liked one or two of his teachers, but if he did, he never told me about them – only about the incompetent, ignorant and pompous ones.

He focused on what was wrong with his educational environment because that was a lot easier to speak about openly than the humiliation he had experienced at the hands of his classmates. He was almost certainly as sexually inhibited as I was, although he never spoke of such things to us children. He once recounted to me a story of how an innocent boy had been beguiled by three 'forward' teenage sisters; and tricked by one of them into an early, forced marriage. The message was clear: just as crime did not pay, so illicit sex led to disaster. Moreover, confidence (forwardness) was a dangerous quality to possess. Far better to be quiet or reserved. I was not temperamentally quiet or reserved, but that story left a deep impression on me. Fearful people are easily scared.

As adults, Albert and Ethel's children did not remember their parents sleeping in the same bed, or even in the same room – though of course they would have done so once. What Ted, the second born, remembered was that his mother had occupied the main bedroom, which the girls shared with her when younger; the three boys slept on an enclosed veranda (the sleep-out) and used Father's room to dress and undress. Ian remembered that when he reached what his parents judged to be the appropriate age, his parents had entrusted Dick, his oldest brother, with giving him a birds and bees talk. Ian was keen to learn about the facts of life but, to his disappointment, Dick just 'beat around the bush' (!) and never got to the point. Ian ended up as unsure of the details as he had been before – and as I would be at the same age.

Shamed people fear to be seen

It is in Beth, the second daughter and fourth child of Albert and Ethel Crago, that the family themes of fear and shame appear most dramatically. Beth was very attractive and, from childhood, she stood out from her brothers and sisters for that reason. Within the family, she was seen as beautiful (just as Dick and Ted were seen as 'brilliant'). But Beth was also extremely shy. Her looks attracted admiring attention, yet instead of feeling buoyed by this, she shrank from it. She notoriously resisted being photographed, and would hide under the bed when a photograph was being arranged – just as she hid under the bed or under the house when strangers or people she disliked arrived at the front door.

Beth's fear and shame would have been compounded by the teachings of the church within which she was raised. Like the Puritans of the seventeenth century, John Wesley had warned his followers in the eighteenth against the display of female beauty, because it tempted people to sin. Young women must dress modestly, eschew cosmetics and avoid anything like dancing, where their endearing young charms might lead them astray.

From the time that Gwen Sanders met my father's family, sometime in 1944, Beth remained my mother's *bête noire*. Gwen Sanders (as she then was) deeply disliked Beth, and wanted nothing to do with her – a feeling that Beth reciprocated. Gwen had felt judged by Beth on her first visit. Gwen knew that her worldly values offended her husband's devoutly Methodist family, and that 'Beth was the worst' – meaning, the most openly evangelical of the Cragos, and the most puritanical. Mum saw herself as a broad-minded career woman, well-educated, confident in her work and convinced (like her own mother) that religion was all a lot of nonsense. She would never have thought of herself as having anything in common with her husband's cripplingly shy (yet, in Gwen's eyes, smugly righteous) second sister.

Yet Gwen disliked being photographed almost as much as Beth did. She did not literally run away, but she made her self-doubt evident by maintaining a poker face for the camera, refusing to smile or relax into a spontaneous expression. She looks sullen in some of her teenage photographs, and in others, wary and unsure of herself. Like Dick's wife May (whom Gwen also disliked), Gwen hated looking in the mirror. Though a tall, handsome woman with a good figure, Gwen craved reassurance about her attractiveness and, late in life, said bitterly that her own mother had praised her school results, 'but never a word about appearance'. She wanted to be like other girls, like girls were supposed to be – pretty, flirty, confident in their ability to attract a man. Where Beth hated and feared the effect of her attractiveness on others, Gwen hated her own looks and doubted her attractiveness. After all, Gwen had had no father during her early childhood, and no father at all after her sixteenth year. The man who might have supplied some warmth and admiration as she came into her first bloom was dead. And her mother, grieving, lonely and proud, could not make up for the deficit.

Eva herself was a person as fearful and socially unconfident as Beth, though she would never have seen the parallel. Eva – just like Beth's mother Ethel Crago – found it easier to express affection to her son than to her daughter, and could not give the warm hugs and the words of praise that Gwen needed. When Gwen was a schoolgirl, she told us, a man next to her on the train had tried to put his hand up her skirt. Gwen was shocked and probably froze in horror, just as I would later do (with far less provocation).

Despite her façade of feminine confidence as a young adult in the early 1930s, Gwen shrank away from the opportunities for casual sex that her mildly risky behaviour had put in her way. She knew that her mother, Eva, would be horrified, for despite her lack of religion, Eva's values around sex were as puritanical as Beth's. In Beth, Gwen had encountered the same personality type as her mother, and her visceral reaction to her husband's younger sister led her to unexamined, harsh judgements that were as extreme as Beth's judgements of her.

What We Need to Know

What's in a name?

As anthropologists remind us, names are powerful things. Our given names seem to embody our selfhood, and if we do not like ourselves, we wish we had a different name. It has become increasingly common for adults to actually change their given names, in search of a new identity that seems to offer them a sense of security and belonging. At six, I thought that being called John might gain me more acceptance from the other boys. When, at twelve, I found myself called Crago instead of Hugh, I heard it as a kind of insult. Of course that was a wild overreaction – yet not completely without foundation. The use of my surname by teachers did merge my identity with that of my father's family, make me into a representative of a species instead of an individual. But, significantly, I took particular exception to being called by a name that, to me, conflated me with my father – for that is exactly what my father himself had felt, some thirty years before, when his headmaster called him Albert. I did not hate my father, as he had hated his – in fact, I felt respect and affection for him – but I followed the same pattern, even though I did not know then that he had felt the same as me.

There was, I now see, a further dimension to the pattern. Did I want to be called Hugh because 'Crago' automatically aligned me with my father's family, not my mother's? For in my first twelve years of life, I had absorbed my mother's assumptions about the relative importance of the Crago and Sanders families: to her, Dad's people were a threat, people to keep at a safe distance. By repudiating the use of my surname, I was, in my own way (and completely unconsciously) choosing my mother above my father – exactly as Dad had done, a generation earlier.

Just as names embody individuality, so the deliberate altering of a name by others asserts power over the person whose name is taken. Nicknames and diminutives are part of many languages, and Australians are notorious for their insistence on altering or shortening names even when they are perfectly easy to say in their original form. This often starts within the family: my father's elder brothers Richard and Edward immediately became Dick and Ted; Gwynneth was shortened to Gwyn (but pronounced Gwen, which must have led to feelings of awkwardness when my father chose to marry a Gwen), Bethel became simply Beth and Cherie was pronounced to rhyme with cherry. But at school, the renaming process takes on new dimensions.

Nicknames (and mangled forms of existing names) become badges of belonging to a peer group – or ways of excluding others from it.

Hugh was a relatively unusual name when I was growing up, and (although I didn't realise it) had vague connotations of status and Englishness. I doubt my mother considered such things in choosing to call me Hugh – it was after all her brother's name, and her family were far from aristocratic, though her mother's father, Robert Kirkham, had been very comfortably off – but her choice of Hugh for me reinforced my difference from most of my peers at Grafton High. And so I became Hughie, or 'Craggs' (for Crago). Although I didn't analyse all of this then as I have done now, I was certainly conscious that my renaming was in part a process of being required to conform to the majority, to give up my prized specialness. Accepting that I was not special was a hard lesson for me to learn, and I resisted it fiercely.

Silence, difference and narcissism

Sex was not a subject of discussion in the family I grew up in, nor in many other families at the time. As we have already seen, silence leaves a space which children inevitably fill with ideas of their own. My parents left my sex education to books, and the books themselves omitted key things – such as the fact that nature ensures the continuation of the species through making sex intensely pleasurable. To my knowledge, no 1950s 'facts of life' text included this information, presumably out of fear that telling children that sex was fun and highly enjoyable might cause them to try it out. Of course many children experimented nonetheless, but I did not, and I automatically shrank in distaste or fear on the tiny number of occasions on which other kids invited me into such explorations. Sexual inhibition was just one part of a more general inhibition – 'we (my family) don't do lots of things that other people do'. 'Rough' and 'wild' were the two adjectives my parents used when describing such people, marking their own status as middle-class (and respectable). I don't think I was actually told not to play with rough children, and I did have occasional contact with them, but I knew this contact ought not to extend too far. Sexual inhibition and clean language were one way that middle-class families (the anxious class[1] as some scholars have called them) distinguished themselves from those of lower station who were seen as both wild and rough in their language and their actions.

And so, despite the fact that my father was liberal-minded by comparison with many Methodists of that time, and despite my mother's dislike and distrust of the restrictions imposed by any kind of religious beliefs, the taboos on sexual pleasure, bodily display, alcohol and unnecessary spending in which my father had been brought up survived almost intact, and were transmitted, albeit in a somewhat milder form to me. Felt difference meant silence about many things, but especially about sex and (in my case) about faith as well, as we will see in chapter 9.

I concluded that sex was not a topic for discussion with either of my parents, and I filled the yawning gaps left in my knowledge with information derived from self-chosen adult fiction. The convictions that I arrived at from such reading were convictions shaped by fear. To be sure, I received the message that sex could be enjoyable, that adults sought it out almost compulsively – but for me, this message was trumped by anxiety. My mind selected the scary, foreboding things about sex, and it was these that made the most lasting impression on me. Even when, at around seventeen, I read the historical romance *Angelique*, its glowing portrayal of sex left my fears intact. My way of reading adult fiction had been shaped by my anxious, sensitive genetic temperament, reinforced by the values in which my parents had raised me, and my sense of difference and specialness kept me apart from other sources of information. I never experienced anything physical with a real girl, and the only occasion on which a much older girl touched me (to stroke my face in the dark) I had been around ten years old, and recoiled in shock. I knew there was such a thing as pleasuring oneself, but I shied away from it, and never learned how. Hence, I would reach adulthood with little sense of the responsiveness of my own body – let alone anyone else's.

In my extreme reaction to being renamed and to being teased verbally, I was simply demonstrating the power of my genetic heritage. Sensitive, fearful, socially awkward children do not 'take such things in their stride' as more confident children do. Instead, they retreat within themselves, reaffirming their specialness – which must now be kept hidden from the common herd. Two thousand years before, the Roman poet Horace had written *Odi profanum vulgus et arceo* (I hate the common throng, and shun them). From around the time I entered high school, I began a conscious re-imagining of myself as not like the rest of the crowd, a European in exile, not a dinkum Aussie, a scholar and a dreamer, not an athletic, rough-talking, insensitive male like so many of the boys I knew at school. (My grandmother's cousin Henry had done much the same at much the same age, but at the time I knew nothing of that.) No wonder the other boys were sure I must be a poofter. I must have radiated distaste for the activities that were proper to adolescent males. Much of this re-creation of my identity drew its inspiration from my reading, which I experienced with great vividness, and re-enacted in my fantasy play. My imagination was peculiarly literal, and so when I was called a long streak of shit, I could not hear the words without seeing what they denoted – something amplified by the interior of the boys' ablutions block, with its rank, repulsive smells.

It was exactly the same literal imagination that simultaneously invited me to take fictional descriptions of sex so personally, casting myself as the shocked, humiliated young woman rather than as the triumphantly phallic man. Sensitive individuals are dominated by their imaginations rather than by realities, and their fears dwarf the real experiences that provoked them. I never understood then what Shakespeare meant when he made Julius Caesar say 'Cowards die many times before their deaths', but in the first two or three years of high school, I experienced that death daily. My defence was to create worlds of imagination in which I could work out my rage and heal my battered self-esteem in the form of military conquest. Because I controlled the entire game, I could, like Kaiser Wilhelm II in his pre-war simulations, always arrange outcomes to suit myself. I did not want to share my games with others, because then I would relinquish control. On the rare occasions when, as an adult, I played strategy games with a friend, I usually lost badly. I was no strategist, no field marshal *manqué*. I was simply escaping from a painful reality.

La Belle Alliance

When my father first took my mother to Yass to meet his parents, his sister Beth remembered that she was the only one of the three Crago sisters actually at home. But she would undoubtedly have told Gwyn and Cherie all about her shock and horror at the 'city girl's' behaviour and her careless dismissal of faith. Gwyn, Beth and Cherie giggled together about Gwen and blamed her for taking their adored and idealised brother away from them. Many years earlier, much the same had happened when Dick married May Lepper. In both cases, the alliance confirmed the Crago girls in the rightness of their convictions, and warded off the painful awareness that their brother had preferred his fiancée to them.

When she read an earlier version of this chapter, Cherie (then in her seventies) insisted that her mother, Ethel, had never joined in the girls' condemnation of Gwen, and she may well have been correct. But although Ethel may not have said anything overtly critical, she certainly permitted her daughters to do what they did – tacitly, she too was part of the alliance. Joining with others of a like mind is something human beings do when they perceive a threat. It can of course be a good and useful thing to do. But it can equally serve as a way of denying an uncomfortable truth, and focusing anger and hurt instead on an external enemy who may not really be an enemy at all.

Once more, with genotyping

How much of my sexual confusion and self doubt was simply because I was slower to reach puberty than most of my age peers? For the first two years of high school, I did not feel the rush of blood to my loins that gave my classmates their bodily confidence and their obsession with all things sexual. I saw them only as crude and cruel, and told myself that if this was what 'being a man' entailed, then I wanted nothing of it. I continued, for a seemingly endless time, to inhabit the body of a tall, thin child while my classmates were rapidly becoming young men. I strongly suspect that this late maturation was something I shared with my father's family – in the case of my mother's, I can't be sure. I can remember being relieved when puberty finally arrived, but by then, it was too late to regain all of the confidence and self-possession I had lost.

Like my Auntie Beth, I was born highly sensitive and highly expressive – I displayed my feelings openly (my father on several occasions took me aside and gently counselled me not to show so much on my face). Like Beth and most of her siblings, I was born with a tendency to anxiety, though I was not as fearful as she was. Like my grandfather Albert, who had died when I was around eighteen months old, and of whom I had no memory at all, I was temperamentally prone to express my fear in irritability, complaining, and loud shouting. I was not just different because of my father's Methodist values, or because he happened to be the inspector of schools, and so a prominent figure in the country towns in which I grew up. Nor was I different simply because I was so tall and so thin, with long fingers (the type of body associated with Marfan syndrome, though I do not have the other symptoms). I felt different because I *was* different, genetically, from the majority of my fellow humans.

I may have claimed that I did not want to belong to the 'bewildered herd', but that was a convenient half-truth. Deep down, I wanted to belong, to be accepted, not to be different – all the things I had wanted at six. I had simply learned to conceal it better, even from myself. Other boys, I thought, born with lower levels of anxiety, would be judged fit to fight in wars, and would come back heroes – like Ivan Southall's aviator Simon Black, whose adventures I devoured as an adolescent. They would find partners easily, and have children without problems. They would get promoted at work because others would trust them:

they would be seen as regular guys, who did what was expected. They wouldn't agonise over the problems of the world, or feel somehow responsible for human suffering, and then feel guilty that they weren't doing anything to relieve that suffering. And perhaps some of them did – though Ivan Southall was certainly not among them: as I later discovered, he showed the same temperamental qualities as me.

4

Just a Little Wedding

In My Time

Somebody to Love (Oxford, 1969–1971)

It was 1969, the year of Woodstock and Altamont. Love was in the air, but so was fear. Most of the 60s had passed me by, shapes of things before my eyes, monochrome images on a television screen. When John F. Kennedy was shot in Dallas, our class had been watching a movie in the assembly hall of Grafton High School, and the projector was briefly halted to announce the news. America was far away, and the event made only a brief impact. At university in Armidale in 1965, I was more preoccupied with getting my weekly Latin prose done than with the Freedom Rides and the violent clashes they sparked. University had proved a safe haven for me, and I had made a number of genuine friends. The reality of the Vietnam War hovered menacingly as I finished my degree, but receded when I found that I had escaped the draft. In 1968, as Martin Luther King and Robert Kennedy were assassinated and students rioted in the streets of Paris, I was absorbed in tutoring first-year university students of English literature, pretending an adult sophistication I knew I did not possess.

The one way in which the spirit of the 60s had reached me was through its music. That music – by turns ebullient, angry, visionary and reassuring – became my passport to membership in the 'Class of 63'. Now I knew what others felt because I felt it too. Classically trained, I was initially contemptuous of 'pop', but popular music was rapidly transforming itself. Gone were the anodyne sentiments and bland melodies of the 30s and 40s, the crude early rock and roll of the 50s. The menacing chords and relentless rhythm of Jefferson Airplane's 'Somebody to Love' got under my skin as effectively as Mick Jagger got that unnamed girl under his thumb.

I was no longer six years old, but I still could not have told you why 'Somebody to Love' had such a hold on me, nor did I think consciously about how its words 'Don't you need somebody to love' might apply to my own situation. I just knew that the song somehow belonged to me. As had happened before with 'Little Red Monkey', I could not decipher all the words but I did hear one line as 'Your mind, your mind/is so afraid'. The actual words were 'is full of red' (that is, rage), but I heard fear instead of rage. It was a significant mishearing.

I had found somebody to love, and I was in Oxford reading for a postgraduate degree, and soon I would be getting married. But as well as joy there was fear, a fear I did not want to think about. I had been drawn to Maureen initially because of her academic accomplishments, her study of several languages and her wide reading. She readily embraced some of my own interests, and we lent each other books. I knew she was some seven years older than I was, and that she'd had no previous relationship. She loved me, rarely challenged me, and saw me as having the confidence that she herself, a basically shy person, felt she lacked. It had all happened before, only I knew nothing of that then.

So here I was in the city of dreaming spires, set for a bright academic career and about to be married. My belief in Christianity was already faltering, but I still considered myself bound by the principle that sex must wait until after marriage and so did she. And so we waited. Of course we could have been married in Australia and left for England together. But I thought it more romantic to be married in the chapel of my college at Oxford, and I wanted to be there before she did. I wanted to make my own friendships and networks before she got there. I wanted to hug them to myself – still the three-year-old who hugged *Kindergarten of the Air* to himself, and refused to let anyone listen with him. I did not realise it, but I was arranging things in this peremptory way in order to lessen my own anxieties. I didn't want a big family wedding where relatives would observe me, and so I arranged a tiny wedding on the other side of the world, with no public celebration. I could not have revealed more clearly my sense that marriage was something shameful, something to be hidden away, but I would have been the last one to realise that. I would have said that I was looking forward to it, but just didn't want all that fuss. Beyond that, I did not think.

Maureen's parents, who lived on a property in north-western NSW, would not be able to attend a wedding in England, and nor (I thought) would my own parents – although my mother rapidly decided that they would, combining attendance at our wedding with a trip to Europe. Maureen accepted this unfair arrangement with indignation and a sense of betrayal, which I brushed aside. It was the first of many times that I would minimise the strength of her feelings and dismiss her objections. Her resignation when faced by something she found painful simply encouraged me to charge ahead, convincing myself everything would work out for the best. I had no concept of a shared life, or what relationship would mean. I knew little about the person who loved me, and whom I believed I loved. I was locked inside a little room full of grand fantasies and dark terrors.

So we had our little wedding – very little indeed. I didn't even feel able to invite my Uncle Hugh, who lived in Cornwall, and whose family I'd visited once when I first arrived in England. I was oblivious of the rudeness displayed in this omission. Of course I had a model for such conduct, a model for fear-dictated blindness to the sensitivities of others, but like most people in their early twenties, it would never have occurred to me to compare my own behaviour with my mother's or that of any other relatives: what I knew was all I needed to know.

Despite all my efforts to keep it small and safe, our wedding still felt awkward, wrong in some way. At some level I knew that I had avoided something that seemed too hard. Maureen and I had previously agreed that she would not dress as a bride. Maureen was never one for self-display.

She may well have showed disappointment, but I failed to notice it. No photographs were taken, although one snapshot was taken by an Oxford friend at the earlier civil ceremony, which had to precede the (to me) real wedding, because the college chapel was not licensed for weddings. My father, mother and sister returned to our flat for a meal, because my father would have been uncomfortable in a restaurant, and then they went off to their hotel in London. There was no honeymoon, although we could perfectly well have afforded one, because the whole idea of a honeymoon whispered to me of the unvoiced and the unthinkable. Both of us felt desire, but neither of us had prior experience of sex to assist us, and neither of us had ever discussed the matter in any detail with those who had, let alone with each other. I was not impotent, but I was afraid of hurting her, afraid of what my own body wanted, and she took her cue from my anxieties, unable to cheerfully take control and help me through my ineptitude. Somewhere in my head, I heard the voice of Marjorie Morningstar: 'then shock, shock, shock and it was all over'.

It took months before we actually managed to have intercourse, and all the doctors we consulted assumed that the fault must be hers, a view I was happy enough to shelter behind. But Maureen had been a willing partner – she was not frigid. The problem was mine, but the medicos did not know how to help this likeable but extremely anxious young man to acquire a new physical skill, and to think about his partner's needs as well as his own.

Nobody asked me, 'What exactly are you doing when you try to have sex? Show me on this model.' Nobody asked, 'Hugh, are you afraid of something?'

When, eventually, we did succeed, my relief was only temporary. I could maintain an erection easily, but did not come to orgasm. I could not let myself go, surrender to sensation. Had they been privy to all of this, the long-ago kids at high school would have been even surer that I was a poofter, but that wasn't the explanation. Although I did not think of these things until much later, being anorgasmic might well have had something to do with my fear of sexual experimentation in my teenage years, with my lack of a big brother or trusted male friend, with the moral code within which I had been raised – sex outside of marriage is a sin – and oddly, even with the long years of childhood in which, after waking each morning, I put off my need to pee so that I could spend longer reading in my warm bed and avoid the long trek to the outdoor dunny! Had I, perhaps, trained myself, according to the best behavioural principles, in not letting go?

This frustrating impasse continued for nearly two years. All around me the sexual revolution of the 60s was blossoming, reminding me painfully of my own inadequacy. For some months, I saw a psychiatrist, but became increasingly contemptuous: he seemed completely inept. Eventually, I asked about hypnotherapy, and he referred me to a GP trained in hypnosis. For the first time, I found myself in the presence of a professional who seemed to understand me. He displayed no incredulity, no thinly veiled contempt. Instead he did ask the one question that went to the heart of my aloneness. Which was more important to me: my work, or my relationship? To my own shock, I unhesitatingly answered 'my work' – in other words, my devotion to reading, research and ideas, all of which constituted a vaguely formulated dream of a future as a scholar.

I knew it was a terrible admission that I cared more about those things than about the person I had chosen to be my partner for life, but having admitted it brought relief. Fear had led to my neurotic self-absorption and crippling shame; when some of that fear began to dissolve, so did the immediate problem. I think this had less to do with the handful of sessions of hypnosis than with simply being in the presence of someone who did not mirror my own savage self-judgement. It would not be for another five years that I would seriously think of myself as a potential counsellor, but more than anything else, it was this experience of being accepted and understood which turned me in the direction of what would, within ten years, become my second career.

Quite unexpectedly, I started to function sexually in a normal way. To me this was an enormous relief, a dragging stone cut from my belly (an image long remembered from the fairy tale). It was all too easy for me to forget that someone else had had to live through all of this, through my shame and fear, too often expressed as biting criticism of her. Restored to apparent confidence, I dreamed of a future for myself as a radical educator who would give my students 'freedom to learn' in their own way, in their own time. It was my version of the 60s dream of massive social revolution. And it was another way of denying what was wrong with me, and directing my energy into curing the world instead. To be fair, I would not have been the first would-be radical to be guilty of that.

Despite this turn for the better, the words of 'Somebody to love' still sounded in my mind. Why? Despite all that had marred the first two years of Maureen's and my life together, the joy within me had not died. It was probably her joy in me that I had killed. But why would I need 'somebody' to love – as if almost anybody would do – in order to feel acceptable to myself? Why was it that I could treat so disrespectfully the person whom I had not long since promised to love, honour and cherish? It was as if I was punishing her simply for being herself, for not being exactly what I needed her to be. It was what my mother had done to my father, but although I had witnessed it repeatedly as I was growing up, I did not yet know what had lain behind her cutting words.

In Family Time

1944

There was no wedding photograph displayed in the home I grew up in, and I don't think I ever wondered why. My mother said very little about her wedding to my father. What I do clearly remember her saying was that it was just a little wedding and that she wore just an ordinary blue dress (in other words, she wasn't dressed as a bride). She didn't say it with any apparent sadness or regret, but with dismissive defiance. I took her to mean that she was a bit of a rebel and enjoyed bucking convention. Later, when as an adult I began asking about my family history, a few more details emerged. 'Well, there was a war on' was my father's initial explanation of the smallness of the wedding. Yes, it was 1944, but it wasn't as if he had been on active service, snatching a few days' leave to get married before he returned to the fighting and the possibility of death. Nothing like that. His occupation as a teacher meant that he was in no danger of being sent into combat, and his military service was confined to weekend desk duties for the University Regiment, stationed right there in Sydney. The 'ordinary' blue dress my mother had mentioned was in fact bought specially for the occasion, 'And gee, she looked good in it too!' said my father appreciatively (years later, and not in Mum's hearing).

Then I discovered that the only people at my parents' wedding had been my grandmother, Eva, and my father's elder brother, Ted. Of course my mother's father had died long before, but that in itself does not account for the tiny attendance. It seemed that Eva had refused to attend if Mrs Crago (my father's mother, Ethel) was going to be there, and so Ethel had not been invited. My father had wanted his sister Cherie to be there, but – knowing that her mother was not going – she had declined. Possibly the same had happened with Albert, my father's father, but I can say only that my father would almost certainly have been relieved not to have his father present. Dad may have backed down in the face of Mum's displays of emotion, but there were gains as well as losses for him in this defeat.

The one challenge to the sad pattern came from Ted. He had come uninvited, just pushed in (as he put it much later) because he felt that somebody from the family ought to be there. Nobody else had the courage to go against the tide of Crago antipathy to my father's choice of bride. When Ian had brought Gwen Sanders to Yass to meet his family, she had thoughtlessly switched on the radio to listen to the races on Saturday afternoon. For the Cragos, gambling was a sin, and even listening to the races was viewed with suspicion. And then Gwen had told Ian's younger sister Beth that religion was just a lot of nonsense. She took an instant dislike to her prospective mother-in-law, whom she saw as a 'matriarch' who wanted Ian all to herself. As far as

Gwen was concerned, it was a competition between her and Ethel to secure Ian's loyalty – a competition Gwen was determined to win.

And so a wedding was held in which the bride was not dressed as a bride, and in which there was no reception – after a cup of tea at a café with Eva and Ted, my mother and father departed for a short honeymoon in the Blue Mountains. The wedding was a small, private event, shadowed by the couple's uncomfortable awareness of the others who should have been there – not just the other Cragos, but Gwen's brother Hugh (then serving overseas), and any representative of her dead father's people – like Gwen's Auntie Ruby. Eva disapproved of Ruby and her mother, Gwen's paternal grandmother, and there had been little contact between Eva and Victor's sister after his untimely death. The pattern of dislike and emotional distancing was not confined to the Cragos.

I am not sure that my mother felt any regret about all of this, but I know my father did – long afterwards, his sister Cherie showed me a letter he had written to his parents the day before the wedding, thanking them for all they had done for him. It was graceful and tactful, but implicitly, it was an apology for his failure to secure them a place at the wedding, an acknowledgment of his own feelings of guilt. Ethel kept his letter for the rest of her life, and Cherie kept it for the rest of hers.

If any photographs were taken on that day in 1944, no copy was ever displayed in my parent's home, nor kept in their albums. My parents' wedding had foreshadowed my own and Maureen's – even though when I was married, a quarter century after them, what I've just described was completely unknown to me. My mother never talked directly to me about her sexual relationship with my father, and for his part, he mentioned it only once in the years that I was growing up, although what he did say indicated enjoyment and appreciation ('It's well worth waiting for!'). I am told that my mother once said (to a trusted listener) that 'at first it [sex] is all very exciting, but then nothing happens'. She may, of course have simply meant that she was disappointed that my father had wanted to turn over and go to sleep, instead of lying close to her and whispering intimacies as she had hoped. However, I wondered then, and still wonder, whether this meant that she had been anorgasmic, as I had been? I wondered whether this had remained the case, and whether this might have had something to do with her apparent dissatisfaction and disappointment in my father. Eventually, though, I would realise that even if this were true, there were more compelling reasons for her attitude to him.

Once my parents were married, contact between my father and his own family of origin dwindled rapidly. In 1947, my parents took their first child (me) around to show Dad's parents and siblings, but his father died the next year, and there were only two later visits to my grandmother, Ethel. The first of these took place when I was around six – the visit I later recalled with memories of awkwardness. No doubt there was far more awkwardness than I was aware of! The second visit came when I was fourteen, and Ethel was temporarily living with Dick and May at Bowral. I noted (in the diary I sporadically kept that year) how surprised I was to find that Grandma Crago (as my mother called her) was 'a very nice old lady' and that my earlier impressions had been so wrong. The only Crago relatives we visited regularly, once a year, were Uncle Ted and his wife Beryl – and that was no accident. Ted was the one who had felt confident enough to attend my parents' wedding despite not having an invitation. He was also mild-mannnered and normally unflappable – unlike several of his excitable siblings.

In striking contrast, we visited Mum's mother Eva – Evie to me – every year, beginning just after Christmas, and lasting most of the summer holidays. It was abundantly clear that my father had become, effectively, a member of my mother's family. One family had taken over the other. 'Taken over' was a phrase my mother used on a number of occasions to describe such processes – almost as if a military conquest had occurred.

1908

Just as my own wedding to Maureen in 1969 had followed the template of my parents' in 1944, so theirs followed the template of Eva's 1908 wedding to Victor Sanders. Once again, it had been 'just a little wedding', held not in a church but at Eva's family home – the sizeable terrace house her father Robert Kirkham had built in Cleveland Street not far from Sydney's Central Station. Here again was a bride not dressed as a bride, and one whose choice of partner met with family disapproval. To some of Eva's family, Victor was just a junior reporter with no money and no prospects – and, as they discovered, far too young for her to boot. In fact, Eva's older sisters had disapproved of most of the women who had married their brothers – a pattern very similar to the way the Crago sisters felt towards my mother. Whether Victor's mother was present, I do not know; his father had died when he was sixteen. Perhaps wedding photographs had been taken (the Kirkhams went in for quality studio photographs taken by professionals) and perhaps they had once been displayed in Eva's home, but if so, they had certainly disappeared by the time I knew her. No wonder I did not consider the lack of a wedding photograph in my own parents' home as something of any significance. We don't know what we don't know, and so what we know is all there is to know.

Three generations of one family (Eva, her daughter Gwen, and Gwen's eldest son, Hugh) had been married in small ceremonies that embodied awkwardness and embarrassment, a pervading sense that something wasn't right. So what about the wedding of my other grandparents, Albert Crago and Ethel Stear, in 1904?

1904

When I asked Uncle Ted what he knew about his parents' wedding, he responded by telling an odd little story. He said that his parents had been married in a small country church at Bowning (the village near Yass to which his six-year-old brother Dick had tried to run away), but that the church had subsequently been pulled down 'because it was built on the wrong piece of land'. This anecdote has all the hallmarks of a story heard (or overheard) in childhood, and only half-understood. Without added details, it makes little sense. Yes, the church was demolished at some time after the wedding. To whoever passed on that story to Ted (presumably as a boy) it may well have seemed a bit of a joke. But why would anyone pass on such a story at all unless in a way it was an oblique comment on something much more significant? If you can't say something nice, don't say anything – or tell a story that seems to be about something else. And why would Ted have recounted that story to me when I asked him about his parents' relationship? Was it, by implication, the *marriage* that there was something wrong with, as well as the land on which the church had been built?

Despite most of my Crago relatives' reluctance to paint anything but a positive picture of their family, I gradually learned that Albert and Ethel (despised Father and adored Mother to my dad) had had a stable, but not particularly fulfilling or happy, life together. Ethel, the eldest daughter of Richard Stear, a successful small businessman and former mayor of Gulgong, was outgoing, sociable, a capable housewife, and practised at looking after her younger siblings. She was also prone to tears and headaches when under stress. A romantic, she clearly craved a soulmate, who would whisper loving words, share her dreams and act gallantly – like the handsome heroes in the popular novels she read compulsively.

Albert, the youngest of eight surviving siblings, could never have been that soulmate. He was shy (to the degree that would now earn him a diagnosis of social phobia) and governed by irrational fears. He kept his feelings to himself except when thrown into panic, which he would express in outbursts of shouting. Albert was socially inept, and gallantry was not in his repertoire. He would have expressed his feelings for his bride in actions, not in words. The wedding night story told by Ethel many years later to one of her children focused on the fact that Albert, believing his bride asleep, had 'tenderly tucked in her blanket'. That is all I know about their first night together, but it speaks volumes. She wanted to believe that he cared about her, and he did – but in his own way, and her need for overt affection, expressed in words, seemed impossible for him to fulfil. After he had tucked in her blanket, she said, she lay wakeful, but did not want him to know.

This is only one of several stories of Albert and Ethel's failure to understand each other. Albert's grandson John once said that his grandfather had been 'dominated at the mill' by his responsible eldest brother Will, and 'dominated at home' by Ethel, a responsible eldest daughter. She was the one who arranged things, sang solos in church on Sundays, planned future marriages for her daughters, gathered the family around the piano for singsongs, and dreamed of careers for her brilliant sons. Albert just got on with the daily routine – physical work in the flour mill of which he was joint owner; more physical work on the ten acres that surrounded their home. When she invited guests home to dinner, Albert often pleaded weariness and went off to bed before the guests left. He wasn't one for parties, however genteel and non-alcoholic, and maybe his tiredness was as convenient an excuse as his wife's headaches.

Albert continued to behave towards his wife in the only way he knew. He was a practical man, and 'practical' was his term of approbation. Each morning he got up first, lit the stove and brought a cup of tea to Ethel, who was still in bed. Albert's nephew Ralph, who thought Ethel 'a lady' and Albert 'obnoxious', scornfully claimed that his uncle once thought it perfectly appropriate for Ethel to travel in a cart that had earlier been used to transport a load of muck (that is, manure). To Ralph, that signalled his uncle's lack of breeding and his total failure to understand his wife's true nature. Ethel and Albert got on, and they had six children together, but their relationship was not a companionate one. It clearly was not a partnership of equals and, though nobody ever said so, Ethel was almost certainly more intelligent than Albert, and better educated (albeit not in the academic sense) and no doubt that difference too played out in the form of misunderstandings and resentments that could not be talked about.

1866

Albert and Ethel's was far from the only marriage in that extended family to have been built on the wrong piece of land. Ethel's cousin Henry Lawson (born in two years before her, in 1877) captured in writing the miscommunication and loneliness of two very different people yoked together by an impulsive decision to get married. At their wedding in 1866, Henry's Norwegian-born father had been thirty-four. His bride was just nineteen and desperate to get away from home. Henry's story 'A Child in the Dark, and a Foreign Father' is partly based on memories of Henry's parents, Louisa Albury and Niels Larsen (anglicised as Peter Lawson). In the story, Henry's sympathies are clearly with the quiet, long-suffering husband, and he depicts the wife as histrionic, manipulative and self-centred – probably drawing on the conduct of his own wife Bertha (who at the time he was writing was having a psychotic episode) more than on childhood memories of his real mother. Louisa separated from Peter in 1883 and moved to Sydney. Peter, prone to depression, lived a lonely life, earning a living as a house painter. Louisa, in Sydney, went on to live out her dream of making a difference to the lives of women all over the country, and published the pioneer feminist magazine *The Dawn*. Peter and Louisa remained on reasonably good terms, but never reunited.

The Stears (Ethel's family) and the Cragos (her husband's family) were simply and sincerely religious. They found Henry Lawson's grittily realistic stories – to say nothing of his very public alcoholism, his republican politics and his lack of Christian faith – a major embarrassment. Cousin Henry was a topic Ethel's family – including my father – were encouraged to avoid. Even though Lawson was long dead, my father simply told me, as a child, that I was Henry Lawson's 'third cousin' (more accurately, he was my cousin twice removed). My parents possessed plenty of books, but not one of them was by Henry Lawson. When, as a teenager, I did read some of Henry's stories, I found them boring (which I would now interpret as meaning depressingly realistic). Many among the Cragos would probably have made very similar judgements – if they brought themselves to read his work at all. The only fan Lawson had among the Cragos was, not surprisingly, Ted. And it was not until the next generation of the family that anyone could think of naming a son Lawson in Henry's memory (as Gwyn's second son, Murray, did).

1896

Henry Lawson's marriage to Bertha Bredt in 1896 followed a similar pattern to his own parents'. She was a wide-eyed, passionate nineteen-year-old, he was ten years older and already gaining a reputation as a talented ne'er-do-well who kept sabotaging his own chances of success. Neither Henry's family nor Bertha's approved of the match and no relative on either side attended it. The ceremony was a hole-in-the corner affair in Sydney, solemnised by a maverick minister who did not belong to the Methodist mainstream. The two witnesses were simply passers-by, roped in off the street. From that rocky beginning, Henry and Bertha's relationship lurched forward through seven years of disappointments, failures and mutual recriminations, producing two children before it eventually came to an end. Henry and Bertha returned from their abortive time in England in 1901, in which Bertha suffered her breakdown, and separated soon after they were back in Australia. Lawson's story 'Joe Wilson's Courtship' looks back with melancholy and carefully restrained cynicism on the bright days that would never come again.

1946

Lack of intimacy and communication, rather than lack of sexual fulfilment, is the theme of the 'little wedding' stories I have told so far. But there is one story which provides a context for my own miserable ineptitude and insensitivity in the early years of my marriage, and that is the story of my father's younger sister, Beth. As we saw in the last chapter, Beth seemed scared by her attractiveness rather than given confidence by it. When she grew up, she trained as a teacher, but she dreaded being on show in the classroom (as her beloved father dreaded being on show in front of the congregation in church) and after one holiday at her parents' home, her sisters had virtually to coerce her into returning to work. She retrained as a nurse, but the change of occupation did not solve the problem. Then, against the odds, she got married. Her mother, Ethel, had helped it along a bit. Semi-arranged marriages were not uncommon at the time, especially in rural areas. Roy Plumb was a churchgoer, a quiet, pleasant man, then in uniform but about to return to his secure job in banking. Early in 1946 he and Beth (then aged twenty-seven) were married. There were photographs, and most of Beth's family attended – though Albert, her father, was notably absent, pleading illness; he would die two years later. It was not exactly the little wedding of our earlier examples. But the curse was there, nonetheless.

When she wrote to me in her seventies, Beth observed tartly, 'it was very different from choosing a partner in peace time, I can tell you.' The implication is that she didn't have much choice and had to settle for Roy because there were no better offers. Widespread strikes were occurring, and the Chifley government (whose left-leaning policies were anathema to the conservative Cragos) seemed unable to control them. Beth acted as if the striking workers had deliberately chosen to go out in order to spoil her wedding – her extreme sensitivity resembling the egocentricity of a very young child. With less than three days' warning, the caterers cancelled the reservation that had been made for the wedding breakfast. Cherie, the youngest sister, stepped in to help, and all the food was prepared in Yass. Gwyn, the eldest, offered to drive everything to Sydney, and did so. But, in the words of the Yass newspaper,

> Now a wedding wouldn't be a wedding if something didn't go wrong at the last moment – and so it did in this case. A bottle of tomato savoury was found to be missing, and although a most careful search was made, it could not be found.[1] It was thought to have been lost on the road, but when the bride's brother returned home after the wedding, lo and behold this very choice savoury filling was found in the refrigerator. In the hurry and scurry of despatching the food, it had been overlooked.

The newspaper reporter called the item 'Love Will Find A Way', and the message was that Beth's reception had managed to be a success despite the strikes and disruptions, thanks to the loyalty and hard work of her family. But the inclusion of the lost bottle of tomato savoury is significant. Something had been left out. Something intended to give relish to plain food. Are we being told that Beth went into her marriage lacking a key ingredient? Beth's siblings would have laughed scornfully at such a far-fetched interpretation. But why on earth include such a tiny, trivial detail, if the telling of the tale were not being organised unconsciously by an awareness that something vital was missing?

All I know for sure about Roy and Beth's marriage is that no children were conceived, and that as far back as their adopted son Graham could remember, his parents had slept in separate beds – as indeed Beth's own parents did (presumably because it was a form of contraception) as far back as Ted could remember. After seven years of marriage, Roy and Beth adopted a girl and a boy through a church agency. Beth found the experience of motherhood sorely trying, to the extent of demanding that her adopted daughter be 'sent back' (which of course was not an option). Even normal child behaviour would have seemed overwhelming and uncontrollable to Beth, whose anxieties rose sky-high on the slightest provocation. Her strong reactions were not confined to her children.

To her, as to her father before her, visitors to the home were experienced almost as an invasion – a violation of the small, private space in which she felt secure. As an adult, she would speak to visitors through a locked screen door, and she refused to allow her children to invite their friends to her house. To highly anxious people, staying within boundaries means safety. The crossing of boundaries is fraught with risk, and brings with it heightened fears and (often) odd behaviours. When relatives arrived at her door, Beth was capable of telling them 'You can come in, but you'll have to get your own tea – there isn't any food in the house!' When her adult children sent her presents, she was known to send them back, explaining 'We've got too much junk in the house already – we don't need any more!' Beth seems to have modelled herself on her father Albert's tendency to paranoia and, like him, was deeply suspicious of Catholics, unionists and 'people who work for the government' (that is, public servants, whom Beth regarded as lazy). In the 1960s she formed the idea that a 'conspiracy of young people' sought to destroy the institutions and values she held dear.

In families like my father's, sex was not talked about at all, or only very obliquely. So it is impossible to know for sure what happened with Beth and Roy; we can only speculate. Either Beth and Roy's marriage was never consummated (because Beth was paralysed with fear of the physical act) – or there was a sexual relationship at first, but Beth found it distasteful and repulsive. A gentle man, Roy would not have wanted to force himself on her in the face of her terror. To both of them, perhaps, that would have felt like a rape. With some professional help, and much patience on Maureen's part, I was eventually able to overcome my own sexual inhibitions, and to function normally thereafter. No such options were available to Beth and Roy, in a family context where Beth, at least, would have found talking about her anxieties, even to close relatives, utterly impossible. Those anxieties may even have included the acknowledgment that she felt no physical desire for Roy or any other man, something she would (I imagine) never have dared to disclose to anyone.

In fact, frankness about sex was increasing in the 1930s and 1940s, when Beth was a young adult. Van der Velde's *Ideal Marriage: Its Physiology and Technique* had been published in 1926, and went through forty-two reprintings thereafter. It openly talked of shared sexual pleasure and was explicit about how this could be achieved. I can remember my own father recommending it to me before my own marriage as a good book to read – and I also remember that, with a mulish determination not to be advised by anybody, I refused to do so. I might have managed far better if I had! It is not hard to imagine Beth similarly rejecting any attempt by a well-meaning relative to help her to see the sexual side of marriage as something potentially enjoyable. But of course, Beth's attitudes to sex and attractiveness had been formed from early in her life by the teachings of Methodism's founder, John Wesley, whose feelings about the union of man and woman were profoundly ambivalent. Her genetic anxiety had been powerfully reinforced by Methodist teachings.

Beth and Roy remained together until his death, and their adopted children remember him as a caring, affectionate father. But the couple's lives were ruled by the stern dictates of Beth's inner terrors, which led her at times to extreme rudeness, savage judgements and punitive actions. Those actions simply mirrored her own self-loathing. It was only her Christian faith that kept in check both her self-hate and her judgemental attitudes to others. From time to time, she would feel remorse and try to make amends, but it did not last, and she seems always to have reverted to fear. My mother, who had met Beth on only a few occasions, believed her husband's sister was 'mad'. It would never have occurred to her that Beth's extreme introversion, fear of strangers and hermit-like existence strongly resembled those of her own mother, Eva Sanders, because Eva would 'talk and laugh like anything' when surrounded by her own relatives.

1751

All his adult life, John Wesley had had a powerful attraction for women – and felt powerfully attracted to several of them himself. His struggles with the 'lusts of the flesh' are well documented; his long celibacy was a matter of conviction (and self-doubt) rather than something he lived easily with. On several occasions, he had almost decided to marry a woman for whom he felt deeply, but held back. The first occasion was the relationship with Sophy Hopkey in Georgia, in 1736 (see chapter 6). The second had been his almost-marriage to Grace Murray, a devoted follower who by nearly everyone's estimation would have been a soulmate for John and an ideal partner in his life work. Finally, in 1951, when he was forty-eight years old, John made up his mind to marry Mary (Molly) Vazeille, a widow of Huguenot descent, past childbearing age, with whom he had only recently become acquainted. He must, one might imagine, have been desperate.

Having often maintained that his own celibacy was necessary for his mission, John now had to retract his stance and justify his decision. Few of his friends and relatives were convinced by his arguments and his brother Charles (who had previously opposed his brother's intention to marry Grace) was implacably hostile. Mary hated Charles, resenting his closeness to John, and he, no doubt, felt that Mary had 'wanted John all to herself'. John married Mary in virtual secrecy and, astoundingly, made no reference to the occasion in his private journal. Unsurprisingly, perhaps, the couple's relationship soon deteriorated, with John acting towards his wife in a controlling fashion, and Mary becoming pathologically jealous of her husband's close relationships with female adherents.

What We Need to Know

Opposites attract

Had I been asked in 1969 what attracted me to Maureen, I would have said that I felt able to be myself with her. I felt accepted. Safe (as a word to describe a relationship) was not then in my vocabulary, but it is the correct word for what I felt then. I had picked someone who seemed compatible, who shared many of my interests, and who (I sensed) would put my needs ahead of her own. Like my father (as I later discovered), I had not been passionately in love when I married, but I felt affection, care and delight in Maureen's company. I had made a choice more reminiscent of the semi-arranged marriages of two of my father's sisters than of the impulsive love match of my mother's parents, Eva and Victor. Yet I, like Victor, was years younger than my bride; like Victor, I would often act like an irresponsible child; and like Victor, I would often experience my wife as a disapproving, critical parent, whom I would then resent for raining on my parade.

In Maureen, I had also chosen someone who bore a considerable resemblance to my father. Maureen rarely showed the depth of her feelings; like my father, she was disciplined and organised in almost everything she did; like him, she preferred solving problems to talking at length about them. Maureen was governed by strong ties of loyalty and obligation, and had difficulty in asserting her own needs when confronted with a panicky, controlling partner – exactly as Dad had.

Although I had little knowledge of my father's brothers and sisters then, Maureen also resembled the Crago personality generally. In particular, she resembled Cherie: shy, yet determined; capable, yet self-effacing, willing to subject herself to another's will, probably because at a deep level she doubted her own worth. Cherie had been my father's favourite sister, and he her adored big brother. And so, as with my paternal grandparents Albert and Ethel, my maternal grandparents Victor and Eva, and so many others in the extended family, my marriage brought together the expressive, irresponsible Cavalier (slow to grow up, impulsive and selfish) and the inhibited, over-responsible Roundhead (prematurely adult, wary, planful and self-abnegating). The dynamics of our marriage reproduced the dynamics which, I discovered much later, typified my extended family on both sides. We coped better than some, and worse than others: such marriages endure and (sometimes) mature, if at least one of the partners is patient enough (or unconfident enough) to wait until the other grows up emotionally. Maureen had to wait a very long time for me to do so.

Truth to tell, few marriages are really made in heaven and few are entirely free of sadness and resentment. Even those who start off passionately in love usually find that their idyll does not last more than a few years. A comfortable coexistence between two people with common interests and values, based on compromise and mutual respect, has a longer shelf life than most 'romantic' unions, and that has been true in the case of my own marriage.

Fault lines in families

Many of the marriages in both my mother's and my father's family were not particularly happy, and quite a few of them were deeply troubled.[2] In this, my family was in no way unusual. But I want to draw attention to the pattern that I followed without any consciousness of it, a pattern that goes back several generations on both sides. In the cameo of the 'little wedding', the seeds of later trouble are clearly visible.

Families tend to fracture along predictable fault lines, and the two most predictable occur in connection with funerals and weddings. Funerals involve someone leaving the family permanently, through death. Weddings also involve someone leaving (a grown-up son or daughter), while simultaneously, someone (their partner) is joining the family. At weddings and funerals, emotions run high, and things are said which cause offence – aided, in the case of most weddings (and wakes) by the amount of alcohol consumed, but the absence of alcohol does not prevent hurtful exchanges. At weddings, hope soars (at least for the couple) and any reference to the realities of married life is seen as inappropriate. Grief is also present, especially in the parents of the partners, but by social convention, that grief cannot be expressed openly. Aggressive feelings may be expressed towards the new member of the family, cloaked in humour. Alternatively, parents may feel that their daughter or son has 'betrayed' them by choosing so unsuitable a spouse. That spouse may openly display qualities that parents fail to recognise (because they are less openly displayed) in their own son or daughter.

Neither family is prepared to have its young adult offspring 'taken over' by their chosen partners. Disapproval and dislike are expressed visibly through the absence of one or even both families (or significant family members) from the ceremony – as in 'The Sleeping Beauty', where the wicked fairy who was not invited to the wedding curses the happy couple and the wedding guests. The in-law problem stems from this conviction that love cannot be shared: our children belong to us, not to anyone else; their leaving of our family for another seems a repudiation of this belonging. The parents (and siblings) who feel most strongly that love cannot be shared are typically those with the most fragile sense of self-worth.

People who feel secure in the knowledge that others love them and care about them can usually allow their children to form attachments to other people, without feeling rejected themselves. They know they have done their best, and that it is now time to trust their children's judgement. Love can be shared if you have had plenty of it. But if you have not had enough love, if you secretly worry that you have in fact failed your children while outwardly claiming that they have failed you, then you will resent – even hate – the people your children seek out and marry. Curses (as in the fairy tale) attempt to take away happiness from others, and in real life, we curse others when we ourselves feel we have missed out.

La Belle Alliance

My mother's view of Ethel Crago as wanting Ian all to herself betrays the reality that families can generate emotional battlefields as bloody as any national or ethnic struggle for dominance. Time after time, when two families come temporarily together for the marriage of their respective offspring, such power-struggles play out, sometimes loudly and publicly, sometimes tacitly, in whispers and rolled eyes. Family bonds are enormously strong, and families don't let go of them easily, sometimes punishing their own 'disloyal' relative, more often waging a war of attrition with the spouse, a war that may continue for twenty years or more after the marriage. In this war, the affine (the person who has joined the family through marriage) is criticised or joked about behind her/his back, and routinely blamed for anything that goes wrong in the relationship. The radioactive half-life of such contested marriages can last a lifetime. Family members who have faced down family disapproval at their own wedding may subsequently weaken in the face of such strong feelings, and their spouse, in turn, then feels undermined: 'You care more about your family than you care about me!'

Because families can exert such powerful influence over their members, any family member who is able to rise above the jealousy and possessiveness of the rest marks him or herself out as emotionally more mature than they are, able to see both sides and unwilling to blame one and defend the other. In my father's family, this person was Dad's next-older brother, Ted. Ted had already seen the eldest brother, Dick, marry a woman (May) of whom his mother and sisters disapproved. When it came to Ian's turn to choose a bride, Ted could see the same pattern occurring again, and took a stand against it. To do this meant risking his mother's displeasure, and stepping aside from his sisters' unthinking antagonism to Gwen. But Ted was able to avoid taking sides, and it seems he was forgiven for it – probably because he spoke tactfully and did not take it personally when others in the family told him off for his stance. His easy-going genetic temperament, in a family of sensitive, reactive, anxious individuals, no doubt contributed to his ability to stay neutral in their conflicts, as he had done when, unlike both Dick and Ian, he was able to see that his father's roaring was just his way of expressing himself, and not let it deter him from asking Father for something all the others wanted, but were afraid to ask.

A funny thing…

My father, like many people of his era, used to distinguish between funny ha-ha (amusing) and funny peculiar (odd, inexplicable). The fact that I was born in the same year that Beth and Roy were married, and then went on to experience sexual dysfunction in the early years of my own marriage, is of course just a coincidence. Yet such coincidences keep occurring, not just in my own family, but in many families, so often, in fact, that it is tempting to regard them as meaning something. Perhaps it is also significant that, of the three Crago sisters, Beth was the most strongly opposed to my mother, and my mother felt equally antipathetic towards Beth. Such antipathies generally indicate that each person sees in the other things that remind them uncomfortably of parts of themselves – the same process that led me to dislike 'Little Red Monkey' and 'When Fear Came'.

When I was around six or so, it seems that my mother told Beth that of all her three children, 'Hugh is the one who most reminds me of myself.' Beth's response to this was to be deeply distrustful of me thereafter. In fact, she hardly knew me (possibly a couple of visits that I was too young to remember), but she was sure that I must have become a dangerous atheist, like my mother. When at last (at a family funeral in 1988, I (now an adult in my early forties) was in the same room as her, she deliberately crossed the room to avoid having to talk to me.

Did I, under the influence of my own anxiety in 1969–1970, temporarily 'become' Beth? Who knows? But certainly it was a case of funny peculiar.

5

Authenticity and Innovation

In My Time

'Don't Know Who I'm Gonna Be' (Wagga Wagga, 1972–1979)

The 60s didn't come to an abrupt end in December 1969. For many people, including me, much of the 70s was a continuation of the 60s. Only now, I felt in a position to do something to promote what some of us, in our cloudy way, still thought of as 'the revolution'. I was twenty-five when we returned from Oxford – an apprentice adult if ever there was one. I had been offered a lectureship at the College of Advanced Education that had replaced Wagga Wagga Teacher's College, in south-western NSW. At one time I had dreamed of a university position in Britain or Europe, but I never applied for one. I believed I was not gifted enough. More likely, I was not confident enough.

A not-quite-university in the hot, flat country of the western plains was not what I had planned for myself, but a job at a brand-new institution, its courses still being set up, offered me the chance to act out on a real world stage the educational ideas and practices – John Holt, Carl Rogers, open classrooms, Summerhill – that I had read about. Staid, conservative Wagga, a country town of around 50,000 people, might seem like no place for a street fighting man, and I was no street fighting man anyway. But for the next seven years I operated on a vague, semi-conscious image of myself as engaged in some heroic struggle with the forces of convention and repression. I saw myself as a rebel, a pioneer of change. As with my high school fears of violation, these fantasies bore little resemblance to the reality of my day-to-day existence, but they shaped my conduct anyway.

On the voyage back from England in 1972, Maureen and I had read a persuasive and intelligent book called *Animals, Men and Morals*, and decided we must be vegetarians from that time on. We also decided that to live without a car was the responsible thing to do. Pollution from motor vehicles was starting to drown our planet – quite apart from the fact that cars posed a real risk to life. These decisions, taken with a sense of pride and moral rectitude, would prove to be damaging to us in more ways than one, and our families could not understand them. We might just as well have joined the Communist Party or started practising transcendental meditation. Having felt different all my life, I now chose to be even more different. At twenty-six, I surrendered the remnants of my Christian faith – I had felt like a hypocrite in claiming to be a believer. It felt more honest, more authentic, to adopt what Christians at the time called secular humanism – a wish to do good, and to be a good person, but without these things being tied to a belief in God.

For me, the early 1970s were a period of experiment in which I searched restlessly for who I was going to be. It seemed that almost every day would bring a new idea, a new set of possibilities to try. I didn't know the clinical term then, but I can see now that I was hypomanic, living in a state of mild elevation and able to push away any thought that might interfere with that state. Frequent cups of coffee, which I had become fond of at university, fuelled this not-quite-manic state, keeping me energised and excited, but also uncentred and irritable. When Maureen, or someone else who mattered to me, got angry and confronted me with my failings, I felt shame and remorse for a day or two, and then simply went back to feeling fine about myself. I remembered that I'd felt bad, but the memory was shallow. It failed to teach me anything.

Like many academics at the time, I adopted the uniform of dissident young people. I stopped wearing a tie and went to work in jeans. I grew my hair longer and a straggly beard as well. I didn't often get around to mowing the lawn (I used a hand mower for ecological reasons) and the fringe of long grass waving around our little house became a metaphor for the state of my inner world – untidy, unruly and, ultimately, unsatisfying. I had become the same sort of headstrong, unthinking young adult as (I later realised) my mother had been at the same age, and like her I was convinced I was right, and that those who opposed me were ignorant and stupid.

I was supposed to be teaching English literature, yet increasingly, teaching literature seemed a contradiction in terms. Great novels, poems and plays offered powerful experiences, but once you started dissecting and evaluating them, they lost most of their power. 'Teaching' them did not work, I concluded; it was not *authentic*. Most of my efforts went into a new and vaguely defined subject called Communication. Much influenced by reading a book called *What's the Use of Lectures*, I was convinced I ought to allow my students to discover important principles for themselves, without my interference. I believed that if I gave them freedom to pursue their own interests, they would learn more. By doing things and reflecting on their own experiences instead of merely learning about what others had done, they would, I believed, learn more profoundly and lastingly. I had read about encounter groups in the US and about group learning in British primary schools, and with the arrogance of youth, believed that I could provide such experiences without any specific training. I knew that groups offered something very significant, but I did not have the knowledge or the skills to unlock their potential.

The communication experiment lasted seven years. I learned a lot, but the majority of my students did not. I believed I was doing it for them, but I was really giving *myself* experiences and replicating my own ill-disciplined enthusiasms. The many disappointed, frustrated and disaffected students who went through my groups testified to that – thirty years after, at a college reunion, and they were still angry and puzzled. Eventually, I was summarily instructed by my superiors to cease teaching communication altogether and return to lecturing in literature. I had become the naughty boy I'd never been at school. My adolescent rebellion had finally happened, only ten years later than normal. Physically, I'd matured late, and now it seemed that I lagged in other ways too.

I knew I wanted to be a teacher, yet I had nothing to teach. I wanted to write, but the only thing I knew how to do was to write academic articles about literature, and I began to do so. I started many more pieces than I finished, and my files bulged with half-completed papers on a wide range of topics. I would start writing with excitement and purpose, sustained by fantasies of reaching a wide audience (in fact, most academic publications only ever reach a tiny audience). But as soon as I hit a difficulty, I would grind to a halt. I believed that writing should be easy and gratifying. I did not have the self-discipline to work through the block, or the capacity to surrender to my own process and allow the writing itself to show me what the article was about, and how it needed to develop. As with teaching, I was aware of a potential, a space within me that needed to be filled, but I had nothing to fill it with. Later, I would realise that this is part of young adulthood for many of us: in our twenties, we don't know who we're going to be. But life, as Joni Mitchell observed in her haunting song 'Woodstock', was for learning.

From the age of thirty, I began moving towards counselling and therapy, but there too I thought I could leap ahead of myself and master a complex craft without first paying my dues. Maureen and I commenced training as marriage counsellors in 1976, and I discovered all kinds of things about myself – though not the things I most needed to discover. I found I had natural empathy, that others could trust me – even people who I would never have imagined I had much in common with. It was heady stuff. But, just as with my teaching groups, I did not know where to go next. I was still in thrall to the fallacy with which so many counsellors begin their careers – that it was my job to figure out what had caused the problem and to somehow 'make' people change. I got ahead of my clients, anxiously imposing on them my own need to seem wise and skilled. And so most of my clients did not come back after the first session. I was as impatient with them as I was with my failed pieces of writing. What I did realise, though, was that I wanted to be a counsellor, not an academic (even a radical one). Counselling seemed to offer the authenticity that teaching had not offered. I was working with real problems, with human beings in pain. As a counsellor, I could make a difference.

Both of us agreed that we would do more training. Maureen sensibly argued that we could find a course in Australia, that maybe I could keep my job at the college too, and we could complete our training part time – after all, we now had two children. But, as sure of my rightness as ever, I insisted that to find a really satisfying course, one that conformed to my belief in radical education, we had to go overseas. In New Hampshire, I believed, I had found just that course. I would shake the hot dust of Wagga from my feet, we would go to the cold north of the world, and we would learn what we needed to know. I was thirty-two.

In Family Time

1972–75

Just as I was starting my career at the college in Wagga, another academic career was coming towards its end at a college in Newcastle. My Uncle Ted had been among the first students at Sydney University to complete an Honours degree in geography under Griffith Taylor, the foundation professor of that subject. Griff Taylor had been inspirational for Ted, and Ted remembered many details about him. By now, Ted had been teaching geography to trainee teachers for many years. He'd been 'doing a bit of reading', and he'd come across some stuff on student-centred learning that he'd quite liked the sound of, so he went off to Florida to see it in action. On his return, he instituted a very different program for his students. It ran for only a few years, and after Ted retired, a few months short of his sixty-fifth birthday, the Crago plan (as it became known) was abandoned. But for those few years, his students had been free to research and prepare assignments on any aspect of geography that appealed to them. Instead of lecturing in the conventional manner, Ted sat at the front of the room and waited for students to come to him with questions or problems. 'My colleagues thought I was on a pretty easy wicket!' he laughed later. Yet the project left a deep impression on the students who had been part of it. Years afterwards, some of them told Ted, 'You know, we still call ourselves "the Crago kids"!'

Griffith Taylor had come to Australia in 1893, at the age of thirteen. Like Ted, he came from a dissenting, teetotal family, and his parents lived (much like Ted's) on a ten-acre mini-farm near Adderton. The patronage of the eminent Edgeworth David enabled the young Taylor to become a member of the scientific party that accompanied Scott's Antarctic expedition, and Edgeworth David seems to have had much the same inspirational effect on Taylor as Taylor himself would later have on Ted Crago. When Taylor was appointed to the staff of Sydney University, he had to fight hard for geography, which was seen as a new-fangled subject of questionable academic substance. He did not help his cause by willingly embroiling himself in public controversy (like Ted, who was prepared to speak out when others preferred to remain silent). He argued, realistically, that the desert heartland of Australia could not readily be transformed into 'a million farms' to support ex-servicemen – a popular vision at the time. His willingness to shatter comforting illusions like that one (via letters to the *Herald*) earned him a reputation as a traitor to his country, and partly because of this, Taylor retreated to a position in the US in 1928, bitter that his ideas were better received elsewhere than in his own adopted nation. Ted shared Taylor's laconic humour, and both of them argued against retaining Latin as a compulsory subject for matriculation. There were more than a few reasons why Griff Taylor was so important to Ted.

Of course, Ted had been influenced by the same radical turn in education that had influenced me. I knew nothing of this until many years later, when long-retired Ted told me about it himself. In the early 1970s, it would never have occurred to me that any member of my father's family might have been doing something similar to what I was trying to achieve at Wagga. Had I known then that Uncle Ted and I were on a similar path, I might have absorbed some of his wisdom, and run into fewer troubles with my superiors. Ted had been the family diplomat, and had carried this role into his entire teaching career. Everyone respected him, and he was able to persuade others to try things without creating antagonism. Indeed, his quiet, steady presence was very close to that of a counsellor – only I did not see that then.

I had not thought to keep up contact with Ted's family once I was adult myself. Like my mother, I had placed little value on family relationships. I had dismissed my father's relatives, as she had, judging them to be conservative country people with puritan values, and certainly nothing to offer that we could learn from. Perhaps the only reason I eventually found out about Ted's innovations was that my parents had taken us on those childhood visits to his home in Newcastle every year. Ted had remained, for me, a safe person in the Crago family, just as he had been for my parents following their marriage. When, eventually, I realised I needed to know more about the family into which I'd been born, I felt confident to ask Ted. And so, in my late thirties, when my days as an educational reformer were well in the past, I finally found out about his.

1934–1942

Though not as radical as his older brother, my father, too, had been an innovator in his twenties. Smarter and more creative than the average classroom teacher, and having successfully taught children with learning difficulties, Dad had been assigned the opportunity class at Artarmon Primary School between 1939 and 1942. Given this chance to stretch academically gifted kids, he had met the challenge with flying colours. He'd had his class construct a scale model of a medieval English manor, he learned to play the flute and set up a student flute band, he bought a small hand-operated printing press and showed his students how to set type. He bought a colour wheel, and taught them about complementary colours. Dad was good with his hands (in another age, he might well have been an artisan), and he passed on his own high standards to the children. He played them records of classical music and showed them what to listen for. In arithmetic, he took the time and trouble to work out exactly what mistake an individual child persistently made, so that the child could learn to do it differently. There were little science experiments from *Living Things for Lively Youngsters*. He read aloud to his class John Ruskin's long, sombre fairytale *The King of the Golden River*, pointing out to them the power of well-chosen words. His pupils loved him, and afterwards, when he was promoted to school counsellor and then to inspector of schools, he always said that he missed the classroom. He resented some of his superiors at times, and deplored the average teacher's lack of vision and self-serving attitude to the job. But unlike me, Dad had kept most of his feelings inside. *If you can't say something nice, don't say anything.*

My mother, too, had been an outstanding classroom teacher. With characteristic bluntness, she said later that she had probably enjoyed being a teacher 'because of the power it gave you', but I know there was more to it than that. If Mum put her hand to something, she was determined to succeed in it, and teaching was no exception. Not as inventive or wide-ranging in her interests as my father, she nevertheless did some innovating of her own. She taught her pupils how to write poetry (metres, rhyme schemes and all), rightly perceiving that by doing it themselves they would develop more appreciation of the poet's craft. She was an effective and popular teacher. Yet she was stunned to hear, when she attended a reunion of her class towards the end of her life, that her long-ago students had admired her and thought her good-looking. She could not quite believe that they meant it. Perhaps she did not trust that she was worthy of anyone's love?

Both my parents were embarking on their teaching careers at a time of radical change and experiment in education. John Dewey's and Rudolph Steiner's ideas had reached Australia. The notion that learning should be fun, personal and experiential had taken hold. Overseas, the early years of schooling were being revolutionised. In America, it was the time of the *Here and Now Story Book*, the time when teachers began to realise that preschool children's play was not just idle amusement, but a powerful way of learning.

May Lepper, who married my father's oldest brother Dick in 1930, had trained at Sydney Kindergarten Teacher's College. Many years later, she spoke of her excitement at 'going out into all those congested areas' – by which she meant bringing the fun and freedom of kindergarten to Sydney's slum children. For her, it had been a crusade, a form of social activism. After their marriage, May and Dick bought a historic house in Bowral, distant in every sense from the congested areas of Sydney's inner west where May had taught. In her new home, May discovered the gardening principles of expatriate Englishwoman Edna Walling, and embodied them in the sloping hillside garden which surrounded the couple's home in Bowral. Walling gardens were ahead of their time – artful blendings of natural and artificial, of native plants and northern hemisphere imports. May's commitment to her garden was as fierce as any farmer's to his land; she worked long and hard, year after year, to create something that would measure up to her own ideals. Her attitude to her weaving was equally serious. Dick's sisters, who judged May an arty, self-indulgent woman 'with her head in the air', did not see how her attitude to the garden paralleled the relentless work schedule their own father Albert had followed lifelong.

May attended church with Dick each Sunday, but would 'bowl up to the minister afterwards and deliver a critique of his sermon', which Dick found deeply embarrassing. May was always interested in novel and marginal philosophies, particularly spiritual ones, and welcomed into her home Christian Scientists, Theosophists and even ex-Communists. These rebels and intellectual fringe-dwellers must have appealed to her sense of herself as a rebel and a seeker after truth. May's ideas on education strongly influenced her older son, John, who as an adult went on to send both his daughters to Steiner schools so that they would be free to pursue their own talents and not be forced to study a non-negotiable academic curriculum.

In May's pursuit of interesting people and new philosophies, I can see now a wish for *authenticity* – for a lessening of the gap between institutionalised religion and her private quest for meaning, for a faith she could wholeheartedly embrace.

As well as a doctrinal innovator, John Wesley had been an educational innovator. Disgusted with the half-hearted practice of Christianity that was common in the established church of his time, he introduced his fellow students at Oxford to the methodical habits of study and prayer which he had learned in childhood from his intelligent, assertive mother, Susanna. His method would later give a name to the evangelical movement he founded. Wesley even evolved a version of what we would now call experiential group learning – small 'cell groups' that met in college rooms to discuss questions of faith and doctrine with honesty and self-disclosure. Of course these things were a world away from the secular educational experiments that I had engaged in at Wagga, but they, too, constituted a search for authenticity, for a spiritual practice that would inspire emotion as well as simply impart dogma. John was duly ordained but, almost from the beginning, determined to carry out his priestly duties differently.

In his thirties, Wesley was responsible for more innovations – instead of accepting a parish, he decided to preach on a much wider scale, travelling from place to place and preaching wherever he found an audience willing to listen to him. His choice was reinforced when more and more churches refused to allow him to preach from the pulpit. John kept up this itinerant ministry well into old age, reading while he slowly rode his horse from one town to another (later, he had a coach fitted with shelves and a desk, so that he could still work while on the road). He devised novel methods of organising his followers, and novel ways of ensuring that new converts were cared for and watched over. His entire enterprise was designed to breathe new life into the staid, complacent Anglican church of the time, to make faith a living thing – authenticity.

At a time when British roast beef was the linchpin of the English diet, and vegetarianism almost unknown, Wesley opted not to eat meat very early in his ministry, long before he became an itinerant preacher or broke with the established church. He seems to have done so, initially, for reasons of concern for the suffering of animals, birds and fish, stating that the eating of flesh was at odds with the vision of Isaiah's vision of the Peaceable Kingdom (in which all creatures lived without fear). He returned to eating meat two years later, but then abstained again, this time for good, on the advice of his physician. He claimed that his health was permanently influenced for the better as a result, and advocated vegetarianism for health reasons thereafter, rather than for moral reasons, recognising that his position had upset many of his followers. At a time when drinking alcohol was universal, and the poor were being decimated by cheap gin, Wesley abandoned strong drink altogether, although for a long time he was addicted to tea.

Wesley never faltered in his conviction that he had been born to accomplish great things for Christianity. His work – as itinerant preacher, as organiser of his followers, as prolific writer on doctrinal matters – always took centre stage in his life, and relationships had to wait in the wings.

What We Need to Know

Opposites attract: conservatism marries innovation

In Dick (conservative local pharmacist) and May (freethinking ex-teacher and craftswoman), we can discern one variant of the pattern of pairings in my father's family: one conformed, the other rebelled; one accepted, the other questioned; one was dutiful and routine-governed, the other impulsive and spontaneous. In Dick and May's case, the partnership was not unsuccessful. Despite their differences, the couple shared key common interests – May enthusiastically supported Dick in promoting Scouting in their chosen township, Bowral, and acted as Bagheera for the local Cub pack (her granddaughters knew her as Bargie because (like Eva Sanders) May could not stand the idea of being called Grandma or any other name that announced her status as a grandparent). Dick himself had been one of the first in Yass to join the Scouts, Baden-Powell's exciting new youth movement, and in founding the first Bowral troop, Dick declared himself an innovator too. Dick may have been conservative in many respects, but he married radicalism. He was a believer, but he married doubt. He was pragmatic, but he married aesthetics. He was generally satisfied with what he knew, but he married a restless quest for something more.

What's in a name

Just as May's granddaughters knew her as 'Bargie', so I and my siblings knew my maternal grandmother as 'Evie'. I believed then that we had chosen this name for her ourselves, but I wonder now how true that was. There are other examples of grandparents in the family avoiding role-specific names like 'Grandma' or 'Grandfather': my father's older sister Gwyn was 'Mother Bird' to her grandchildren, and my own mother initially asked to be 'Gwen' or (a compromise) 'Grandmother Gwen' to my own children, although she eventually accepted 'Grandmother'. I know that in her case this was because 'Grandmother' made her feel 'old', which she did not like. I felt a similar resistance to a role-specific name like 'Grandpa' when I eventually became a grandparent myself.

At the root of it, I think, is resistance to having one's individual identity 'swallowed up' in something or someone else – as in my father's dislike of being called 'Albert' and my own loathing of being called 'Crago' rather than 'Hugh'. Maybe all of us wanted in some way to hold onto our 'specialness', our individuality, in the face of a new 'name' that merges us with something or someone who was 'not us'?

Social revolutions co-opt youth

In just five years between twenty-three and twenty-six, I had embraced socialism, student-centred learning, vegetarianism and group therapy. Simultaneously, I had abandoned car ownership, Christianity and teaching English literature. Like many young adults, I believed so passionately in my causes that I refused to compromise and so, like many others within my father's family, cut off my nose to spite my face. In my choices, I was more influenced by the social currents of the times (the late 1960s and early to mid-1970s) than most members of my father's family, but several of them had also innovated and broken with tradition – they had simply done it in different ways.

Youth fuels social idealism and drives social revolutions. Boundless energy and optimism, combined with a sense of invulnerability and immortality ('nothing can harm me, I can live forever'), makes young adults the most persistent and devoted of revolutionaries. They don't dream it – they do it. Youthful energy propels them into a search for authenticity – for a way of life that enables them to be who they really are for the first time in their lives, to live their dream of autonomy, of creativity, of professional competence, of social confidence. A big part of this drive has to do with gaining a sense of themselves as individuals separate from their families.

To understand family patterns, we need to compare like with like, and we need to see individuals in the context of their own place and time. What seems like conservatism to us may have been radical in the time of our grandparents, or even our parents. What seems surprising and different to us can seem predictable if we know enough about the time in which it occurred. I never thought of Uncle Dick as an innovator, because he spent nearly the whole of his whole adult life living in one small town and working at the same job – I was judging his career by the standards of a later era, when changes of occupation were becoming increasingly frequent. I did not think of Scouting as an exciting new youth movement because I was thinking of Scouting as it had been in the 1950s, when I was a boy, not as it had been in the first quarter of the twentieth century, when Dick was growing up. And because May was my relative only by marriage, I did not think of her as bringing innovation and authenticity into the family – let alone bringing those things *back* into the family (after all, only two generations earlier, Albert's father Petherick Crago had been the first of his family to emigrate and to build a successful career in a strange country).

Similarly, when I eventually came to know my Aunt Cherie's

farmer husband Bob Adams, I realised that here was another in-law who had in his own way been an innovator, whose local community saw him as eccentric because he insisted on ploughing in his stubble at a time when others customarily burnt it off. 'Adams has the best crop, but I don't advise you to follow his methods!' joked one of his contemporaries in a half-admiring, half-aggressive way.

Innovation and gender

Among my father's siblings, it was the boys (Dick, Ted and Ian) who appear as the obvious innovators. The girls, once they married, did not return to their careers – which of course was the norm for most women in the first half of the twentieth century. My mother was an exception, though she was not permitted by the Education Department to return to teaching nearly as early as she wanted to. Louisa Lawson was also an exception. It demanded persistence, self-confidence and courage for women to pursue careers – and Louisa had to create hers, for nobody would ever have offered her a job editing a magazine for women: she had to invent that magazine, and self-publish it. It is short-sighted and lacking in empathy to accuse the parents of the 1920s of being sexist or patriarchal when such concepts were confined, at the time, to a tiny minority of radical feminists.

But there is more to it than historical relativity. My father's mother, Ethel Crago, invested emotionally in her sons rather than her daughters. She 'took over' Dick and Ian (as my mother would have said) and made them into her creatures, as unquestionably loyal as if she had been their feudal overlord. They would fulfil for her the dreams she herself had felt unable to follow. Her investment in her daughters was much less total. Her own choice in young adulthood had been marriage and children – even though she possessed a talent that could have enabled her to pursue a professional career (see chapter 8). How easy would it have been for her to encourage her daughters to deviate from the hard choice she herself had made? Instead, she was relieved and pleased when Beth and Cherie eventually got married, and did as much as she could to help them to that end. But both these younger daughters were also socially anxious and unconfident – unlike Ethel herself. She worried about them, rather than celebrating their achievements.

Gwyn, the eldest of the three girls, was different. She was not obviously fearful or over-sensitive – yet instead of her temperament winning Ethel's approval, the two of them clashed. Deprived of the opportunity to shelter and protect Gwyn in the way she sheltered and protected Beth and Cherie, Ethel seems to have experienced her eldest daughter as a rebel and a rival, rather than a protégé. And Gwyn's closeness to her father, Albert, would have cemented that impression. Significantly, when it came time for Gwyn to plan her adult life, she planned it with a friend rather than with her mother.

Gwyn never doubted that she wanted to be a nurse, and she and her friend Furner Baker had chosen this career for themselves while still at high school. No academic achiever then, Gwyn shone once she started her nursing training, ending as a triple-certificated nurse, the highest level of qualification the profession could then offer. For Gwyn, the years of nursing in Sydney were (her son Peter thought) the high point of her life. She enjoyed her work, she enjoyed exploring Sydney, she had lots of fun with her friends, and she felt confident and competent. 'She could always find her way around,' said Peter, his words implying more than Gwyn's good sense of direction.

As a young adult, Beth's fears dominated her attempts at a career. Trained initially as a school teacher, she was (so my father reported) highly thought of, but she lasted only a short time in that career. The feeling of being on show, the tensions of managing a classroom, the need to adopt an enthusiastic, positive attitude even when she did not feel it – all these are enormously stressful for any person born fearful, sensitive and socially withdrawn. At around the same age as I married Maureen, Beth gave up teaching and retrained as a nurse.

Cherie, who shared a similar genetic temperament to her sister Beth and their father Albert (though she exhibited it less intensely) was able to break new ground in her hitherto sequestered life as a young adult. As the age of twenty, in 1942, Cherie volunteered for war work at the National Standards Laboratory in Sydney. For Cherie, whose entire life had been spent in a small country town, it was a massive venture into the alien world of the big city. She had uncomfortable and even frightening moments, but she coped for thirteen months, and afterwards spoke proudly of the skills she had acquired. Given the chance to work and master the requirements of a job, Cherie shone. But for her, as for both her sisters, marriage marked an end to that young adult adventure, and in 1950 she returned to an existence on a farm, with limited contact with people in the local community and limited chances to travel. Her practical skills and ingenuity would be largely restricted to the world of the homestead and the property.

Difference and dissent

Just as I did, many young adults choose values and ideologies that confirm or intensify their existing genetically-rooted personality traits. Young adult energy and ebullience can temporarily override innate fearfulness, but it rarely lasts. If (like Beth and New Zealand novelist Janet Frame) shy, sensitive young people initially choose careers that escalate their anxiety, they tend to abandon those choices in favour of life structures that offer less intimidating challenges. More often, fearful individuals will, from the beginning, choose jobs and belief systems that will shield them from too much fear.

Young adults may also choose positions that create distance between themselves and their families of origin, especially likely if they have experienced their families as conflictual, or themselves been in conflict with parents and/or siblings. In my father's family, both Gwyn and my father exemplified this pattern. My own choices in my early twenties follow this pattern too. I adopted vegetarianism on our voyage home from England, as if to say, 'Well, now I'll be back closer to my family, but let's make sure that I can keep them at a distance!' Our choice to give up a car (which we made in England before returning to Australia) was very similar. And of course we had chosen to live in Wagga, a day's travel away from my parents, and had to rely on a once-daily train to get us to them, which inevitably created a more distant relationship than would have occurred had we lived in a nearby suburb, a short drive or even a walk away. We imposed this distance from their paternal grandparents on our children, as my mother had imposed distance from my surviving paternal grandparent on me. My mother's younger brother Hughie imposed distance on his children in a much more extreme way, by marrying a Scotswoman and joining the British army at the end of World War Two.

In my early twenties, even before our decision not to own a car, I had avoided learning to drive. Though all of my age peers wanted to drive and soon learned to do so, I never joined them. The thought of being in control of a ton of machinery travelling at high speeds on roads crowded with other vehicles alarmed me, and I doubted that I would be able to cope with it. I must have known that Evie, my mother's mother, had never learned to drive either, but of course I did not think about that in relation to my own avoidance. Much later still, I discovered that my great-uncle Will Crago, elder brother of my grandfather Albert, had also 'failed' this benchmark of autonomous adulthood. He had begun learning but after a minor mishap, had dropped the whole idea of driving (exactly the same thing had happened to me). Of course Will's decision was made in the days when cars were still relatively new and regarded as dangerous, but the pattern of giving up after a single attempt, of being unable to 'get back on the horse' is, to me, a clear sign of a fearful temperament. Of course, Evie was notoriously a shrinking violet, but Uncle Will was seen in my father's family as one of the confident ones. Confident he no doubt was, but this one telling example makes it clear that he shared at least one aspect of the family's genetic heritage. Fear can take many forms.

In many ways, my young adult value choices simply reinvented the customs that had made the early generations of Methodists so different from the mainstream of English (and Australian) society of their day. My choices ensured that I would continue to be regarded by others as weird, or (worse) smug and self-satisfied. Maureen and I took our positions on the issues of our era very seriously. We did without many of the devices and machines that most people relied on to lighten their labour. We wanted to limit our family to two children ('zero population growth' as it was known before the world forgot about overpopulation all over again) and this too would have seemed to most people as ridiculous as the early Methodists' abstention from alcohol.

I was *born* different (genetically), I *felt* different (in part due to Dad's Methodist heritage) and, as a young adult, I consciously adopted positions that would ensure that I would be *regarded* as different lifelong. I did so in a more extreme way than my parents or their siblings, but in a range of ways, they too had made choices which distinguished them from the rest, and displayed their determination to be their own person. For they too were genetically 'different', just as I was.

Spaces and substance

I dropped into teaching easily, almost as if born to it (both of my parents had been teachers, and I had absorbed many aspects of the role from them). Yet although I was good at explaining complicated things in simple language, and although I was patient and caring with my students (despite often being impatient and insensitive in my intimate relationships), I deliberately turned away from doing the very things that made me a born teacher. I did not want to be an authority figure. Though a confident speaker, I refused to lecture. I insisted that my students discover things for themselves (which of course is also a position of authority, even though I did not see that at the time). I can see now that I was denying my likeness to both my parents, insisting to myself that although I was a teacher like them, I wasn't the same kind of teacher; in fact, I wasn't really a teacher at all!

I discovered quite early (while still a senior undergraduate) that I had the capacity to inspire enthusiasm in a community, and to speak out things that others felt but could not voice as openly. I was, in fact, a somewhat charismatic individual, with my mother's (apparent) social confidence and my father's warmth (and, I might add now) my grandfather Victor's 'word of command' and my grandmother Ethel's ability to hold an audience so 'you could hear a pin drop'). Yet in a way very reminiscent of John Wesley, I was suspicious of those very traits and, when temporarily in the limelight, behaved almost as if I were embarrassed by the regard of others, and by the way I seemed to attract would-be followers.

I possessed the capacities and the charisma, but I did not, in my twenties, ever feel that I had the substance. Somehow the charismatic exterior concealed a hollow at the core of my self. At some level, I knew that I could fill the space of a wise man, or even a prophet – and already, some of my students regarded me this way – but my ideologies were too shallow, and my social confidence only a thin veneer over a level of fearfulness and self-doubt which, though less than Beth's or Cherie's, was still quite real. My favourite 60s band, the anarchic Jefferson Airplane, had sung 'I don't know where I'm goin' yet, I don't know who I'm gonna be.' Many young adults have felt very much the same (one might almost say that it goes with the territory). But I was now beginning to have answers to the questions in the song: 'the other side of this life' would unfold soon enough.

6

Loyalty and Betrayal

In My Time

Angel of the Morning (Keene, New Hampshire, 1981)

Music reaches us at a deeper level than words, going straight to the emotional core of our being. Grand opera relies on this. The actual words of many famous arias are corny, even fatuous, but the soaring vocal lines, the emotional colour of the orchestral accompaniment, 'lift us up where we belong'. For me it is just the same with popular songs about love. Provided that there is a good tune, no matter how clichéd the words may be, I have never been able to prevent them from affecting me deeply. Neither my critical faculties nor my resentment of being 'taken over' in this way have ever stopped those clichéd words from sneaking in, under my guard. And the trouble with clichés is that they have a habit of coming true.

When Maureen and I set off for the small town of Keene, New Hampshire, in 1979, our relationship had seemed to me in fairly good shape. We got on well much of the time, and had worked together, not without some fierce disagreements, on a research project that had lasted six years. Our decision to retrain together for a career in counselling was a genuinely shared one. Sexual difficulties were a thing of the past. Criticisms, quarrels and tears were not, but we always seemed to bounce back from them and things went on in their accustomed way. Our relationship was again on an even keel, mainly because she had resigned herself to putting up with my sureness that I was right and my tendency to criticise her when I felt bad in myself. I half-knew (but didn't want to know) that she was more distant than she had once been. I had trampled on her sensitivities too many times for her to experience the unconditional love she had once felt for me. I was not easy to live with – though of course, neither was she. She could be mulishly stubborn, rigid in some of her habits, and sententious at times when I needed her to be loving and accepting. She was (though I never saw it then) a true representative of the less attractive side of Methodism – a bit dour, overly serious, wary of spontaneity and joy. She deeply doubted her own worth, and often found it hard to stand up for her own needs and to express her feelings. Her upbringing by a mother who made no secret of her disappointment at not having 'a pretty little girl with curly hair' to show off to her friends had not helped.

When we left Oxford for Wagga in 1972, I had been twenty-five. When we went to America to study counselling, I was thirty-two. The earlier decision had been propelled as much by fantasy as by reality, and so was this one. Maureen was the voice of reason: were we sure that our foreign qualification would gain us employment when we returned after two years of study? Were there counselling jobs for which we would be eligible to apply? What about our girls, then aged three and seven? How would they cope with a new country, and with both of their parents studying? I was sure that things would work out for us, so sure that I did not take her concerns seriously.

From our first days in the humid New Hampshire summer of 1979, I fell in love with Keene. The dignified red-brick buildings of Keene State College along Main Street, the quiet, shady streets, the Revolutionary War soldier on his pedestal in the square, the small, grey-blue timber building that then housed Antioch New England Graduate School (it has since become Antioch University New England, with a proper campus of its own) even the number plates on the cars, which proclaimed 'Live Free or Die' – everything fed my fantasies about the home of the brave and the land of the free. All around Keene were the wooded hills of southern New Hampshire –

softly green in summer, flaming into umber, gold and scarlet in fall, bare and startlingly patched with snow in winter. In that strangely familiar landscape (for it matched the book-derived landscapes of my own imagination), I felt safely enclosed in a way I had craved all my life. The America I knew from media coverage was a frightening place of big cities, racial tensions, crime and violence. No doubt many of the townspeople in Keene owned a handgun, but in two years we never saw one. Nobody we knew ever referred to guns.

The course in which we were enrolled lived up to my dreams too, for Antioch New England was a far-flung outpost of Antioch College in Ohio, a private university which had become wildly popular in the 1960s as radical educational ideas temporarily swept all before them. That wave was receding by the late 1970s, but Antioch still clung to some of its notoriety as 'Flake City' – a place where 'anything goes' and where all the rules of conventional education could be broken. We took classes and completed assignments for assessment, but there were no grades and, essentially, no failures. Direct clinical experience occupied four days of each week, and formal instruction only one. We were taught by practising counsellors and therapists; teaching was only a sideline for them. Class discussions were lively; students drew constantly on their personal backgrounds and shared their personal feelings. Here, alive and flourishing, was the experiential learning I had idealistically tried to impose on my students back in Australia. I loved the freedom of being a student again, engaging with new ideas and (in the phrase we used) 'working on myself'. At least, I believed I was.

Antioch students at the time were mostly white liberals, fired by the ideals of the 1960s: pro-feminist, conscious of ethnic diversity, environmentally aware. They were true believers, outsiders like me. From that first day in infant school, I had known I was different, and although I had made friends as an undergraduate in Australia and then again at Oxford, I had never experienced the feeling of being acceptable to a community. Now, at Antioch, I did. My classmates liked me. The things that Australians had regarded as weird or slightly risible were positive attributes to them. I saw my own good qualities – warmth, enthusiasm and sensitivity – mirrored back to me in the faces and words of my fellow students. They believed in me, they trusted me. I felt closer to some of them than I'd felt to anyone before – except for Maureen. Yet her experience of Antioch was not as positive.

Less willing to adopt American attitudes, to modify her phrasing and even her accent (as I almost immediately began doing), her politely cautious personal style seemed to some of her fellow students to lack warmth and to hint at judgement. She worked hard at her internship, saw lots of clients, used her supervisor's wisdom productively and was well-regarded by the staff at the community mental health facility where we had both gained student placements. By comparison, I was lazy as an intern, sometimes seeing only a single client in a day, and spending much of my time reading in the library of Keene State College next door, or scribbling in a manic flight of ideas at my table in the Keene State coffee shop. Needless to say, I was always behind with writing up my client notes. It was a repeat of my behaviour at Oxford, where I'd researched topics that had nothing to do with my thesis, and failed to finish it before we came back to Australia. Street-fighting man that I was, I simply had to rebel against any system I was a part of. Only in classes at Antioch did I feel able to conform to expectations, and I could do so there because I felt that I belonged. I felt a deep sureness that this new career direction was right for me – indeed, that America was right for me. One of the (previously lacking) certainties of adult life had fallen into place.

And then, towards the end of our second and final year in Keene, I went to a Valentine's Day dance at Antioch. The dance had been organised by the dance movement therapy students, few of whom I had met. To the counselling students, including Maureen and me, the DMT students seemed like free spirits, full of New Age talk, a bit flaky. Maureen didn't dance and (I suspected) was a bit embarrassed by my dancing, which was energetic and enthusiastic. So I went alone. I wasn't looking for adventure. I wasn't looking for romance. I just looked forward to enjoying myself with people I liked. But then, for the first time in my life, I had the experience of *something happening to me*.

I found myself dancing with a woman with blue eyes and ash-blonde hair. It was as if her body, her whole energy, ebbed and flowed with mine, echoed mine, mirrored mine – she was attractive (in my eyes, beautiful); she was a dancer and, like me, studying to be a therapist. That was all I knew. As the dance came to an end, I asked her name. She said, 'It's Susan.' We met again a few days later, while Maureen was away in Boston at a conference. I knew I was playing with fire in issuing this invitation, but I just pushed those thoughts away, and went ahead. She came round, we ate supper and I put our daughters to bed. We talked, we danced, we kissed. I said how special she felt to me. She said, 'Hugh, I feel the same way.' I had found a woman who lived and expressed herself through her body, where I (most of the time) ignored and despised mine, a person who trusted her intuition where I overrode mine, who followed a spiritual path, something hitherto alien to me. I wanted those differences. But it was all happening too fast, and something in me held back, as if I knew already that I would turn away from this invitation to a new relationship, a new life, a new country.

Maureen returned and I told her what had happened. I could never lie to her, but my compulsive honesty was also an indication of just how insulated from reality I was. At first she kept her feelings under control. When I told her I wanted to go on seeing Susan, she became angry, implacably angry. She made it clear that if I took the next step, she would ask me to leave, that our marriage would be over. She would return to Australia with our daughters. I knew I could not allow that to happen. I would be a distant dad whom the girls saw only at long intervals, for short periods. I would be the worthless, irresponsible father who had betrayed their mother. But Maureen's anger also meant that she cared enough to fight for me. We had disappointed each other, and I had often enough trifled with her feelings, but I was deeply attached to her. We were held together by twelve years of shared happiness and shared suffering, by two children we loved. Why didn't that count?

Susan and I met several more times, but the joy of being together rapidly gave way to guardedness. As I held back from commitment, Susan began to distance herself. I glimpsed the person she really was, eerily like Maureen for all that she was seven years younger than me. Like Maureen, Susan was disciplined, organised, responsible – and prone to depression. Once she realised that Maureen and I were not washed up, that our marriage had not broken down irrevocably but had merely hit a rough patch, she no longer felt right about seeing me. We hadn't had sex, but it is not necessary to have sex to have an affair. I had fallen deeply in love, I had entrusted a very vulnerable part of me to the hope of a new beginning with her. Now I had to mourn that hope.

And so it ended, as it had to end. We danced together for the final time, we said goodbye. It was a fantasy ending to a relationship that had shrivelled like a butterfly that dies before its wings have hardened enough to fly. I had hurt and disappointed Susan. I had hurt and angered Maureen, forfeiting her trust – perhaps for good this time. Yet I did not entirely regret what I had allowed to happen. When we first met, I had liked Maureen, felt safe with her and loved her, but I had not felt the 'in love' that other people sang about, wrote about. Now, at thirty-three, I had felt it. Yet I had also damaged the woman who had loved me and accepted me for who I was. I had damaged her respect for me. For most of my life so far I had been a selfish, thoughtless child. Perhaps, if I had experienced the average young man's late adolescence and early adulthood, I might have grown up earlier? Perhaps.

'Angel of the Morning' seemed to be playing almost every time I switched on the radio in those last months in New Hampshire, reminding me constantly of what I had done, and how I felt. The woman in Chip Taylor's song (written, of course, by a man) is a gratifying fantasy-figure – a lover who offers herself without demanding commitment or loyalty from the man. 'There'll be no strings to bind your hands, not if my love can bind your heart', she sings. But clearly, she doesn't really expect her love to bind his heart. She is the eternal other woman, almost *expecting* to take second place in her lover's affections, almost expecting that, sooner or later, he will turn away. Pathetically, she sings, 'Just touch my cheek before you leave me' – that's all she asks. Susan had seemingly played this part, at least initially. But then, as the reality of the situation became clear to her, after she spoke with Maureen, it was she who 'slowly turned away', because I was unwilling to commit. And I was the one who craved that farewell touch, a clear indication (I see now) that it was *acceptance* I craved, rather than a new lover and a new life.

At thirty-four, I had come to a crossroads in my adult life. I had taken the path of duty and caution, not the path of danger and adventure. I had acted in accordance with my fearful, wary Crago relatives. The circle of my life had begun to swing back in the direction of values and principles that I had earlier flouted. From now on I would cease to entertain fantasies about being happier with a different partner. I would opt for what I had originally chosen, and make the best of it. I had lacked the courage to risk everything, and must now live with the knowledge that I had done so. It would all start to make sense when, within a year or two, I started my quest to find out more about my parents, my grandparents, and their families.

In Family Time

1944

When my parents were married in 1944, my father had been twenty-eight, and my mother thirty – both were older than the average age at which people were married in Australia in the 1940s. Years after Maureen and I returned from New Hampshire, my father confessed, 'See, when I met your mother, I wasn't, um, deeply in love with her at that time.' It was a significant disclosure. Perhaps he had, in his own way, sensed what had happened to me in America, even though

I'd never said a word about it. At all events, his statement came as a revelation.

My parents had never shown open affection in my presence, and I remembered vividly my mother's frequent, sharply worded criticisms of my father. He was too tight with money, he put a damper on her enthusiasms and his ideas about education were all wrong. She had once burst into angry tears when she opened her Christmas present, and found that he had bought her an expensive toiletry item, but not the one she had told him she wanted. Despite all this, I had always assumed that my parents had started off in love, still loved one another, and stayed together because they did. I had once found a very old letter from Dad to Mum, in which he addressed her as 'Honey' – an American endearment that I'd never heard him use and which seemed quite uncharacteristic. That had confirmed my conviction that they had been in love when they married. Now I could no longer be sure. Dad also told me (though not on the same occasion) that Mum had previously been courted by another man. This admirer, apparently an academic, was very keen on her, and gave her presents (one of which, to Dad's evident discomfort, my mother had insisted on keeping for the rest of her life). Despite this evidence of an attachment on her part, I somehow assumed that the professor's devotion to her had not been reciprocated. I guess I did not want to think there had been someone else before my father.

Tight-lipped about her past, Mum was perfectly capable of blunt honesty if she trusted the person she was talking to. She once confided to such a person that the man who had been in love with her was already married but she had been very serious about him. The man who had been so keen on my mother was already married, but my mother had been very serious about him. He had promised to leave his wife and marry my mother but (as so often in such situations) that did not happen. It is possible that my mother's decision to marry my father was a reaction to this betrayal of her hopes. If all of this was true (for Mum was capable of enhancing the facts), it would certainly explain why my mother acted as if Dad were deeply disappointing to her, and why she had felt entitled to criticise him despite his (to me) obvious devotion to her – which is exactly how I had behaved to Maureen (though with no backstory to excuse it).

But there was more. My father also cherished the memory of an earlier attachment. He once told me that, as a teachers college student (he would have been eighteen or nineteen), he had taken part in a musical theatre production and been 'very smitten' by his leading lady. He had been invited to her parents' home, only to be given the cold shoulder. Even though the relationship with that young woman had barely started to form, he had clearly felt embarrassed and betrayed. Typically of him, Dad told this story only the once and never mentioned it again, but his behaviour – to feel both shamed and insulted – was certainly behaviour that I had observed in him in response to other (very minor) slights. Could it be that my father, too, had married someone else (my mother) as a way of numbing the blow he had once been dealt by another woman? My father and my mother had freely chosen to marry one another – indeed, they had chosen in defiance of their parents' wishes – yet they had ended up behaving as if their marriage had been arranged for them. In the words of another song, 'What's love got to do with it?'

1919

When I fell in love with Susan in New Hampshire in February 1981, I was just thirty-four. When my mother's father Victor Sanders fell in love with 'the beautiful nurse' in England he was thirty-three. Why did he do it? He had clearly been disappointed and dissatisfied in his marriage, and his affair in England had meant enough to him for him to wish to turn it into a novel later. Victor was a romantic – he longed for life to conform to the gratifying patterns of daydream and fiction – and it would have been in character for him to choose romance over duty. Yet (like me) he chose duty – perhaps influenced by rediscovering six-year-old Gwen, the daughter he had left behind as a toddler in 1915, perhaps hoping that he and Eva might enjoy a new beginning now that the war was finally over. Eva turned him out when he confessed to the affair, but she took him back. He would have been thirty-four then. Thereafter, their relationship was shadowed by his betrayal. Self-centred and impulsive Victor may have been, but he clearly felt that he did not have the right to abuse or criticise her. She had been loyal to him for eleven long years, including nearly four when he had been absent overseas, and he had let her down.

Was it not simply combat-induced trauma, but also a nagging feeling of guilt at this betrayal that led Victor to shift restlessly from job to job in the ten more years that remained to him, that drove him to rely more and more on alcohol to restore the bonhomie and optimism he had displayed before the Great War? Was he, in fact, depressed? There is no way of knowing now, but I think it is likely. My soldierly grandfather, a man's man if ever there was one, completely lacking in the Christian faith that guided my father and his family into the ways of duty and obedience, was probably as capable of self-doubt as I. And, like me, having struck out impulsively for a romantic new beginning with another woman, he turned his back on it, choosing obligation and loyalty instead. Was he, deep down, fearful – just as I was, like so many on my father's side the family?

1900

The apex of Henry Lawson's writing career came in 1899 when, as a young man of thirty-two with his wife Bertha and two young children, he embarked for London, sure that he could find fame and fortune in the Old Country, and convinced that Australia was no place for an important writer such as himself. Henry was favourably received in London, but his work did not sell as well as it had done back home, and he resented his publisher's (accurate) opinion that some of what he submitted was not up to his usual standard. Henry found it difficult to meet deadlines and, though he worked hard, there was very little money. Bertha loathed the seemingly endless cold, sleet and fog, and felt imprisoned in the tiny apartments that were all Henry could afford for his family. Bertha suffered a complete breakdown, becoming delusional, violent and paranoid – although some have argued that it was Henry who became violent, not Bertha.[1] After just two years away, the couple returned from the Old Country in 1902 with their marriage in tatters, and though for a time Henry spoke of returning to London where, he fancied, he had been on the brink of major success, he never did. Bertha requested a judicial separation in 1903.

During the bad times in England, Henry seems to have clung to the memory of a woman called Hannah Thornburn, whom he had met before he married Bertha. If we can believe the several fictionalised versions of Hannah in Henry's later poems, there was a strong sexual attraction, but it did not go further than that: he depicts Hannah as a lily of purity, an idealised girl he loved from afar and who inspired him. To the extent that they had a relationship, Hannah seems to have offered Henry comfort and praise – which, by the time of their abortive stay in England, Bertha was no longer supplying, though she had certainly done so in their first years together. Hannah's big grey eyes were (in Henry's words) sad with sympathy for sufferers and sinners, recalling Victor Sanders's nurse with 'big, sad eyes'. For both men, an idealised woman embodied the feminine, caring qualities that they denied in themselves, the qualities that they no longer saw in their mothers or wives. One semi-autobiographical poem of Henry's gives the impression that Hannah had agreed 'to be his' after his return from England, but it is impossible to know whether this is merely a fictional embellishment.

What we do know for sure is that Hannah had died in Adelaide of complications following a miscarriage, some two weeks before Henry himself arrived back from England. She had been in her fourth month of pregnancy when she was taken to hospital, so Henry could not have been the father (as some people once speculated). For Henry, the shock of landing in Melbourne to learn of Hannah's death was massive. He would not have known of her condition, let alone that it would prove fatal. For Henry, as for many creative men, an idealised woman retained her power to inspire and console even when the relationship was long over: 'She lives in the Marriage that Might Have Been', he wrote some five years later.

1735

In 1735, John Wesley, then aged thirty-two, sailed for the New World to convert the Indians (as Native Americans were then called). In the settlement that would later become the city of Savannah, Georgia, Wesley set about his missionary work with zeal, inventiveness and careful planning – qualities that would distinguish his whole career – but he failed to convert the Creek Indians, commenting that they 'had no inclination to learn anything, but least of all Christianity'. Instead, he met a spirited (and troubled) eighteen-year-old among the English colonists in his school for the propagation of the Gospel. Her name was Sophie Hopkey, and John fell deeply in love with her. Sophie reciprocated his affections – at least at first. Acutely conscious of the strength of his attraction, John fought an inward war between his desire for Sophie and his conviction that he must remain celibate. He saw himself, after all, as a Man of God with a great destiny. In response to his wavering, Sophie too wavered, and eventually rejected his not-quite-proposal, opting to marry someone else. John was so consumed with jealousy of this man that he went to the lengths of declaring their union invalid because the banns had not been properly called (though skipping such steps was common in marriages among the colonists at the time). John had hesitated, and had forfeited his chance with a woman he truly loved through his own inability to commit to her.

What We Need to Know

The language of cliché and the language of art

The right hemisphere of the cerebral cortex in human beings organises its perceptions in the form of gestalts or patterns, patterns that embody both emotion and aesthetic shape. What literary critics call clichés are examples of these patterns; so are commonly used chord progressions in music. Popular songs depend on such clichés, verbal and musical. They appeal direct to the right hemisphere. Despite the efforts of the left hemisphere (which makes a distinction between fresh-minted language and well-worn currency) clichés and formulas continue to appeal to us – even to intellectuals, if they are honest with themselves. They convey what I call the wisdom of the right hemisphere – strong, simple patterns that match how we feel, rather than what we rationally know to be correct. Their images are colourful, dramatic, intense, condensations of experience – dizzy heights and plunging depths. There are no shades of grey. The language of the right hemisphere swings straight from ecstatic joy to deep depression. And so, popular songs echo back to us how we feel inside, and that feels good, even when the feelings themselves are painful. While I listened to it, 'Angel of the Morning' seemed *true*.

Ages and stages

Why would so many affairs take place in the early thirties? Or, to put it another way, why would so many marriages run into trouble when one or the other partner reaches that age? Between the late twenties and the mid- thirties, most of us undergo a period of transition which is driven from within by biological imperatives (the brain matures significantly, while the body is already past its peak and in the earliest stages of a long, very slow decline). For the first time, many people begin to question the lives they have built for themselves – and this includes not only their choice of partner, but their choice of career path. We become more acutely aware of what we may be missing out on by the choices we have already made.

By the age of thirty-two, when Maureen and I left for America, I had already begun retraining myself for a new profession, and embraced new values to go with it. For years, like many people, I had fantasised about what it might be like with someone else. America, with its exciting challenges and new opportunities, simply potentiated these questions and reinforced existing fantasies. I fell in love with America well before I fell in love with an American woman.

Of course it was partly illusion: small-town New Hampshire was very different from mainstream America, and Antioch was nothing like a mainstream American graduate school. But in my brief flirtation with the idea of starting over with a new partner in a new country, I also allowed myself to glimpse the emotional reality that such a new start might involve, the reality of losing both Maureen and my daughters. Emotionally I was still a boy, but I was, for the first time in my adult life, up against a wall. The very values I had rebelled against now made me reconsider my selfishness and impulsivity. The values were those of my father's family: you made your choice and you stuck with it; you did your duty, and didn't run away from it. If you ducked those obligations, then you were a self-indulgent, worthless person, a Cavalier, a Peter Pan. There had been hardly a single divorce in my father's family. The words of the marriage vows, from the Book of Common Prayer, spoke simply and powerfully, in absolutes – much as popular songs did:

> …for better, for worse, for richer, for poorer, in sickness and in health, till death do us part.

For me, what happened in Keene, New Hampshire in 1981 was a turning point. My youthful rebellion had run its course, and I had begun to 'swing back' towards the values and behaviours that I had absorbed in childhood, both from my father's duty-governed, self-denying Methodism and (paradoxically) from my mother's choice – when she decided to marry my father – of a man who she knew would look after her for the rest of her life and never desert her, of a man who had proved himself reliable over one who had not. And of course, that choice had also been her father's. I had followed their pattern, without realising it.

Births and rebirths

My age at the time of my might-have-been new relationship was very close to those of several others (in the family and outside of it) who fell in love in their early thirties. Yet in my case, that age was significant for another reason: thirty-three was my mother's age when I was born. There is a theory – little known, and often derided by those who do know of it – that our adult life crises often occur when we reach the age our mother or father was at our own birth.[2] Here mystery is wrapped in mystery. How could this possibly be real? Surely it is simply coincidence? Or is there some kind of cellular memory, something transmitted in the genes, that triggers such events at those particular ages? Are we, in a sense, giving birth to a new self? I will return to this subject in the last part of this book.

Loyalty and betrayal

Human beings are vulnerable creatures, and it is very easy for us to feel disappointed, disregarded or even rejected by our partners whether or not an actual 'affair' has transpired. My mother felt betrayed when my father picked the wrong present to give her for Christmas. In some troubled marriages, it is impossible for the partners to tolerate the fact that they disagree or differ. Expressed differences of opinion threaten their sense of worth, and lead to endless, destructive bickering, in which one ultimately wears the other down. My parents displayed this pattern, and from my thirties on, I began to wonder whether I had done any better than they had. Perceived betrayals wound our sense of selfhood, and genetically sensitive, fearful, people – like my grandmother Eva, like my mother, and like me – will feel these wounds more keenly than thicker-skinned individuals. Self-doubting people not only doubt themselves, they doubt their partners. In fact, they see their partners through a screen of their own fears of betrayal – regardless of whether or not those partners merely dream it, or actually do it. Paranoia lies not too far off, though many of us never cross that border.

A marriage is one long-established way that human beings seek stability in a life that inevitably involves 'change and decay' (in the words of the hymn 'Abide with Me'). While our popular songs speak eloquently to us of our longing for true love, perhaps what most of us really long for in a relationship is *certainty* – a person we can trust no matter what happens, a life that does not confront us too nakedly with loss and pain, a world that will not disintegrate around us. Whether or not we believe in God, all of us need to believe in something. Not somebody to love, but rather, *somebody to love us*, somebody – or (for people of faith) Somebody – who will accept us just as we are, with all our imperfections and unworthiness.

7

Sanity and Madness

In My Time

We Have Already Forgotten Their Names (Taree, NSW, 1988)

> We did hear, later on, what his real name was but if we ever chance to read it in the 'Missing Friends Column', we shall not be able to give any information to the heart-broken Mother or Sister or Wife, nor to anyone who could let him hear something to his advantage – for we have already forgotten the name.
>
> Henry Lawson, 'The Union Buries Its Dead', in *The Country I Come From*, 1901

'Gidday, *cousin*!' says the small man challengingly, his piercing blue eyes looking straight up into mine. I am startled and wary. He's not any cousin I know about and, to be honest, I feel a bit intimidated. But then I realise that he doesn't really expect a personal response. He's been working his way through the reunion crowds, saying the same thing to everyone he comes across. He knows that many of them are likely to be cousins of some sort, but he's happy to keep them at a safe distance. He doesn't pursue our new acquaintance any further.

The Albury family reunion was announced years ahead of its scheduled date in 1988. Invited by the indefatigable Alison Brooks, whose husband is a descendant of Emma Albury, the massed descendants of John Albury and his wife Ann were to gather at Taree, on the lower north coast of New South Wales, to celebrate the 150th anniversary of the family's arrival in Australia. My father wasn't interested in going, but his sister Cherie, his brother Ted, and Ted's wife

Beryl all planned to attend. It would be, I thought, a great opportunity to find out more about one side of my extended family, and to find out what the Alburys thought about their one famous man – Henry Lawson, great-grandson of John Albury. In that hope, though, I would be disappointed. No conversation that I participated in would contain a single reference to Lawson.

Ever since our return from New Hampshire seven years earlier, I had been consumed by the desire to discover more about my family of origin. Along with my fellow students, I'd been introduced to the exciting but confronting idea of researching our own ancestors and then presenting, in class, our reflections on family patterns and family secrets. I had been captured by the idea of writing an emotional history of three generations of the Crago family, including my own. I'd asked questions of my father and mother, and gotten very little in the way of information. Neither of them felt easy about being asked 'What sort of person was your dad?' or 'How did you parents get on?' Both of them stuck to the safe and superficial ('Mother was a wonderful woman' or 'Well, Dad was away a lot because of his work'). Of course they were guarded – they knew what I now did for a living, and it isn't easy having a son who might be 'trying to psychoanalyse you'. As a youth worker put it to me a few years later, 'I don't want anyone writing a book about what's in my head!'

I had contacted a number of my relatives on the Crago side, and arranged meetings with those who seemed open to the idea – which didn't include my Auntie Beth, Dad's younger sister. It was more than forty years ago that my mother had taken Ian away from the family who adored him, and (so Beth was convinced) proceeded to raise us three children in her Godless ways. There was no way that Beth was going to have me in her home, or in her presence at all. In response to my question about whether she would be attending the reunion, Beth had written back, 'We expect to be in Ujiji, Tanganyika, next year about that time!' Of course she was being sarcastic. The thought of her peaceful haven in Taree being invaded by enormous numbers of relations she had never met must have been terrifying for her. 'Beth doesn't have much confidence,' her brothers and sisters told me. When I arrived at Taree for the reunion, I did walk past her house, though. Perhaps if *I'd* had more confidence, I would have bowled up to her front door and introduced myself? Two of my Armstrong cousins – Auntie Gwyn's younger sons Cam and Lou – had, I later discovered, done exactly that, and got away with it.

Even Dad (who'd always seemed to me quite confident) had grumbled, 'All these relatives – you've got nothing in common with them and you don't know them.' I privately thought, 'But if you knew them, maybe you'd find you did have something in common with them.' It was typical of me at the time to assume that I knew better than Dad, that I was more emotionally healthy than he was – and to miss the real significance of his phrasing. Sure, he didn't know them but, despite that, he 'knew' he didn't have anything in common with them. This could only be because, as a child, he had soaked up his own parents' discomfort at references to unmentionable relatives, people who were way beyond the pale. I did not see this at the time, because I myself had grown up with a similar attitude – tacitly from Dad (who would never talk about his father, while constantly saying what a wonderful woman his mother had been) and more overtly from Mum (who conveyed to me eloquently, without saying it in so many words, that Dad's relatives, with the single exception of Ted and Beryl in Newcastle, were dull people who lived on farms – actually only two of them did – and from whom we stayed as far away as possible).

So now I had finally, in my mid-thirties, become curious about my family and, instead of assuming that what I knew was all I needed to know, was prepared to listen to what they had to tell me. I had little time, for my father's eldest brother, Dick, had already died of cancer while Maureen and I were in New Hampshire, and his wife, my Aunt May, was suffering from dementia. In several years of listening to elderly relatives, I had begun to realise more about the true nature of the family into which my father had been born. The Albert Cragos were a family of quiet people, a family that didn't want any fuss, who didn't like to be a bother, a family who tended to be wary and even resentful of people more confident or more outspoken than themselves. But since the family code was 'If you can't say something nice, don't say anything', their strong suspicions and resentments were rarely voiced except to each other – or perhaps a trusted friend. Of course, they were not all fearful and anxious. Though sensitive and emotional, their mother, Ethel, was a confident woman in many regards, and so was her daughter Gwynneth (Gwen, to the family). All three of Ethel's sons possessed some social poise, albeit coupled with anxiety in the case of Dick, the eldest, and my own father Ian, the youngest. Other Cragos, descendants of Petherick Crago's younger brother, Frank, also seemed more confident. But the personality of Albert Crago, that fearful, socially awkward man, seemed to have shaped the culture of the family I had begun to know.

My elderly aunts and uncles, most of them in their seventies by now, had a range of carefully understated adjectives to describe those family members they didn't like. 'She was a bit of a bird', 'They were difficult', 'She wasn't an easy person to love', 'Oh yes, May and her funny little ways', 'He got quite wound up about it.' They didn't want to judge others harshly, yet their dislike and their incomprehension leaked out anyway. What all those tactful expressions actually signified I was only just starting to discover.

I began to see that much of what I'd learned from my Crago relatives was only part of the truth, a truth that was more complex and ambiguous than I had originally thought. My father's family were not just anxious and quiet, but highly sensitive – easily hurt and slow to forgive. They could not – at least until many years afterwards – even talk about what had gone wrong, let alone sort it out with each other and reconcile. They handed down the conflicts of one generation to the next, unquestioningly accepting their parents' version. Theirs was not the kind of sensitivity that would have enabled them to put themselves in someone else's position. The men held forth in a heavy-handed, sermonising way, addressing even their adult listeners as if they were children. The women's gnomic pronouncements ('That's just the way she was') permitted no requests for elaboration. Had *Game of Thrones* been around in the late 1980s, the words 'You know nothing, John Snow' would have been very apt for them – not that any relative of my father's would ever have watched a show as brutal, dark and confronting as George Martin's fantasy.

The three days of the Albury reunion passed quickly and, for the most part, I stayed with the relatives I already knew. I felt a bit cowardly doing so, a bit unadventurous – until I realised that this was what most people were doing. They stayed with known relatives in preference to making contact with those they didn't know and 'had nothing in common with'. No doubt a lot of family stories were retold, and no doubt many people found out more about each other, forging stronger bonds as a result. The reunion had been a resounding success, and wonderfully well-organised, but the upbeat tone of the proceedings did not permit the acknowledgment of death, pain or shame. And I was beginning to realise that the Albury family, overall, might have had more than their fair share of those in their 150 years in Australia. Drinking problems, mental illness and eccentricities were not mentioned.

A reunion concert had been advertised for the final evening, and everyone was invited to offer items. Hardly anyone put their hands up. It seemed the Alburys – like most of my Crago relatives – were not natural performers. Two middle-aged men in blue tuxedos sang some of the old standards, like 'When You Come to the End of a Perfect Day'. To provide a nod in the direction of the Albury family's one celebrity member, I had offered to read 'The Drover's Wife'. I think most of the audience would have preferred 'The Loaded Dog', but they sat through my choice without visible restlessness. Afterwards my younger daughter, who'd come with me to the reunion, told me wonderingly that Cherie 'had tears in her eyes', and that 'Ted blew his nose'. Lawson's stark picture of what life had been like for a pioneer woman had touched them. Ted always talked as if he valued his family connection with Lawson, but to most of the audience, the great

Genogram 3

Paternal grandparents and their families of origin (see especially chapter 7 and Theoretical Considerations)

Henry Albury (Harry) 1825–1908 — **Harriet Winn** 1825–1895

- Emma 1845–1954
- Elizabeth 1852–1860
- Susanna Gertrude (Gert) 1854–1927
- Pece 1857–1963
- Ann 1859–1940
- Joseph 1861–1943
- Frances 1864–c. 1950
- Ellen 1866–?
- Blanch 1869–1926

Louisa 1848–1920 — Niels Larsen (Lawson)
- Charles b. 1869
- Peter b. 1873
- Gertrude b. 1877
- Annette (died in infancy)

m. 1866: Henry Lawson 1867–1922

William CRAGO 1799–1894 — **Elizabeth Tamblyn** 1810–1892
m. 1832/33

- Francis Justin 1837–?
- Elizabeth 1841–?
- John 1845–1934
- Francis (Frank) 1848–1907
- William Henry 1851–1936 — Alison Hattersley

Petherick Tamblyn 1833–1907 — **Ann Stephens** 1838–1919
m. 1858

- Mehetabel (Met) 1860–1914
- Elizabeth Ann 1861–1940 — William Henry 1863–1945
- Frances Julia 1865–?
- Frederick 1867–1884
- Sadonia (Doan) 1871–?
- Helena Jane 1873–1948
- Ada 1878
- Elsie*
- Frederick*
- Edward*
  *all died in infancy

Richard STEAR 1853–1929 — **Phoebe** 1850–1926
m. 1875

- William 1876–1957
- Herbert 1877–1901 died of diabetes
- Mildred 1880–1956
- Ilma 1882–1966
- Olive 1883–1959
- Gertrude (Gert) 1885–1915
- Clarence 1887–1908 died of diabetes
- Muriel (Mune) 1889–1952
- Miriam (Pink) 1892–1929 died of flu

Albert Cecil 1879–1948 — **Ethel Wyn** 1879–1963
m. 1904

Australian author remained beyond the pale. He was unsafe, a reminder of things in the family that were better left in decent obscurity.

On the bus on the way back home to Wagga, I thought about family histories that left out the bad bits because if you put them in, someone was bound to be offended – even if the black sheep in question was someone who had lived several generations ago. Maybe it wasn't just our family that was so sensitive to hurt and slight. Maybe most families were? Once a family history is published, nearly every family member seems to find something to offend them in what the author has recorded.

What I didn't think about, then, was my own behaviour at the reunion. I had not confidently gone out into the assembled throng and introduced myself – even though Alison, the organiser, had made it much easier for all of us by having everyone wear colour-coded badges that showed which of the many children of John and Ann Albury each of us was descended from. I considered myself confident, but I had acted like a shy person. I had got up in front of everyone and read Lawson's story, in order to ensure that he was not forgotten – but public performance distances performers from their audience, and can be a safe substitute for making personal contact with individuals. I had asked my own immediate relatives some questions, and listened to them talking about the family, but I had acted almost as if I did not quite belong in the big gathering, and I had felt as though I had little or nothing in common with most of them. It was exactly what my father had said – 'You don't know them, and you don't have anything in common with 'em.' I was no more confident, no more emotionally healthy, than he had been.

In Family Time

There were four family members who were not talked about (in my hearing, anyway) at the Albury reunion. Apart from the long-dead Henry Lawson, two were siblings of my father: my aunt Gwyn, whom I had not met since I was a child, and my aunt Beth, who actually lived a few blocks away, but who felt unable to be present and where, once again, long-ago antagonisms had meant little contact. The fourth was my eldest cousin John, son of Uncle Dick. On a visit when I was around six, John (then an adolescent) seemed to me grown-up – he was thirteen years older than me and, although there was nothing intimidating about him, it seemed an unbridgeable gap. By the time I myself was an adolescent, John was no longer discussed in Dad's family. There were muttered mentions of 'breakdowns'. That was all I knew, until I began asking questions about all of these mysterious relatives whom my parents did not visit and rarely talked about. In my late thirties, I finally initiated contact with John, liking his honesty and directness, and also seeing hints of the behaviour that I knew had alienated others.

In the lives of these four individuals – Henry in the generation of my grandparents, Gwyn and Beth in my father's generation, and John in my own generation – the murkiness of the distinction between sanity and madness becomes apparent. Henry, Gwyn, Beth and John had two important things in common. All of them, in their own ways, said openly things that most people would not say and did not want to acknowledge. And all four of them were deeply unsure of their own worth – though some of them could produce enough apparent self-belief to convince people otherwise, at least some of the time.

I shall introduce them in chronological order, beginning with Henry, focusing on the behaviours that caused problems for their relatives, and for themselves.

Henry Lawson (1867–1922)

People who don't read much (or at all) don't judge writers by the quality of their writing but by the quality of their lives, and Lawson's life was, by any standards, a mess. Alcoholism is something that everyone (except perhaps lifelong non-drinkers) understands. But what my father's relatives did not know was that Lawson also suffered from a mental disorder, most likely manic-depressive illness (now known as bipolar disorder). His drinking was secondary to what was in all probability a wrongly diagnosed mental illness.[1]

Henry had been a shy, anxious, sensitive child. In 1883, after his mother Louisa separated from Peter Lawson and moved her children to Sydney, Henry, the eldest, was sent out to work to help support the family, and there experienced the same sense of alienation from his peers, and the same kind of teasing, as both I and my father had experienced in early adolescence. He was already composing verse. Louisa was herself a poet – proud of her son's precocity, but also critical of him when he failed to live up to her own high standards. Hoping to attend university, Henry studied at home for the matriculation examination, but failed it. He failed again on a second attempt. Initially, he made a living helping his often-depressed father, Peter, as a builder and house painter. After Henry began to publish, he gained as a journalist but found it difficult to accept the restrictions of the role (just as young Vic Sanders, my mother's father and also a journalist, did). As his writing gained him increasing fame, Lawson was well supported by his publishers, but he rapidly spent his advances, failed to correct his proofs promptly, and demanded additional payments over and above the generous royalties his publishers had already paid him. He shamelessly resold the rights to several of his works. Repeatedly, his publishers indulged him, but his spending always ran ahead of his earnings and he seemed incapable of saving and organising his finances. Wild schemes took the place of rational planning.

Already successful in Australia, Lawson, by then married to the much younger Bertha Bredt, took his family off to London, convinced that he would achieve far greater success there – but he soon became disillusioned. With Bertha in a precarious mental state, the couple retreated in disarray back to Australia, where they separated. From that time on, Bertha had to keep pursuing Henry for the child support payments which he had promised. When things were bad, Lawson drank more – even if he had to borrow money to do it. When things temporarily improved, he became over-confident and grandiose. And so it continued. Lawson had many loyal and patient friends, but wore out his welcome with most of them eventually. He became more and more dependent on others to pick him up (literally, sometimes) and re-establish him in some kind of secure living arrangement. He was jailed on more than one occasion, and 'dried out', only to start drinking again. Most of the time, Henry was more or less depressed. He worked hard at his writing, but he had become a hack, producing short, mediocre pieces simply in order to get enough money to keep going for another week, and painfully conscious that his best work as a writer lay in the past.

People have some understanding of depression, although relatively few have experienced a depression so severe that it feels impossible to get out of bed in the morning (let alone shower or go to work). Mania, by contrast, is something that only a small minority of the population have experienced (though individuals who use cocaine or methamphetamines may experience a temporary, chemically induced version of it). Mania is a high that lasts not for hours but for weeks, a state in which the manic individual feels capable of anything, unstoppable – yet also driven, irritable and unable to rest or sleep. While they are manic, sufferers have poor judgement, take huge risks and are largely oblivious of the effect they are having on others. But they generally enjoy it. When the mania ends, however, the sufferer slides into a dark night of the soul, a 'black anguish' in which death beckons as the only relief.

It is the alternation of the two extremes or poles (hence *bipolar* disorder) that distinguishes manic-depressive illness from depression proper. The highs – in a way – protect the sufferer from the lows, but inevitably, the highs come to an end and the person crashes into what some depressives call 'the black pit'. No sufferer wants the lows, but (at least at first) manic-depressives prize their mania (which is why so many refuse to take the mood-stabilising medication that could alleviate their condition – medications which are available to us but unknown when Lawson was alive). Understandably, they fear that if they were medicated, all the joy within them would die and they would become dull, half-dead, incapable of creativity or purpose.

Both then and now, those who suffer manic-depressive illness often become alcoholics too. Lawson relied on alcohol both to create temporary highs and to medicate the depression that came upon him when he faced the truth of the failure of his marriage, his inability to handle money responsibly, and his descent into a hobo existence in which he relied on asking well-wishers for 'two bob' (equivalent to about a dollar in today's values) to get him through the day.

Even now, some people suffer lifelong from bipolar disorder without ever being diagnosed or treated. Often, as in Lawson's case, they numb themselves with alcohol or other drugs, and so are treated for the addiction rather than the underlying affliction. If they exhibit the hallucinations typical of the most severe form of the illness (bipolar I), they may be misdiagnosed as schizophrenic and receive inappropriate medication. If they manage their mania by focusing on a business or political career, their frenetic pace and soaring ambition often draw admiration in a society that hero-worships self-made millionaires and driven entrepreneurs. If they channel their mania into creative work – painting, sculpture, musical composition or writing – their illness is often regarded simply as an inescapable aspect of an 'artistic temperament'. As Kay Redfield Jamison (herself a sufferer) shows us in her splendidly honest yet scholarly books, being manic-depressive does not, in itself, make you creative, but it certainly provides those who are already creative with intense experiences that almost demand expression.

So Henry Lawson was not just a drunk. Nobody knew it when he was alive, but Henry was descended through his Norwegian father Niels Larsen (which he changed to Peter Lawson) from a family of manic-depressives. From his mother Louisa Albury's side he had also inherited genes that predisposed him to emotional disorders. He was never diagnosed with mental illness (as his younger brother Charlie was), though his friends recognised that there was something badly wrong with him, and his roller coaster life continued until his death at the early age of fifty-five.

Gwynneth Stephens Armstrong (1913–1988)

Gwynneth Crago was the third child and eldest daughter born to Albert Crago and his wife, Ethel, née Stear. Gwyn's second name was for her Crago grandmother, Ann Stephens – Albert's mother, to whom he had been deeply attached. In her turn, Gwyn was as deeply attached to Albert, her father. Through Ethel's mother, Gwyn was descended from the Albury family, and Henry Lawson was therefore her cousin, once removed.

Gwyn's early adult years were marked by her single-minded determination to become a nurse. She was confident and competent in her professional role, and it was in performing it that she first met her future husband, Harold Armstrong. Yet her marriage began under difficult circumstances, which required the young couple to live at Harold's family home, and Gwyn, who had previously clashed with her own mother, did not take kindly to being treated as a kind of serving maid (as she saw it) by Harold's father, a successful grazier. We need to remember that a woman who has occupied a professional role becomes used to being treated with respect. Once she marries and stays home to raise her children, she is often – even now – treated as if she knows nothing, and her self-respect crashes. When Gwyn married Harold, this was even more prevalent than it is today.

Gwyn was blunt and uncompromising in her opinions. Some of her adult relationships with family members led to clashes. When fired by the unfairness or wrongness of something, she got 'wound up' and talked compulsively, much as her sister Beth did. The aggrieved, argumentative talk was Gwyn's equivalent of the intense, repetitive ranting that unmedicated sufferers from bipolar disorder can so easily be caught up in – Gwyn was not mentally ill, but normal individuals can sometimes behave in odd or extreme ways, just as mentally ill individuals may at times appear completely normal.

Despite enjoying material security, Gwyn and Harold were not particularly happy together, and at times it seemed that they were held together by a kind of exasperated loyalty – and of course, by their four sons. 'Shut up, Harold, shut up! What would you know about it!' Those are the words her then-daughter-in-law Helen recalled Gwyn saying in the course of a family argument – though others in the family denied she would ever have said such a thing. Gwyn was hugely popular with her neighbours, for she showed her cheerful and ebullient self to friends and acquaintances, while keeping her moroseness within the family circle. 'Whenever I complained about something,' said her daughter-in-law Wendy, 'Gwynny always had something worse that had happened to her.' 'Difficult' was the word that some other family members used about her – the same word they had used of her father Albert and of her sister Beth, the same word that in a previous generation had been applied to Henry Lawson's grandfather Harry Albury and to Elizabeth Anne Granger, her father's much older sister.

Beneath Gwyn's combative manner lay considerable vulnerability and acute sensitivity to slight. She remembered all her life how, in childhood, her 'own brothers' had called her 'Pug' because of her flat nose. Like her sister Beth, she found it hard to forgive such unthinking childhood cruelty and, as she grew up, she knew that she was plain compared with 'beautiful' Beth. Later, in middle adulthood, Gwyn dressed without regard for how she looked, as if to deny people the satisfaction of seeing her try desperately to look attractive when she knew she was not.

In this way, she displayed something very similar to the behaviour of her Auntie Elizabeth Anne, for Gwyn was old enough to remember Auntie's visits better than younger siblings like Ian, Beth and Cherie. Elizabeth Anne would insist on travelling second-class on the train 'because there isn't any third' (as if to say that she was not worth spending money on), and on arriving at Albert Crago's ten-acre block would immediately remove her boots and walk barefoot 'to feel the good earth'. Elizabeth Anne was regarded in the family as 'obnoxious' because she said what she thought and delivered judgemental opinions instead of sensing the need for tact. Eventually both Albert and his older brother Will banned Elizabeth Anne from their homes – an extreme measure indeed, indicating that, for them, her behaviour had crossed the border between 'difficult' and 'obnoxious'. Gwyn would never be called obnoxious, but her bluntness would ensure that, within her own family, she would be regarded with wariness by some – including her younger brother Ian. My impression was that he was actually scared of her and stayed away from her for that reason. When he heard of her death (according to my mother), Ian became very agitated at the thought of attending her funeral and seemed relieved when I offered to go instead.

Even in her garden, Gwyn cared little for how things looked: 'She'd have a sea of weeds waist-high, and little patches scratched in the ground for this thing and that, and in each of them there'd be some plant growing, but every one of them was in the right position for sun or shade or water…' Washing up was a nightmare because of the way Gwyn kept her kitchen. What Gwyn valued was practicality, as her father had done. Behaviour that matches our own values is 'practical'; behaviour that doesn't, constitutes 'funny little ways'. Gwyn was not manic-depressive like Henry Lawson; she did not suffer from social phobia and paranoia like her father Albert and her sister Beth, but her forthrightness disguised (from others and even from herself) her own lack of self-worth. This is 'counter-phobic' behaviour: we act the opposite of how we really feel inside, because our vulnerability may (in our eyes) leave us open to devastating attack.

Gwyn had more than a little in common with her younger brother Ian's wife Gwen – whose name was so similar to her own, who was almost the same age and whom she cordially disliked. Soon after her marriage to my father, Gwen made two drafts of a letter thanking Gwyn for her wedding present, awkwardly worded attempts to balance gratitude with honesty. Sadly, it seems that she never sent either.

Bethel Marion Crago

In Hebrew, Beth-El meant 'place of God', and it was a name sometimes given to non-conformist chapels. There can be little doubt that Beth knew what her name meant, and certainly her faith was central to her whole life. For Beth, God's love provided her with a sense of worth and belonging that she seems not to have felt in her earthly relationships. It would have been very easy for Beth to experience herself as 'an imprisoned spirit' (Charles Wesley's words) 'fast bound in sin and Nature's night'. She tried valiantly to be good, but her passionate, entitled, judgemental nature got in the way, alienating others, including her siblings and her own children. In Beth, the genetic temperament she shared with many of her relatives was wound to a high pitch. Her extreme avoidance of society led her to an almost hermit-like existence and would now have earned her a diagnosis of social phobia – yet she would set out on long trips alone, provided her two boxer dogs were with her in the car.

Much of her apparent rudeness was simply a manifestation of the overwhelming fear she (like her father before her) felt when confronted with strangers or people she disliked. Her strongly held beliefs about Catholics, public servants and (as the 60s advanced) 'young people' verged on being delusional, yet she was never diagnosed with any kind of hallucination. She alternated between near-despair ('It's only when you're at the end of your tether that you really need a God') and righteous anger, lashing out even at those who cared about her – yet no psychiatrist labelled her a case of emotional dysregulation for, like most people at the time, she would never have dreamed of consulting a mental health professional. She sought her solace, and wrestled with her demons, within the trusted framework of the beliefs in which she had been raised. She lived to a ripe old age, while her patient partner, Roy, declined into dementia. She refused offers of help from her brother Ted (prompting him to say, uncharacteristically, 'And for that I can never forgive her!') and returned presents sent to her by her adopted son Graham's family. 'Your mother's mad!' one of Graham's school friend had exclaimed when Beth had refused to admit him to her home. Was she mad? Not psychotic, no, but surely more than just eccentric.

Psychiatry has a term – personality disordered – that signifies an individual who never qualifies for a diagnosis of mental illness, but some of whose actions, thoughts and feelings are nevertheless beyond the pale. For most of us, after all, madness or 'craziness' involves actions that simply do not make sense to others, which seem extreme, gratuitous and uncalled for. In a sense, Beth simply expressed what others in the family also manifested – she just expressed it more intensely.

John Tamblyn Crago (1933–1988)

Dick Crago, Beth's oldest brother, had two sons, John and Richard. John, the elder, was the one people noticed – he was tall, good-looking and apparently brimming with confidence. Like his mother, May (whom the Crago sisters had thought 'a bit of a bird'), he was full of ideas and enthusiasms, where his younger brother seemed reserved and tentative. May was a fine weaver and a creative gardener and, early on, she saw herself in John. John, she felt, would do great things (exactly what Ethel Crago had felt about Dick). John showed an early talent for painting, but Dick refused to tolerate the possibility that his son might be an artist – 'There's no money in art,' he would say. Though Dick would never have admitted it, it was exactly what his own father would have said.

There were hints, while John was still a child, that something might be amiss. While he and Richard were alone at home, John persuaded his brother that they should light a fire in the grate, sending flames roaring up the unswept chimney. The chimney promptly caught fire and the family's lovely old weatherboard house could easily have burnt to the ground, though their father got home in time to put the flames out. That may just have been an example of 'boys will be boys', but there were other indications. One mealtime, the boys' mother impulsively offered her family the chance to do something different from sitting down to eat together, and told them they could take their plates anywhere they wanted in the house or garden. What exactly had prompted May to make this strange suggestion is unclear but, in any case, Richard remembered how John chose to eat his meal sitting on the rubbish heap. May, who had her own 'funny little ways', did not seem to see the danger signs. John hated his years boarding at Knox Grammar and, despite his intelligence, failed the Leaving Certificate examination (as Henry Lawson had failed the equivalent Matriculation exam) and had to sit for it again the following year in order to get into university. Eventually John went off to London to study industrial design – a new start in the Old Country to which both his parents were fiercely devoted.

But while John was living alone in London in his early twenties, it seems that he overheard a boarder in the next room trying to kill himself. John had a breakdown (the vague term that people still use to cover anything from temporary collapse after a stressful event to a psychotic episode). It is common for families to blame particular, dramatic occurrences for the onset of mental illness in one of their offspring, but it seems more likely that the trauma simply triggers a first episode of psychosis in an individual who is already predisposed genetically to that illness.

John married the forthright, pragmatic Jenny Wilson and they had two daughters. John was in most ways a loving, gentle man. He was a seeker – engaged lifelong in serious explorations of spiritual paths outside the purview of Christianity. He was also eager to support and encourage the enthusiasms and talents of his children. John had long periods of stability in which he was capable of holding a job, but from time to time would sink into depression and paranoia. He was not a regular drinker, having been raised by a teetotal father, but as an adult he would go on occasional binges. Like Henry Lawson's, John's drinking probably served as self-medication for a sensitive, introspective individual who was anything but a conventional man's man. There were episodes in which John impulsively 'spent money he didn't have' (a typical manic behaviour also displayed by Lawson). He would run up debts and then write 'terrible letters', pleading with his brother Richard (in general practice in Wagga Wagga) to loan him money. John became obsessed with the dangers posed by electrical wiring, and Jenny had to wash the family's laundry by hand for a long period because John was convinced that their electric washing machine posed a danger. Sometimes he would be gripped by uncontrollable rage, terrifying the young daughters whom he dearly loved. Interestingly, in the light of Dick's lifelong antipathy to Albert, John cut himself off from both his parents for an extended period of time, though at the very end of Dick's life, there was a moving reconciliation when John visited his father on his deathbed.

After many years of suffering, John was diagnosed with paranoid schizophrenia after an attempt to drown himself in Sydney Harbour. It is true that John occasionally experienced hallucinations and delusions, but these can also occur in the more severe form of manic-depressive illness (bipolar I in today's terminology) and the latter diagnosis would have fitted better with the fact that John experienced both depressive lows and manic highs, in which he sometimes claimed that he hadn't slept for a fortnight – something that may not have been a total exaggeration.

The circumstances in which John died, just a few months before the Albury family reunion, remain unclear. He had been out shopping and had bought pawpaw, a fruit that he tended to buy when he felt 'down' – perhaps another form of self-medication. But he collapsed, apparently from a heart attack, without having removed the fruit from his shopping bag. John was fifty-four years of age at his death – very close to the age at which John's twice-removed cousin Lawson had died. If any member of the family had been aware of it, they would almost certainly have dismissed it as a simple coincidence, 'just one of those things'.

Bad Uncle John?

Of the four Crago brothers who emigrated from Cornwall to Australia in the mid nineteenth century, three enjoyed considerable success. Petherick, the eldest (my great-grandfather) bought the existing flour mill at Yass and built a larger one – the mill that his sons Will and Albert Crago inherited. Petherick's third son Francis (Frank), also a flour miller, became mayor of Bathurst and then moved to Sydney and built the large mill that still stands (now converted into apartments) near Newtown in Sydney. Frank and his family owned a large, comfortable home in Strathfield. William, the youngest of the four brothers, became a prominent Sydney physician and was instrumental in founding the *Medical Journal of Australia*. Only John, the second brother, who had been preceded by two siblings who'd both died in childhood, seems to have brought shame on this otherwise respectable, high-achieving family. John lived out his life in obscurity, often turning to his successful brothers when in need of money, and seemingly an embarrassment to the family. The other three brothers 'went up in the world'. John went down. Like Lawson, he was an alcoholic – and most alcoholics become alcoholics because deep down they lack a conviction of their own worth.

Did John Tamblyn Crago know of his father's Uncle John? I don't know, but I can guess, on the basis of how such things were handled by my father in my own childhood. If John heard the elder John's name mentioned, it would have been a minimal reference ('Oh, yes, I believe there was another brother called John. I don't know what happened to him' or 'There were four brothers came out from Cornwall, and I think one of them was called John, but I've never heard anything about him'). In this way, the older John's name would have been associated with an empty space in the family and, as we've seen already, spaces where information is lacking breed fantasies, and children's fantasies are inevitably going to reflect either their wishes or their fears.

What We Need to Know

What's in a name?

Their thinking still dominated by the older parts of their brains, children tend to have a special relationship with others who they know bear the same name as their own. They may consciously compare themselves with those people ('No, I'm not like her'), or they may simply feel like them, *belong* to them in some strange way. This can happen with historical figures from the past and with fictional characters too. For many younger children, the two are probably in the same category. But most of all it happens when the other person who has your name is, or once was, a member of your own family.

How much was John Crago I influenced by survivor guilt – the fact that he himself had survived to adulthood, while his two sisters, born before him, had not? Could my grandfather Albert Crago (who had also survived while an older brother and three younger siblings had not) have experienced something similar?

Did John Crago I and his great-nephew John Tamblyn Crago both feel confirmed in their low self-esteem when they read or heard about Bad King John (as he was known in the kind of 'kings and queens' histories of England that were still current in Australian schools right up to the 1950s)?

John Plantagenet, a younger son of Henry II, was not expected to inherit the throne, and was known as 'Lackland' because he had not inherited the lands and castles assigned to his brothers Richard and Geoffrey. When he did become king, after the death of both his older brothers, John acquired a dire reputation at the hands of the monks who first chronicled his reign. Gleefully, they pointed out how John had lost important lands in France, how he was forced by his barons to sign Magna Carta, and how he even lost the crown jewels while his baggage train was crossing the Wash. John was described as prone to rages, selfish and traitorous. John Lackland took advantage of his older brother Richard 'Lionheart', yet was forgiven by him. No subsequent king of England has sought to call himself John. Nor has any subsequent king ever been called 'Bad', although plenty of others could have qualified for that dubious distinction.

The truth is that John was no better, but no worse, than many rulers of his time, and arguably no more irresponsible, selfish and cruel than his older brother Richard 'Lionheart'. The whole Plantagenet clan were notorious for their ill temper. But, aided by the Robin Hood legends in which a tyrannous John was allied with the bad Sheriff of Notthingham, John retained his tarnished reputation until relatively recently.

In the Crago family, the name Tamblyn was reserved for eldest sons. John's father Dick had borne it, and John most certainly was told why he too was named Tamblyn, to commemorate Elizabeth Tamblyn, the wife of his great-great-grandfather William Crago. Knowing that you are the oldest in your generation of the family, with a special given name to mark that distinction, is likely to confer high expectations on a child. As John's sister-in-law Roslyn said, 'Great things were supposed to flow from John.' For some children, those expectations could have led to pride and confidence, as it did in John's father Dick, whose full name was Richard Tamblyn – even to a sense of entitlement. But it seems to me that John Tamblyn Crago did not, deep down, feel sure of his own worth, and so may have needed to lose his position of primacy, just as John Lackland may have needed to lose Normandy – and the crown jewels – in order to live up to (or down to) his nickname.

Freud's disciple Carl Jung proposed that people tended, as adults, to enact the literal meaning of their surnames, something that is now called nominative determinism. To supply a contemporary English language example, a man called Trump may grow up to score an unexpected triumph over his more favoured rival, and become president of the USA. We now know that the still-developing brain of a young child does respond in a concrete, literal way to words (including given names). As a girl, New Zealand writer Janet Frame (whose personality was strikingly similar to Beth Crago's) pronounced the word island as 'is-land', and continued to think of it in that way in the opening volume of her autobiography, *To the Is-land*, contrasting it with 'Was-land'. When Ethel Stear married Albert Crago, she remarked later that 'she didn't mind' having a new surname – in other words, she had (understandably) felt uncomfortable at being a Stear (albeit spelled differently from the castrated beast). When her son Dick married May Lepper, it is more than possible she felt similarly – but how much might her maiden name have influenced the process by which, within quite a short time, she was regarded with wariness and derision within the family she had joined?

As a child, I knew that my name was also the name of my mother's younger brother, Hughie, a man who had disappeared out of her life before I was born and whose story I only found out as an adult. Later, I discovered that, as a child, my mother had disliked and resented her male rival for their mother's affections. However, in my growing up years, my mother flatly denied that I'd been named after her brother. Instead, she claimed, both my sister Katherine and I had been named for characters in 'a good book I'd been reading at the time'. This book was the historical novel *Katherine*, set in the reign of Richard II. Of course I read the novel as a teenager, curious to know what the Hugh in it was like. As I explained in chapter 3, this character was the brutish, insensitive Sir Hugh Swynford (his name suggesting swine) who treats the heroine so callously on their wedding night. I did not realise then that *Katherine* could not possibly have been my mother's source for her children's names: Anya Seton's novel was not published until 1954, several years after my sister's birth in 1951. I must have wondered why my mother would have chosen such an unpleasant character to name me after, but it never occurred to me to question why she might have needed to fabricate this story instead of telling the uncomfortable truth – that she had named me after a brother she had disliked, yet felt guilty about disliking. It was exactly the same kind of irrational, contradictory action that Beth (Crago) Plumb had so often displayed in her life, and which I personally experienced from her – refusing to see me, and then, months or even years later, sending me a conciliatory letter, or a small gift.

The 'spectrum' of mental illness

Genetically fearful, sensitive and reactive individuals are, almost by definition, more prone to develop emotional disorders than their easy-going, thick-skinned peers. This particular genetic bundle can display itself in a wide range of symptomatic behaviours from mild anxiety through to obsessive compulsive disorder, from mild to clinical depression, from mere eccentricity (as A.N. Wilson says in his biography of Queen Victoria,[3] 'it is the mark of the true eccentric that she does not see the world as others do') to the extreme isolation, hallucinations and bizarre actions typical of schizophrenia. Some members of the family, who miss out on all or most of this genetic heritage, may be completely normal; others will experience mild to moderate levels of difficulty, yet manage to achieve a stable and reasonably fulfilling life; others again will be dominated by their genetic legacy and suffer full-blown mental illness or personality disorder.

In practice, the separate disorders distinguished by psychiatry shade into one another, and individuals who will never be diagnosed with a mental illness will nevertheless share some behaviours and thought patterns with those who are. What is in question is a kind of continuum, a spectrum of mental health, in which, as we've already seen, the genetic bundle of fearfulness, sensitivity and reactivity often (though not inevitably) results in an individual who, even as a baby, will be perceived as 'difficult'. Such infants invite more frustration, anger and adverse judgements from parents than their genetically more fortunate siblings, and so their genetic potential for being troublesome, difficult or even 'bad' is reinforced by their upbringing.

The social defeat hypothesis[4] proposes that when individuals are repeatedly dismissed, devalued or shamed by significant others in their lives, they are more likely to develop schizophrenia. I strongly suspect that this hypothesis should extend to other forms of cognitive and emotional dysfunction. And it seems persuasive that an ideology like that taught by John Wesley would support and reinforce such early experiences of defeat. Implicit in early Methodism was a conviction that human beings were helpless in this life, and that only in the redeeming power of Christ could they hope for justice and appreciation – and then only in a Heavenly afterlife. This belief faithfully reflected the social realities of Wesley's England, when the poor had virtually no hope of ever rising above their station.

Dysfunctional individuals keep popping up in each new generation of the Crago family and its associated lines – John Crago I (my great-grandfather Petherick's brother); Elizabeth Anne Granger and Albert

Crago (in Petherick Crago's own immediate descendants), Beth in Albert's line, John in Dick's. In the Albury–Stear line, there are Harry Albury, Henry and Charlie Lawson, and Gertrude (Gert) Stear. No doubt there more than I know about, since dysfunction of any kind tends to be passed over in silence as families close ranks around their black sheep and weak lambs.

In almost every instance within my own extended family, the genetic source of emotional impairment is found *not just in one parent's family, but in both*. Henry Lawson inherited his not only from the Alburys (through his mother Louisa, Harry Albury's daughter) but from the Larsens (through his father, Niels). Beth inherited hers not only from the Cragos (through her father Albert) but from the Stears and the Alburys (through her mother, Ethel). John inherited his not only from the Cragos and Stears (through his father Dick) but from the Leppers (through his mother May), and so on.

Opposites attract; gene pools replace themselves

By the principle of assortative mating, young adults tend to be attracted to individuals who they consciously or unconsciously recognise as similar to themselves in key ways. It is well attested that people tend to partner with those whose class background, level of education and physical attractiveness roughly match their own. But I believe it goes much deeper than that. In my view, young adults are drawn to partner with those whose *genetic potentials* are similar to those already present within their own families. And so, various degrees of emotional disturbance, including mental illness, are reintroduced into the family line, even when the couple themselves may be located at the normal end of the spectrum. This is because it is possible for us to carry genes which do not express themselves in us, but which do express themselves in one or more of our offspring.

In each married pair, one partner tends to be seen (by relatives; even by the couple themselves) as more normal, stable and dependable, the other as different, unreliable and irresponsible. Family opinion focuses on the differences not the similarities. It suits families to locate problems in one spouse rather than the other, and there is a strong tendency to blame one's brother's wife (or sister's husband), rather than one's own sibling. This kind of judgement helps families to feel better about themselves, but it fails to reflect the full truth. Rather than seeing people as choosing individuals with whom they feel comfortable (though that is true enough in itself) we would do better to see *families* as choosing other *families* in whom they recognise a similar genetic mix to their own. Of course this choice occurs at a deep, biologically driven level, of which the two partners are unaware. But it occurs, nonetheless.

The power of silence

In Henry Lawson's story 1901 'The Union Buries its Dead', the narrator briefly encounters a young man – the two do not introduce themselves. It is only later, at a graveside funeral service in a nearby town, that the narrator recognises the deceased (who has recently drowned in a nearby billabong) as the same cheerful horseman he met only the day before. Nobody knows anything about the stranger – his union card is the only thing that identifies him. But, with the despairing cynicism that was Lawson's trademark, he ends his bleak little tale with the comment that by the time the man's relatives place newspaper advertisements seeking to know his whereabouts, those present at the little funeral will 'have already forgotten his name'. In Lawson's fictional world, lone individuals (usually men) wander, cut off from their families and even their friends: they live alone much of the time, and they die alone – something that could also be said of Lawson himself. By the time the Albury reunion took place, sixty-odd years after his death in 1922, Henry had achieved the very fate he assigned to the dead union man – others would not even remember his name. In this way, families often obliterate shameful or embarrassing ancestors, simply by never talking about them, and by giving only evasive answers to their children's questions. Silence perpetuates shame while attempting to conceal it. I have little doubt that the same thing happened with John Crago I. Two generations on, few in the extended family would even have known of his existence.

Extraordinary sanity and ordinary madness

Most of us have a vested interest in staying well away from mental illness, and in minimising the possibility of its occurrence within our own families, because it might reflect badly on us. If we were secure in our own worth, truly accepting of ourselves, would we so easily feel 'contaminated' by a relative we might not even have met? Might it not be, then, that many of us inwardly share at least some of the insecurity, the lack of belief in our own worth, that these odd, 'funny' individuals display more openly? And so, when we're honest with ourselves, the comfortingly clear distinctions, the solid barriers that separate 'normal' people from those who live beyond the pale begin to blur alarmingly. Gwyn Armstrong was no more mentally ill than I am, but both of us might easily enough be classed as 'funny peculiar' by others who observed our unashamedly unconventional behaviour.

We view sanity as normal and madness as an aberration, but surely the reality is that many normal people are abnormal to some degree, and some mad people can be more in touch with the harsh reality of human existence than the rest of us allow ourselves to be.

As psychologists are now starting to acknowledge, depressive people actually see the world more accurately than the rest of us do, simply because they are less well defended. The truth is that life is often unfair and cruel, and many people never get a chance to achieve their potential. But for those who are 'born without a skin' (or at least, born with a very thin one), the dark reality of life impinges upon them constantly.

If people with depressive disorders acknowledge the sadness and unfairness of life more fully than the rest of us, are they not 'saner' than we are? If they find themselves asking, 'What is the point of all this?', and answering that life is essentially meaningless, then might they not be braver, in some ways, than those who are simply and sincerely religious? And if a few of them capitulate after years of struggle, and take their own lives, can they be judged so harshly for that?

Henry Lawson, Gwyn Armstrong, Beth Plumb and John Crago

all, to varying degrees and at different stages of their journeys, looked upon the void and felt the smallness and essential isolation of human life. All of them felt different, felt as if they did not belong. And a felt sense of inadequacy, a sense of not belonging, leads, more often than not, to a sense of injustice – and a conviction of one's own entitlement.

8

Injustice and Entitlement

Du mein Freund,
Mir war auf dieser Welt das Glück nicht hold!
Wohin ich geh? Ich geh, ich wandre in die Berge.
Ich suche Ruhe für mein einsam Herz.
Ich wandle nach der Heimat, meiner Stätte.
Ich werde niemals in die Ferne schweifen.
Still ist mein Herz und harret seiner Stunde!

O my friend,
Fortune was not kind to me in this world.
I'm going back to the mountains,
To still the loneliness
Of my heart.
I'm going back to where I came from,
And I'll not stray again.
I am at peace now, for
I know my time has come.

> 'Der Abschied' ('The Farewell'), after poems by Wang Wei and Meng Haoran, German text 1907, further adapted by Gustav Mahler for *Das Lied von der Erde*, 1912, and freely translated here

In My Time

Life has not been kind (Southport, Armidale, Sydney, 1994–2000)

When I gained an honours degree in English at the age of twenty-one, my father exclaimed, slightly too heartily, 'Well, now the world's at your feet!' Dad's words may have carried a trace of envy, but the strength of my own reaction shocked me – as if he'd insulted me, not praised me. 'It means nothing of the kind!' I snarled. 'I've got a long way to go yet!' I did not realise it then, but my ungracious, scornful reply was a way of covering an unanticipated vulnerability. In that moment, I had been my Auntie Beth, angrily returning a lovingly intended gift or compliment that had probably triggered her into feeling bad and worthless.

Brought up with a horror of 'skiting', I wanted to be admired, but when (in small ways) I found myself a success, I longed to get out of the limelight and sought a quick getaway. I was perfectly capable of relishing my success when I felt alone with it, but if anyone else intruded on it, even with the best intentions, I would somehow feel compromised, shamed. I was still that three-year-old boy listening alone to *Kindergarten of the Air* on ABC radio. Even then, it seems, I was unable to share intense experiences, needed to hug them to myself. If anyone else intruded, I felt out of control. But being in control is a lonely place to be. You are alone with your fears, not just with your triumphs.

Though I was not conscious of it at the time, I made strenuous attempts to disown my competence throughout my twenties. At Oxford, I turned down the chance to convert my thesis into a doctorate. I thought I would go straight to writing books without the need for such boring preliminaries. And I thought the bright red-and-blue DPhil gown showy (perhaps, in this city that had been a Cavalier stronghold during the first years of the Civil War, I thus displayed my Roundhead leanings?). In my first academic job, at Wagga, my initial philosophy of teaching literature was not to teach at all. I retrained as a counsellor and family therapist because that work seemed more real, more useful to the world than 'tearing books to pieces' (as my students had called literary criticism). I continued to think about literature, and to write about it, but I had given up my licence to practise as a literary scholar and from now on, would be an outsider in the literary world – no longer part of the club. By paying close attention to children's responses to literature, I puzzled and alienated most of my fellow enthusiasts for children's books (who considered children almost irrelevant to the serious business of analysing the books adults had written for them).

Once I had requalified as a family therapist, I sabotaged myself again, by aligning myself with confronting theories which ran contrary to the generally optimistic spirit of my professional colleagues, and retaining a strong interest in psychoanalysis (which family therapy had rejected). My ideas were unconventional and mostly unfashionable, so I was grateful to find editors willing to accept my articles at all. I published in peripheral journals, and thus ensured that my articles would remain unread by the very people I most wanted to be noticed by. Yet I maintained a dream of being an independent scholar and some day being valued for my work.

I obtained a book contract with reputable publishers in Melbourne for *A Family in Time,* the big family book I'd begun after our return from New Hampshire, but when they requested substantial cuts, I stubbornly refused to sanction any at all. I eventually withdrew from the contract. I was still terrified of success, and so (without consciously realising it) ensured that it did not eventuate. Like several of my relatives in the past, I had cut off my nose to spite my face. But even though I now knew about those relatives, it did not occur to me that I was doing exactly what they had done.

By the time I returned to academic life after two years as a student in New Hampshire, seven years as a counsellor in Wagga, and two more in charge of a small youth refuge in Southport, I was forty-five, and had done some growing up, at least within my work life. No longer did I need to deny that I knew something of potential value to my students, and could legitimately offer it to them. By 1992 I was teaching within the School of Education at Griffith University, on Queensland's Gold Coast, starting again at the bottom of the academic ladder as a junior lecturer. I threw myself enthusiastically into my one year contract position. I enjoyed tutoring in an evidence-based subject (human development), mentored by a psychologist colleague who became a good friend. Then, after two renewals of my contract and the hope that I would soon gain a permanent position, there was a change of leadership. Our new dean made all the right noises but clearly wanted to get rid of the dead wood on his staff (which meant anyone without a PhD). In the twelve years I had been out of the academic world, things had changed dramatically.

Despite my truculent rejection of my father's praise in 1968, I had always been proud of my first class honours degree. Back then, firsts were few and far between, and could not be earned by hard work alone. I was disgusted to hear our new dean announce a strategy of recruiting an honours class from undergraduates with above-average grades, 'coaching them intensively so they all got firsts' (his exact words), and then funnelling them 'straight into a PhD program'. He wasn't being generous to less-than-brilliant students. He just knew that he and his department would get brownie points for the number of doctoral students they'd enrolled – not for the quality of those students, or their appropriateness for the long grind of researching and writing a doctoral thesis. It didn't matter if most of them dropped out, disillusioned, along the way – it was the initial head count that mattered.

I must have made my disapproval clear, though I can't now recall what exactly I said. Despite loud public assurances, the dean axed my position at the end of my third year. Should I realistically have expected any other outcome? But then, I wasn't being realistic. I was hanging onto the academic standards that I had experienced in my own youth, and a notion of 'academic freedom' to speak out frankly that had already slipped into legend. But before that, I had grown up with a Methodist conviction that if asked a question, I must answer with the truth, even if I suffered as a result. It was that radical innocence – an inability to conceal my true nature – that I shared with more than a few members of my family of origin.

Less than a year later, I gained another contract lectureship, this time for three years, teaching counselling in the School of Health at the University of New England in Armidale – and the same thing happened again. The senior academics who had appointed me were replaced by a new head of department and a new dean, both mouthing the rhetoric of economic rationalism. Superficial charm and charisma (like Napoleon's) masked their ruthlessness. They never apologised, never explained. Like Hitler, they were convinced that the normal rules did not apply to them, and that they were entitled to 'total loyalty and obedience' from their staff.

I had wanted to stay in Armidale, stay teaching for my old university. But, in a blind repetition of my earlier pattern, I sabotaged any chance I had of that. I might be an outstanding teacher and a prolific publisher, full of ideas and energy, but those things now counted for very little without the all-important PhD. The letter mattered, not the spirit. And I had antagonised my new department head. I'd been advised to stroke his ego, but could not bring myself to do so. 'We've got to get rid of Hugh,' he exclaimed in a meeting (I was not present: others told me about it later). My contempt for him, and my own sureness that I was morally right, were as much signs of narcissistic entitlement as his contempt for 'these fifty-year-old men struggling to finish their PhDs', his dedication to his way or the highway. But I did not see that, and found myself, predictably, on the highway.

For months I was preoccupied by the injustice of it all. 'Oh, so you're all bitter and twisted, are you?' asked a woman recently appointed to a lectureship in the same faculty that had dispensed with me. She was on a contract too, but confident that she wouldn't lose her job at the end of it. I burned at her remark, but perhaps it did me good: I realised that it was useless to seek justice from the system that had extruded me, and that the longer I fancied myself as a Count of Monte Cristo who would one day gain a delicious and grandiose revenge, the more I risked deserving the bitter and twisted label.

I wasn't, in fact, one of 'those fifty-year-old men struggling to finish their PhDs' whom the head of my department so despised. I had never wanted to enrol for a doctorate. I had lots of reasons for this, not all of them irrational or silly. The sorts of books I wanted to write were old-fashioned ones – addressing substantial questions and ranging much more widely than the narrowly focused research-based investigations required of a PhD candidate. But underneath all this, I still believed that the quality of my teaching and my thinking was such that I should not have to complete a doctorate (when I'd been an undergraduate in the 1960s, it was still possible for outstanding scholars to gain promotions, even professorial chairs, without one). Just like the little Hitlers I had joked about with Maureen and my friends, I was convinced that the conventional rules should not apply to me.

Jansen Newman Institute, in Sydney, was, in 1998, a small private college that offered training to would-be counsellors and psychotherapists. Like Antioch, it struggled financially, employed contract staff to do much of its teaching and admitted mostly mature-age adults – the kind of students I most enjoyed working with. I was offered a position as head of the academic program, and, as I had done before at UNE, I began to refashion the existing curriculum into something with shape, purpose and integrity. An important part of that integrity, for me, was not to take on students whose personalities did not fit them for the demanding role of counsellor and psychotherapist.

My superiors claimed they wanted proper academic standards, but clearly felt uneasy when I imposed them. They did not openly question my assumptions until I'd written the submission that would gain the institute accreditation from the Higher Education Board. Once the accreditation came through, the executive officer appointed by my employers made it clear that I was stopping the institute from enrolling students in sufficient numbers to assure the institute's continued existence and growth. I was no longer welcome at JNI. I saw the writing on the wall and resigned.

Three times in ten years I'd been appointed by idealistic superiors who recognised themselves in my honesty and my capacity for hard work – as well as in my conviction of my own worth. Three times in ten years, those employers had been replaced with others, who, by contrast, viewed me as a dangerous whistle-blower whom they must get rid of. At each institution in turn, almost everything I had worked tirelessly to put in place vanished within a couple of years of my leaving. The standards were watered down, the innovative subjects and imaginative set texts pulled back into line with what everyone else was teaching. Nearly all the students who had trusted and believed in me adjusted their values to the new regime – after all, what choice did they have?

Thirty years after my first teaching position in Wagga, I was still playing the teenage rebel. I began to admit to myself that it was not just a matter of being discriminated against by unfair bosses. Perhaps they'd have gotten rid of me anyway, but I'd been making it easy for them. I'd neglected my wife and my children in favour of my own quest to break back into an academic world I'd gaily rejected in 1979. Now the ones who could have loved me and supported me through the dark wood were thoroughly exasperated and wary of another of my fantasy-inspired 'new starts'. I was depressed, I was angry and I had reached the middle of the journey of my life.

I first heard Gustav Mahler's *Das Lied von der Erde* as a young adult. I could not really say that I felt comfortable with its wild swings between drunken elation and deep melancholy (I did not know it then, but Mahler suffered from manic-depressive illness.) The lyrics of its six songs, originally Chinese but freely translated into German, spoke of the beauty and fragility of life, of loneliness, and of the ever-present looming threat of death. At twenty, one does not relish such a perspective. I reacted to *Das Lied* much as I had to 'Little Red Monkey', whose minor key and talk of loneliness had so affected me at six. Over many years, I grew into Mahler's music, but for me the highlight of the entire symphony came in its final and greatest movement, where the poet farewells a friend who admits that 'Fortune has not treated him well', and is now heading back to his homeland in the mountains, where he will wait for death with a peaceful heart. As the departing friend sings his final lines about how the earth renews itself in the spring (added to the original by Mahler himself), the yearning sadness of the music shifts into the major and the melodic line soars upwards, like sunlight breaking through clouds. These few bars took me over, reached me in a way that I could never describe or explain.

I was fifty-four. My cousin John had dropped dead at fifty-four. By fifty-four, Gustav Mahler, too, was dead, and that other, distant cousin whom nobody had wanted to talk about at the Albury family reunion had died just months later than Mahler, at fifty-five. It was time for me to admit I was in trouble, and seek the help I'd needed all my life.

In Family Time

My father sang. He sang each Sunday in the church choir, nervous that he might fail to get the high notes, although he almost always did. He sang at home, too, sometimes sitting down at the piano and accompanying himself in the parlour songs he remembered from his own childhood (when in her turn, his mother Ethel had sat at the piano and encouraged her growing family to sing along). But Dad didn't ask us to join in. Family entertainment had changed, subtly, into solo performance. Not that Dad expected praise or applause from his children – he probably would've been embarrassed by it. He was performing in order to keep alive a part of him that he associated with childhood innocence, with what his family had called 'good, clean fun'. He was taking, in his own family, the place she had taken in hers. My own mother was rarely in the room when Dad sat down to sing. What he showed, indirectly, in those performances was his loyalty to the woman my own mother had stayed away from, and required him to do the same.

It was Ethel Crago's genes that lived on in my father's singing voice. There could be no doubt about that, for her own voice had been good enough for friends to urge her, as a young woman, to make a career as a professional vocalist. Ethel's singing reminded them of Clara Butt, an English contralto of the late nineteenth and early twentieth century whose rich, deep voice won her an international audience. But Ethel famously replied, 'No, my family comes first.' Her voice became a local treasure to her family and to the Yass community, but Ethel's drive to achieve would have to find other outlets.

Ethel disapproved of her Aunt Louisa's radical politics and freethinking ways. Consequently, my father seems not to have been aware that his great-aunt had also possessed 'the voice'. It was not among the small collection of childhood memories that he cherished and passed on to his own children – memories in which his mother was the shining star and his father the uncouth outsider. But as an adult, I discovered that when Louisa had been around seventeen, William Slee, one of the adventurers digging for gold at Pipeclay (as Eurunderee was then called), had gone so far as to get up a collection to enable Harry Albury's daughter – Louisa – to study singing professionally, back in England. The diggers were sure she had a great career ahead of her, but Louisa's mother Harriet would have none of it. Harriet was a reserved woman who believed it was inappropriate for her daughters to enter public life. Perhaps she was thinking of the notoriously promiscuous Lola Montez, who had entertained diggers in Victoria with her provocative dancing in 1855–56? To Harriet and other respectable women at the time, performing in public was little better than prostitution. At eighteen, Louisa Albury married Slee's mate Nils Larsen in haste, to escape from her family and the stifling little world of the diggings. For years she went on writing verse, but she probably felt less and less inclined to sing as the gap between herself and her taciturn, depressive husband widened. Did she ever find herself thinking, resentfully, of the career she might have had as a performer, had her parents been more willing to acknowledge her talent and support her ambitions? Would she have been so critical of her son's verse if they had?

Later, Louisa would patent a new and efficient catch to fasten mail bags, but, though the Post Office adopted her invention, she never benefited financially from it to the extent she should have, and felt keenly the injustice of the way the Post Office had cheated her. She edited the first Australian feminist magazine, *The Dawn*, wrote much of it, and printed and published it herself. She kept up a lively correspondence with women all over the country, advising, encouraging and warning. Her creativity was eclipsed by that of her son Henry, and history has been grudging in its acknowledgement of her contribution. Her wonderful singing voice remained mute, and most of her poems remained unpublished until late in her life. Hard work and campaigning for the cause of women's rights had replaced the emotional, expressive part of herself that had briefly flowered when she used to sing, alone, in the bush, and make up stories and verses.

With professional singing ruled out, Ethel, too, had to find other ways to express herself, to make a difference. She was not a writer or a thinker like Louisa, but she resembled her aunt in being a capable organiser and so she flung herself wholeheartedly into ensuring her children's futures. She promoted the education of her three 'brilliant' sons, and celebrated their triumphs – at least until they got married. For her daughters, she arranged suitable marriages. Two of her three girls – Gwyn being the exception – married men whom Ethel had nudged them towards. But Dick and Ian, the two sons she cherished the most, both chose to marry women whose personalities and values Ethel disliked. Her husband, Albert, frustrated her with his narrow horizons and his fears about spending money – when he roared, Ethel would retire to her room with a headache. She felt misunderstood and unrecognised by the man she had married, probably just as badly misunderstood and unseen as Louisa had felt by Peter Lawson. Did Mrs Albert Crago ever, as she sang 'Land of Hope and Glory' and 'The Lost Chord' at benefit concerts during the Great War, wonder what her life might have been like had she enjoyed better opportunities?

Henry Lawson and Harry Albury

The one Albury descendant who became a celebrity seemed ill at ease with his own fame. He gained success early in life, but perhaps it would have been better if he had served a longer apprenticeship, for when successes did not occur as easily as they had done at first, he sank into self-pity rather than lifting his game. Henry constantly shifted the blame for his failures onto others – including those who had most patiently and loyally supported him.

Henry's blaming out echoed that of Harry Albury, Henry's

grandfather, a confident larrikin who never admitted to any fault, and launched legal actions against those he felt had wronged him. 'It's not fair and I'm not going to put up with it' might have been Harry's motto. As a boy, his grandson Henry Lawson felt drawn to Harry, his only grandfather (he never knew his father's parents, back in Norway), and listened eagerly to the old man's stories, which later formed the raw material for 'Grandfather's Courtship' (not published in Lawson's lifetime). The story is slight, but alive with vivid details of the old man's speech, including his irritation at being interrupted by his grandson, and his frequent use of the phrase 'la-di-da' to denote those who considered themselves as occupying a higher station than his own. Perhaps it is not surprising that the two got on well, for Henry would later display his own version of some of Grandfather's less endearing traits. He not only blamed others rather than taking responsibility for his own problems, but considered himself entitled to loyalty and support, whether he had earned it or not. Had Harry – or Henry – been born into the aristocracy, such an attitude might have seemed understandable. But the Alburys had been a family of peasants.

Henry was the epitome of the irresponsible artist type within the family, the closest to Augustin Meaulnes, the wanderer, or the departing traveller in *Das Lied von der Erde* – always searching, never able to accept the ordinary happiness and unhappiness of life. In Henry's career, the twin themes of entitlement and injustice stand out in high relief. Yet even among Henry's Crago cousins – conventional, dutiful, religious and hard-working – the same themes appear, if in a more muted way.

Albert Crago and Ian Crago

My grandfather Albert was seen by his nephew Ralph (Albert's brother Will's youngest son) as 'obnoxious' – a man who had no idea of how to behave, and no understanding of others. Albert certainly lacked tact and charm. Yet this same man extended credit, time and again, to those who were struggling to pay their bills, and then resented the ones who never bothered to repay him. His religion enjoined him to to give his money away rather than amassing riches for himself. Albert felt obliged to follow that precept. Having low self-esteem, he also had difficulty saying no to people, and he never developed good judgement about whose word could be trusted. He applied the Golden Rule in a mechanical, across-the-board way – and Albert may well have been at the high-functioning end of the autism spectrum, as indeed might Harry Albury.

In a more profound way, Albert experienced himself as unfairly treated by his much older brother Will, with whom he jointly owned the Crago brothers mill. Will – more capable, better educated and vastly more assured – was the 'real miller'. He sat in the office, formally dressed, and dealt with the accounts, while his younger brother worked alongside the labourers, loading, unloading and stacking. Will paid himself the same salary as Albert, but Albert retained throughout his working life the conviction that his older brother could not have built his big house on the outskirts of Yass without having taken more out of the mill than he ought. Unfairness was the theme: like Lawson, Albert felt he had been done down, deprived of what should by rights have been his. I do not believe Will was dishonest or exploitative – he simply felt more able to spend the money that was his to spend (possibly including his wife's inheritance) in a way that his younger brother was too cautious to risk. But Albert did not consider this possibility, and clung lifelong to his belief that his 'la-di-da' brother had diddled him. Probably, his father Pederick, recognising that Albert lacked the capabilities of Will, had tried to provide for him, and also save face for him, by making him a partner in the mill, with the understanding that its real management would remain with Will. This would be consistent with Pederick's leaving Albert, rather than Will, his three rental properties. Albert was the 'weak lamb' who needed additional shelter.

Did my father Ian absorb something of Albert's sense of injustice? He certainly carried on his father's scorn for his older Crago cousins, Will's sons and daughters, whom he regarded as having 'their heads in the clouds'. By contrast, he saw himself and his siblings as hard-working, respectable people, 'not rich, but rich in the things that really matter'. Yet Ian himself was ambitious, more ambitious than I ever realised when I was growing up.

Until close to the end of his life, my father rarely spoke of his early years in the Education Department – quite probably because I did not ask. My own awareness of his career did not begin until I was nine, when, in 1955, he was promoted to inspector of schools, and we moved to Ballina. Before that, I eventually found out, he had been 'a bit of a white-haired boy' in the department, going within a decade from opportunity class teacher to school counsellor to superintendent of special education. Born in 1915, my father was a youthful-looking forty when he arrived in his new job at Ballina, prompting one elderly headmaster to remark sourly, 'I didn't know they were appointing *boys* inspectors these days!' Dad had risen rapidly, and he expected that further advancement would follow – only it didn't. After eight years in the inspectorate, he applied for the next level (staff inspector) without success. He tried again, but saw 'worthless men' promoted in preference to him. He was disgusted. Much later, Dad explained that he had refused to laugh at the 'risqué jokes' made by his superiors. He would stand there with disapproval written all over his face while his peers sniggered. It didn't make for lasting popularity. His lifelong refusal to take a drink didn't help either. He felt different from his peers, different from most of his superiors, too. Different not only because of his Methodist values, but also because he knew he was more intelligent and (I suspect) more ethical than some of them.

As inspector, a role with considerable influence, Dad enjoyed recommending promotion for teachers he considered outstanding, but he hated writing reports that could damage or end the careers of those who underperformed. Just like his father Albert, he didn't like saying no to people. In fact, there were many aspects of being an educational administrator that he did not enjoy. Sitting alone in an office answering phone calls or interviewing complainants did not offer the satisfactions he had gained as a teacher, and at home he would talk longingly of being back in the classroom. He was an enthusiast, a true believer in the power of education, which certainly wouldn't have endeared him to peers for whom educational administration was just a job or a means to personal advancement.

In short, while my father was less overt in his rebelliousness than I was, he too had been a thorn in the side of inept or corrupt superiors, prepared to speak up for what he believed in, even if it hindered his own career. From the time he left home as a fourteen-year-old to complete his schooling in Sydney (and probably much earlier than that), Dad had controlled his emotions and turned the other cheek when necessary. Yet in private, his scorn for anyone who seemed to him incompetent was obvious. He was dismissive of the men who had taught him at Fort Street Boys' High, of those who, at teachers college, had refused to admit him to the choir, of his privileged classmates who had gone straight to university instead of having to complete their degrees through evening classes, as he had. Throughout, he acted like a stereotyped working-class lad with a chip on his shoulder – even though he had been born into a middle-class family. It isn't the literal truth of our upbringing, but what we *believe* about our upbringing that shapes our subsequent lives.

As a beginning teacher, Dad earned praise and promotion more often than rebuke, but like his sister Beth, he remembered every slight he had ever experienced. He may have kept his mouth shut at work, but at home he complained every time a good idea of his own was rejected by his superiors. His disdain for his superiors leaked, and when eventually the ones who had praised and promoted him were replaced by superiors who did not like him and his 'narrow-minded' values, his promotions ceased. It took my father a decade before he accepted that he would not rise any higher.

For the duration of my father's working life (which began in the 1930s and ended in the 1970s), men could expect to remain in a single profession for life. It was very different for women. My mother, too, had been an outstanding classroom teacher. She had enrolled for an MA at a time when the possession of a Masters degree immediately marked out a young teacher for higher things. Like my father, Mum had left the classroom via a sideways move into the role of school counsellor. She had planned to go to America to do her PhD. But then came the war, marriage to my father and, in 1946, the first of three children. For women at the time, marriage and children commonly marked the end of their professional career. Mum's future was now tied to Dad's. Moreover, she had run into trouble with her Masters research. Her supervisor, one Dr Harold Wyndham, had told her that her research design was inadequate, and sent her back to start again with a different research question. Mum was deeply offended, though pragmatic enough to do as she was told. She graduated, but with a second-class degree, and this must have put a dampener on her plans to study for a PhD in Wisconsin.

Long afterwards, when Harold Wyndham had become director general of education for NSW and celebrated as the architect of sweeping educational reforms, my mother used to refer to him disparagingly as 'just a nasty little man who didn't like anyone else to get too far ahead'. Having read her thesis, however, my own sense is that Wyndham had been correct in his evaluation: Mum was an intelligent woman but she was not, at heart, a researcher and she was certainly not an original thinker. Her career went on hold for the better part of twenty years, while she raised three children and (she admitted later) longed for a fourth. In the latter portion of her time as a mother and housewife, she became restless and dissatisfied. Not until 1961 did she gain permission to return to classroom teaching at Grafton High. She threw herself into it as energetically as she had done twenty years before, and when my father was transferred to a Sydney inspectorate, she applied successfully for a lecturing position at William Balmain Teacher's College, where she remained until she retired. She had begun to be seen as a problem by her superiors because, as she said, 'I wanted to fail too many students.' This was at the very beginning of the same moving away from appropriate academic standards, the same belief that every student 'deserved' to graduate, that I ran into much later in my own time in higher education.

Mum would certainly never have failed a student unless there was good reason for it, and her standards were very fair. Like my father, she was scornful of incompetence and considered herself superior to many of her colleagues (which she probably was). She and another lecturer planned a series of primary school English textbooks, but she rapidly became disillusioned with her co-author, saying that all the ideas came from her and that he didn't pull his weight. She wasn't satisfied with the sections for which he had been responsible, and rewrote them. She was probably right about all these things, but (like her husband's older sister Gwyn) she lacked tact and delicacy in how she expressed her views.

Indiscretion was not a new thing for Mum. At Ballina, she had at first relished being 'the inspector's wife'. More sociable and outgoing than Dad, she had enjoyed entertaining local and visiting colleagues. Doors opened and friendships multiplied with the wives of principals and other inspectors. But then Mum thoughtlessly passed on an item of gossip that had been offered to her in confidence. Almost overnight, she and my father were treated more distantly, and erstwhile friends dropped away. 'I didn't know what country towns were like!' Mum said later. 'I wasn't a country girl!' But in fact she had done the same thing much earlier, on that visit to my father's family before her marriage, riding roughshod over the Christian values of her fiancé's family. Both my parents hinted that Mum's indiscretion at Ballina may have impacted directly on Dad's career, though Dad never blamed her for his lack of promotion after 1955.

By the time Mum had retired from lecturing and embarked on an ambitious book about the teaching of reading, her mental capacities had begun to decline. She could not reduce to order the mass of academic material she had to read, and struggled to formulate her own thoughts, even though she had lectured on the subject with such authority at college. Eventually she gave up the project – perhaps an attempt to complete the equivalent of the doctorate she'd been unable to undertake so long before – and succumbed to dementia.

What We Need to Know

Birth order, injustice and entitlement

Birth order may not have nearly as profound an effect on children as used to be asserted – genetic legacies and parental alliances also play an important role – but the difference between firstborns and later-born siblings is still marked.[1] Being a firstborn child (and to a lesser degree, being the first boy or girl child in a family) tends to encourage a certain level of confidence simply because one is always older than one's siblings and has experienced everything before them. Firstborns also tend to internalise their parents' rules more deeply and (often) cast themselves (or are cast by their parents) in the role of rule-makers, policemen or protectors to their younger sisters and brothers – especially in large families. They grow accustomed to telling others what to do. All of this can lend an air of authority even to a genetically self-doubting child and highlight the difference between her/him and another, equally self-doubting, sibling. Such I suspect may have been the case with my grandfather Albert's Uncle Will. To Albert, fifteen years younger (a middle brother, Frederick, having died at seventeen), Will must have been an almost parental presence. Will seemed assured and commanding, so that is how Albert saw him.

Albert himself, not simply the younger brother but the youngest of eight surviving children, got from his birth-order position a powerful reinforcement for his pre-existing level of anxiety. His sense of injustice complemented his older brother's birth-order-conferred sense of entitlement. Will was born to rule, Albert born to serve. Neither seems to have shifted from his position lifelong. When Albert married Ethel Stear – not a firstborn, but the firstborn girl, with six younger sisters – he simply replicated his relationship with Will. As his eldest grandson John memorably said much later, Albert was 'dominated at the mill and dominated at home'.

Back to the future

My father's quiet rebellion against the values of his professional peers and superiors had occurred in the context of a very different social and educational climate from the one I encountered in the 1990s. From 1920 on, schooling to at least the age of fourteen was seen as the right of every child, an entitlement. Higher education, by contrast, was a privilege for a small elite, most of whose university education would be paid for by the government. As an undergraduate in the mid-1960s, I had been part of this elite. By the time I re-entered academic life in 1991, as a man of forty-five, I found universities in the midst of a radical transformation. Education was now a commodity to be marketed and for which the consumer must pay. Higher education was an entitlement of the many. Promotion within the academic establishment came rapidly to those who were prepared to adopt the values of economic rationalism and expediency. Vice chancellors and deans moved rapidly to eliminate those who represented the old values – freedom to speak one's mind, dedication to teaching at the expense of publications and research grants, the right to engage in 'blue sky research' (that is, research motivated purely by the desire to advance knowledge regardless of its practical or commercial benefits).

It was as if I had found myself transported via a time machine to a university system so transformed that I no longer recognised it – and my ability to adapt to that new environment was limited. Exactly as my father had done, I stubbornly maintained the beliefs and behaviours I had grown up with, despite knowing that they were anathema to the institutions I now worked for. There had been many things wrong with the old academic world I remembered from the 1960s. Some staff had been lazy, a few incompetent, many eccentric. But it had been a comfortable, generous-spirited culture, which at its best enabled the disinterested pursuit of knowledge. Now the generosity had gone, and the working conditions were becoming increasingly stressful. Quantity had replaced quality, and staff were rewarded for marketing themselves slickly – even dishonestly – rather than for genuine scholarship. 'You should blow your own trumpet more, Hugh' was advice I received more than once from puzzled superiors who saw how I was failing to 'play up and play the game'.

My father's career path was, on the face of it, very different from mine. But both of us had experienced a dream run early on, followed by repeated failure to reach the level of responsibility and influence both of us felt we deserved. And our career stalemates happened at a very similar age. Dad was forty-eight when he and Mum moved back to Sydney from Grafton and he applied, unsuccessfully, for promotions. He was fifty-five when he was appointed to a staff inspector-equivalent position in charge of teacher training in English as a foreign language, and was able to build and run his own unit until he retired. I was fifty-seven when, in 2004, I was appointed to a senior lectureship at the University of Western Sydney, and had a third and final opportunity to rebuild a counselling program. Dad retired at sixty-two, I worked on until sixty-five, yet both of us had approximately eight years in our final salaried job, and both of us were able to finish it with a sense of having achieved something worthwhile, in part because we had scaled down our original ambitions along the way.

Neither of my parents found it easy to embrace humility, and my mother, in particular, considered herself entitled to say what she felt, regardless of the offence she might cause. My father seems the exact opposite, yet, as for generations of Methodists before him, Dad's behaviour constituted an implicit rebuke to his some of his worldly (and sexist) peers. He did not feel like a rebel, or behave like a rebel, but he was passed over because of the values by which he insisted on living, because he refused to take the easy way out and conform. And I had done the same – resembling Mum more than Dad in insisting on speaking my truth regardless of others' feelings, but nevertheless, following the example of both of them, and, like both of them, experiencing both injustice and (compensatory) entitlement.

Injustice and dissent

John Wesley's preaching elaborated upon Jesus's Sermon on the Mount: Wesleyans must turn the other cheek when insulted or rejected, suffer in dignified silence the slights of others. They must hide their light under a bushel, play down their achievements and disown their triumphs, giving the glory to God rather than to themselves. If they were businessmen, it was acceptable for them make money, but they ought to give away most of their profits, keeping only what was necessary to support their families in modest comfort. Positions of leadership in the government were denied them, yet they must obey the laws of the land and honour their sovereign. By the second half of the twentieth century, when my father was promoted to the inspectorate, most of these restrictions were long gone, yet for a century and a half before that, Wesley's teachings had created a culture in which men and women of talent and ambition would automatically re-experience the same conflicts that had plagued their founder. Loyal Methodists could never feel quite right about excelling or succeeding, yet this left some of them secretly craving what their church had denied them, and resenting the unfairness of being restrained from fulfilling their potential.

Moreover, Methodists understood that they must 'tell the truth and shame the Devil' – which prevented the more literal-minded among them from employing the white lies others regularly used to get themselves out of having to admit to a shameful truth, or saying something that might offend. The best Methodists could do was to remain silent – if you can't say something nice, don't say anything. A sense of injustice (it's just not fair) would fuel their sense of entitlement (I deserved so much better than this).

In most of my professional life, I had ensured that I would be marginalised and my hope of promotion jeopardised. Even when I found professional communities that were compatible with my own personality and interests, I chose roads either less travelled by my fellow professionals, or not travelled at all. I often felt that I was travelling them alone. Did I, in these ways, unconsciously re-create a position that my dissenting forebears had occupied? A strong element in my public stances was one of challenge to conventional attitudes, and I insisted passionately that here were truths that other people could not, or would not, acknowledge. Even if others shied away from these verities, I would espouse them, albeit as a voice crying in the wilderness.

Over the past century or so, my family has included a small number of people who were confidently exploitative (like Harry Albury) or anxiously exploitative (like Henry Lawson) alongside a much larger number who lacked the lasting confidence to stand up for their rights. The same individual could, at different times, display both characteristics. I myself commissioned a harpsichord in my thirties, and discovered that the man I had asked to build it was a perfectionist who found it almost impossible to finish anything (including my commission). He moved interstate, years went by, he had been paid in full, yet the instrument was never finished. I rang him several times to ask him to finish it, or to let me have it, finished or not, but he pleaded for more time, and I could never come at the idea of taking legal action against him to recover what was rightfully mine. As far as I know, it is still in his workshop, faraway in another state. I had, in my own way, behaved exactly as Albert had behaved with his creditors. Yet some in my extended family would see me as always getting my own way, even arrogant.

Talent and narcissism

Few people are able to live their dreams to the full. Most of us have to learn, painfully, that we cannot do what we once hoped we could, cannot live the lives we once imagined for ourselves. But scaling down our dreams bears hardest on those who possess a genuine, genetically determined talent like the singing voice possessed by both my grandmother, Ethel, and her aunt Louisa Lawson. In contrast to abilities that lie dormant until a favourable environment enables them to manifest, such talents are obvious to others from early in their bearers' lives. They draw admiration and (sometimes) envy. Other people tell the talented person, even as a child, that she has a gift, that she is special, that she may go far. Those messages of affirmation come to us from others, including others whose regard we crave. So when we have to give up the dream, confine our talent to a local stage or abandon it altogether, it can feel as great a loss as the premature death of a loved one. It seems unjust because it *is* unjust. But life isn't just and it isn't fair. With the wisdom of maturity, some of us are able to admit that, and we learn to live with our disappointment.

Possessing true talents or abilities that set us apart from the majority almost automatically encourages a kind of self-preoccupation. We do feel different, we do feel special, and early success can certainly generate in us a sense of entitlement. But if for whatever reason we turn away from the achievements that might have been ours, we must live with bitter disappointment. Ethel Crago wanted to be married and have children, and so she did – but in deciding that her family came first, she had to abandon the possibility of being a professional singer. It was only one among the many disappointments and losses she suffered in her long life, and almost certainly not the most important, but it was real nonetheless. Louisa Lawson ended an early marriage that, like Ethel's, had disappointed her, and forged a meaningful career for herself at a time when few women did so – but the voice that had entranced the diggers fell silent. Without societal support for their ambitions, many women at the time suffered the same fate. Would Louisa have been so critical of her poet son, would Ethel have been so scornful of the women who dared to marry Dick and Ian, if each woman had experienced the fulfilment of her own talents?

Henry Lawson was a talented man, but he lacked the humility to learn from criticism and the emotional stability to make the most of his gifts. In such individuals, entitlement becomes entrenched. Instead of pursuing their early dreams, they turn their waning energies to the pursuit of justice – getting even, getting others to apologise, gaining belated recognition. Lawson was delighted when he was finally granted a state pension, but it came only months before he died. He got a state funeral, too, but (as he himself might well have observed) it was a bit late by then.

Once more, with genotyping

There is one more important thing to add, and that is that if (as with so many of my relatives) we are born with genetically determined anxiety that makes us doubt our own worth, coupled with genetically determined sensitivity to hurt (and a corresponding vulnerability to shame), then we may compensate for our felt inferiority to others by feeling special and superior – or by believing that others have deliberately done us down, betrayed us, stabbed us in the back – paranoia. I believe the latter is what probably happened with Albert Crago, my grandfather, and with his second daughter Beth. To locate destructiveness outside of ourselves may not qualify us for a diagnosis of mental illness – but it can have serious consequences, both for ourselves and for those who have to live with us.

9

Faith and Doubt

In My Time

Once More, With Feeling (Currumbin, Queensland, 1960; Sydney, 2000)

As a holiday treat in 1960, our parents took us to a drive-in cinema to see a new Hollywood movie. *Once More, With Feeling* was a comedy based on a successful stage play about a charismatic conductor and his wife. The movie didn't make much impression, and fifty years later I could remember nothing of its plot. 'Once more, with feeling!' is something that conductors say (at least in the minds of Hollywood scriptwriters) when trying to take their musicians beyond mechanical perfection. In the movie, the expression referred to a last try to get the conductor (Yul Brynner) and his wife (Kay Kendall) back together (which involved actually getting married, though everyone has assumed they are). But what is glaringly obvious to me when I watch *Once More, With Feeling* again now is that Yul Brynner's character is a flaming narcissist. Most of the movie's laughs come from his shameless egocentricity, his willingness to manipulate others, the shallowness of his emotional outpourings. Like any true narcissist, he is in love with himself rather than with his partner. Narcissism was not a word I would then have understood. The one thing that I did remember from that otherwise forgettable movie was the words of its title. Even then, the phrase – once more, with feeling – dug deep into who I was, just as its male lead offered me a caricature of who I might easily become and its female lead a portrait of the way I had perceived my mother as a child – shallowly emotional, easily triggered into argument and always disappointed with her partner.

In my growing up years, I loved my parents, but I experienced them as utterly different from me. It would not have occurred to me to hug either of them spontaneously, or to tell them I loved them, no doubt because they themselves were so reticent in both regards. In church each Sunday, I recited words and sang hymns that asserted my love of Jesus Christ, my gratitude to Him for saving me, but no true feeling informed my voice. Deep down, I knew I did not fully believe what I was saying. I was playing the notes accurately, but without feeling. I would have said that I loved Vicki, the girl who had spent just three years in my high school class before her family moved to Sydney. But my feelings, though real enough, were bloodless – longing without physical desire, fantasy that I never expected to turn into reality. The only feelings I truly and fully experienced were fear, in the school playground and the swimming pool; and rage, when I snarled at my brother for spoiling my elaborate fantasy games because he did not understand the rules I had set up (and never properly explained to him). He was only doing what I had done in my brief, hapless time as a player of rugby union – nobody had ever explained the rules of footy to me.

I never related my outbursts to anything that had happened to me as a younger child. As I described in chapter 3, fear and rage began for me when I started high school. And when, some ten years later, I found myself married, snarling at my chosen partner, my apologies and remorse were well-intended, but shallow and short-lived. Once again, I was playing the notes mechanically, more as a way of avoiding pain and shame than as a way of feeling them. It would not be for many years that I would do my relationship, or indeed my life, once more, with feeling.

And so in 2000, forty years after watching that movie, I started seeing a psychotherapist recommended by a colleague. I knew that I had to face my own demons.

The experience of therapy is easy enough to talk about, but not in a way that makes much sense to anyone who hasn't had it. By fifty-four, I had worked as a counsellor for years, and believed in the idea of psychotherapy. I'd done lots of workshops, learned to self-disclose and done bits of personal work, yet I'd never committed to a long-term, in-depth exploration of my inner world. But I was badly stuck in my life and I kept losing my job. I went into psychoanalytic psychotherapy because I sensed that there must be 'stuff' I didn't remember or had pushed away, and this stuff must be driving my adult behaviour. I was a little scared and a lot curious – as I had always done, I was turning my pain into a quest for understanding.

Early on, my therapist challenged my scornful remarks about the boss who had most recently edged me out from the institute. I reacted angrily: suddenly it felt as if my therapist was not on my side, had not really believed my story. She responded to my fierce push-back by avoiding such challenges for a long time. She was right that I needed to feel safer before I would tolerate them, but perhaps she waited over-long. Psychoanalytic therapy is very freeing but it can free a patient like me to perform, distract and control.

Initially, I greatly enjoyed having the freedom to talk about whatever I wanted. My therapist rarely asked questions and generally followed where I led, though her silences sometimes led me to question what I'd just been talking about. I happily *played* in my hour each week, analysing myself and demonstrating to her (I thought) how insightful I was. I roamed unchecked around my private fantasies and fears, no doubt revealing a great deal that I was unaware of, but without her commenting very much. I liked her and felt that she liked me. I valued the fact that she recognised the books and music that meant so much to me, though she steadfastly refused to be drawn into discussions of them. I rapidly became impatient when she did not seem to grasp what was most important to me. I rarely expressed my irritation, though. For the most part, I felt understood, safe and calmed by her presence. All of this was how I had felt, and acted, with Maureen before our actual marriage.

Two or three years in, I started to tell the therapist about my dreams. She responded enthusiastically, as if this was a step forward (as indeed it was), and I disciplined myself to record dreams in writing for the next couple of years. The dreams that seemed most significant involved my being attacked by menacing teenagers, or finding malevolent youths breaking into my house. In the dreams, I would rush around, locking doors and windows in a (usually vain) attempt to keep the frightening intruders safely outside. 'Persecutory feelings' induced by a 'punitive super-ego', she said (to be fair, she hardly ever used such technical language). Initially sceptical, I came to see that I was indeed very hard on myself – a level of self-criticism that fuelled my forthright judgements of others. I didn't feel attacked by her comments, though – instead, they felt like a relief. Yes, here was a key truth about myself, one that I could readily admit to.

At some point, I told her about my mental images of the battle of Midway in 1942. Four Japanese aircraft carriers – *Akagi, Kaga, Soryu* and *Hiryu*, two-thirds of the seemingly invincible carrier fleet that had led the attack on Pearl Harbor – were obliterated by American bombers, their decks torn open, left ablaze and sinking. It was the turning point of the Pacific war. Japan's naval advantage had been permanently lost, and now it was only a matter of time until the war was lost as well. Intellectually, I already knew that my preoccupation with the losing side (in this case the Japanese) reflected not only very strong feelings about being excluded and defeated, but also powerful feelings of hate and a wish to destroy. As a child and adolescent, I had acted out those feelings in my private fantasy games. Later, I had played adult military simulations that re-created battles like Midway – complex and mentally challenging games, but still driven by an obscure wish to smash and destroy. As an adult, I had used sarcasm and scorn to lash others – most of all, those close to me. *Those fatally wounded aircraft carriers were me.* My therapist made it safe for me to admit these things to myself, and wisely did not seek to interpret the 'meaning' of what I had disclosed, although it would have been very clear to her.

After some four years, she suggested that I might progress faster if I came twice a week and lay on the couch, as patients do in classical psychoanalysis. She had realised that as long as I could look at her face for reassurance, I would continue to deny any negative feelings I might harbour towards her. She was right. To recline (as Freud's patients had done), with her sitting behind me, so that I could only hear her voice, left me feeling exposed and vulnerable. When she seemed not to understand me, I experienced her as a critical parent who did not like me or approve of me. Admitting to these feelings was difficult at first, but eventually a huge relief. I could lash out at her, but she remained calm, and when I realised that my anger would not destroy her, I could eventually see how unfair my blaming of her usually was. This is what I had done to Maureen many times, with similar unfairness.

Sometime around this period – or perhaps it had come earlier – she told me that I was 'controlling'. At first I did not realise what she meant. I was a good person – how could I be controlling or manipulative? She explained: I talked so much that there was little room for her to participate. I thought this was most unfair – wasn't Freud's whole idea that the patients do most of the talking and discover things for themselves? She told me I tried to interpret my own disclosures before she did. It took me some time to admit that she might be right. I did talk a lot (Maureen had told me the same) and I did constantly pre-empt what others might say by voicing anticipated criticisms before they did. I felt hurt and aggrieved at what my therapist told me, because I knew I did not consciously want to close her out or defend myself against her attacks. But I gradually came to see that my conscious intentions had little to do with it: I was trying to control her, without realising it. Or was I, perhaps, trying to control someone else, long ago, whom I had once urgently needed to be reliable and loving, and who had disappointed me?

The last big turning point in our therapy was when I told my therapist that I had spoken at a national conference earlier in the year, about my experience of being her patient. Therapists did discuss their own therapy with other therapists – it was not unusual, and of course, I never identified my therapist by name or in any other way. Nor had I talked about specific incidents in therapy or about what I had disclosed to her. So I was shocked by the strength of her reaction. She was angry and told me so. Why hadn't I asked her for permission? This was *our* work, she said – hers as well as mine – that I was describing in public, and I had not even thought to ask her if it was OK! At first I was incredulous. I believed that I had described only my experience of my therapy. I had not talked about her technique, her interpretations, her therapeutic presence – my presentation was not a critique of her professional competence. I had made it clear to my audience that I liked and respected her, felt grateful to her. It seemed to me that in her anger, she was being possessive – maybe even jealous. I let her know that I thought she was misjudging my conduct, but I feared to tell her that I thought her selfish and possessive. I wish I had, because I can see now how fruitful this would have been. These feelings towards her fitted long-buried feelings towards my mother, who actually had been possessive and jealous, although in a different way.

We had to go back and back over this incident for weeks before my feelings (or hers) could settle. I clung to the belief that if my therapist had heard what I'd said at the conference, she would have dropped her objections. I continued to fend off the charge that I had ignored the rights and feelings of others by doing what I felt was justified. I found it incredibly difficult to admit that I had done this.

But if I was such a good person, why would I identify so strongly with images of burning ships, shells tearing through armour plating, planes being shot out of the sky? In those military fantasies I was, simultaneously, both the merciless attacker and the vulnerable prey. In my dreams, I was both the menacing young men breaking into my house, and the terrified, vulnerable me, trying vainly to shut the doors against them. I was the winner and the loser, the bully and the victim, the destroyer and the destroyed.

I think now that my therapist did me a great service in sticking to her conviction that I had behaved unfairly to her. It was not that what I had said was damaging to her in any way – I am still convinced it was not – but what was deeply revealing was my failure even to think of asking her permission, to imagine the potential impact of my action on her. It was a huge blind spot, and, looking back over my life, I realised that there had been other occasions involving other people (mostly women), to whose feelings I had been similarly blind. Other people had been angry with me, but I had dismissed their anger instead of learning from it. 'I just didn't think,' I would often say to Maureen. No, indeed I did not think. Thinking did not come into it – only how I felt. Like Yul Brynner's character in *Once More, With Feeling* – indeed, like my own mother – my point of reference for rightness or wrongness was always myself, not anyone else. What *I* knew was all I needed to know.

My therapist's honestly expressed anger enabled me to tolerate Maureen's anger better. I still flared up and became defensive quickly. But I settled more quickly too and admitted (at least sometimes) that I had been wrong, realised I had hurt or disregarded her feelings, tried to repair the damage instead of carrying on until I wore her down and we were both exhausted and demoralised. I knew that my changes were coming very late. I could hardly expect her to be full of excitement and affirmation. But at least I knew where I had gone wrong and was doing my best to address it. I had scaled down my expectations of her and was less likely to get furious with her for simply being herself, rather than the ideal romantic partner I believed she should be.

Although I had spent seven years in therapy, no trauma had surfaced. I had had an apparently secure childhood in a stable family. But what I slowly came to realise, with my therapist's help, was that I must have been desperate for connection with my parents (and particularly with my mother) from a very early age. I remembered that my mother had once told me (as an adult) that she felt too inhibited to get down on the floor and play with me, my brother and my sister, and so had read stories to us instead. I had loved the stories, and lived in them – but perhaps I had nevertheless got the message: she did not feel connected with me, she could not allow herself to enter my world; I was alien to her. My father, though capable of more warmth than my mother, was also quite inhibited in his expressions of feeling. I must have craved far more spontaneous, demonstrative affection than either of them was capable of giving me.

My therapist identified my need to entertain and perform as the main ways I had found of gaining some sense of connection with both my mother and my father. This fitted with my parents' stories of me, in my third year of life, pacing up and down like a tiny professor or shutting myself away to listen to my program on the radio (in the face of that, could I really deny that I was not controlling?). I don't believe that my mother was unloving or intentionally neglectful: I think she tried her best to be a good mother, but she had little real warmth – her own mother had been incapable of it too. I must have sensed it, and probably felt alone, misunderstood and different long before that day I stood in the school playground and for the first time experienced my difference and my aloneness in the presence of other children.

In one session I had been telling my therapist what Mum had gone through as a child. For the first time in my life, I found myself feeling for my mother – for her loneliness, for her sense of being supplanted by her little brother, for her desperate longing to be praised for her appearance rather than only for her schoolwork. I think I talked, too, of the incident on a train when she was a high school girl, where she'd been revolted and terrified when a man tried to put his hand up her skirt. I burst into tears and said, 'Oh, the poor thing!' I felt as if I was crying, not just for her, but for my grandmother, twice deserted by her husband, and then deserted again by her son, for the generations of sad little weddings where relatives were painfully absent, for the ways that my father had disappointed my mother, and she him, for all the pain and longing and despair that human beings have to live with. And in forgiving my mother, I was starting to forgive myself.

By the time I decided that 2007 would be my last year in therapy, my life had become more stable than it had been for many years. In 2004 I secured a part-time academic position at the University of Western Sydney (as it was then called), with superiors who, in the old style, tolerated my eccentricities and trusted my competence. By the time my original boss had retired and been replaced by yet another corporate-style head of school, my position had become permanent. I wasn't going to throw it away, as I had done twenty years earlier, and I bit my tongue instead of speaking out when I thought something was wrong. Most of my colleagues seemed to like and respect me. For the third and final time, I had the chance to reconstruct an existing curriculum, turning it into something that, I now knew, was going to work better, and graduate future counsellors who were more self-aware and more emotionally intelligent. I knew by now that I would never single-handedly transform a city of brick into a city of marble. I just had to wait, and be content with a little marble and a lot of brick. Besides, I was getting older.

Having been in long-term therapy made me more patient with my own clients, assisted me to avoid confronting them too early. I recognised when they were idealising me (as I had idealised my own therapist), and when they were irritated and angry with me (but hiding it, as I had done). I could stay calm more easily in the face of their antagonism – although I still had trouble with that. I was far better as a group leader than I had been in the past. I could now trust a group to evolve at its own pace, and trust my own instincts as to when to intervene. In the past, I had anxiously rushed in, with very mixed results.

Temperamentally, I was still too sensitive and too reactive to make an ideal therapist, but I learned to play to my strengths and to be wary of my impulsivity. Thirty years after I had first formed the goal of being a counsellor, I felt that I had finally learned my trade. I believed in therapy in a different way – because it had worked for me. I believed in what I was teaching because I had seen the theory work in practice, in my own life. I had found things that I could wholeheartedly believe in – not an immortal, omnipotent God, to be sure, not something absolute and forever, but something that could steady me in the face of life's disappointments and suffering. I had found my own version of a faith. No longer did I doubt that I was worthy of love. Having been present with my father almost to the hour of his actual death, I no longer felt afraid to die, although of course I still feared suffering and incapacity – and most of all, I dreaded the spectre of dementia, which had robbed so many of my relatives of dignity in their final years. Would I, too, one day forget all that had made me myself?

In Family Time

In the first half of the twentieth century, people often remained silent about their spiritual beliefs. If pressed, they would say that what they believed was their own business. Yet in maintaining this silence, many members of my father's family behaved almost as if faith were a dangerous secret – like a terminated pregnancy, an affair or a mental illness. Once more, silence created an empty space, leaving it open to the next generation, as they grew up, to create their own meanings – or misunderstandings – of what faith meant, or didn't mean, to their parents.

My father took us to Sunday school each Sunday, and, later in the morning, to the same church service that he attended. The hymns, the prayers and the regular order of the Methodist service were a given which I did not question. Dad sang in the church choir, and once a year, as the senior local representative of the NSW Education Department, was asked to preach a sermon during Education Week. I found this embarrassing, because my father was always a bit anxious and would sway from side to side as he spoke (of course it never occurred to me that when I was grown up, I might reveal my underlying anxiety just as obviously).

Dad spoke well from the pulpit, but as I grew towards adulthood, I noticed that he rarely said much about the central figure of Christianity. He quoted New Testament descriptions of Jesus's teachings, and made the point that Christ had taught in clear, simple language, using stories to help his listeners connect directly with what he was talking about. Unlike the Scribes, Christ 'taught with authority'. Embarrassed I may have been, but I took on board what my father was saying. He himself was a good teacher, I knew that, and Christ had been a good teacher. John Wesley, who had founded our church, had been a good teacher too – in fact, a famous preacher who could move large crowds to tears, and a writer who explained theological concepts in unpretentious, clearly reasoned prose.

Aside from this, Dad hardly ever talked about his faith. He left it to the Sunday school teachers to explain what 'we' believed. Early in my life, my mother taught us a short prayer to say before bed at night, and she sometimes accompanied us to Sunday services, but it became clearer as I grew up that she doubted the existence of a loving God, or a Heaven to which we would go when we died. Eventually, she openly told me that she was an agnostic (she may have meant atheist). It took me a very long time to realise that perhaps my father might not have believed in the literal truth of the resurrection or the promise of eternal life through Christ's sacrifice. He never said whether he did or not, and his one disclosure of his position (much later, when I was in middle adulthood myself) was ambiguous. He confessed that he had never experienced 'any deep conversion', that his heart had never, like John Wesley's, been 'strongly warmed' by a sudden, absolute conviction of his own salvation. This was the most open Dad had ever been on the issue of his spiritual beliefs, and he did not elaborate, but the hint was there. Significantly, he had recalled Wesley's phrase as 'strongly warmed'; in fact, Wesley had written 'strangely warmed' – it is possible that by strangely, Wesley meant supernaturally – conveying that what he had felt was God's doing, not his own.

John Wesley preached that human beings could earn salvation through faith alone – that is, not by leading a good life, performing charitable acts or engaging in regular religious observances, but by their ability to believe wholeheartedly that Jesus Christ had, by his death on the cross, cancelled out their sins. They need do nothing except believe.

Yet though he espoused a conviction-driven faith, Wesley constantly wavered about his own. He struggled with doubts, craved experiences of certainty, and finally found one on that famous occasion when, at the age of thirty-four, he felt his heart 'strangely warmed'. Even after that he still worried about whether or not this experience had been quite real. Others saw serene assurance in him, yet Wesley was an anxious man. Could God really love mankind enough – love *this* man enough – to save him from death? It was a doubt echoed in the phrasing that John's brother Charles used in his hymn:

> Amazing love, how can it be
> That Thou, my God, shouldst die for me?

Wesley's doubts were not confined to his faith. He wavered over almost every serious decision he had to make: should he break openly with the Church of England? Should he marry, or remain celibate? Should he ordain bishops, as his American followers had requested? Anxious people are anxious about everything.

God's smugglers

As a child growing up with a churchgoing father and a non-believing mother, I had, as it were, parental permission to alternate between faith and doubt. I know that as a child I wanted to believe in the truth of what I heard in church each Sunday, the truth that I believed my father believed in. I found the Christian story emotionally arousing, disturbing and confronting. It contrasted an eternally loving, reliable God with the tiny lives of fallible, sinful human beings. It promised these human beings that death was not the end: God had sent His only begotten son to suffer and die in our place. If we could open ourselves to that great truth, we would, like Him, rise again from the dead and ascend to heaven for ever, in the company of those we had loved in this life. It was a wonderful vision, but almost from the beginning some part of me could not believe it. Could this part of me have come from my mother? Or, in fact, from *her* mother – Evie, the only grandparent I really knew? Of course Evie never talked about belief, and it was only after her death that I found she had been an atheist, telling my mother, 'Religion's all a lot of nonsense.' Her own family, the Kirkhams, certainly contained some committed Christians, like her older brother, Ernest (Ern), who had died in the Great War. But it also contained others whose commitment was only nominal, or possibly non-existent. And Evie had been a considerable, though silent, influence on me between the ages of nine and seventeen, in those yearly stays at her Artarmon apartment each summer. I knew that she never went to church, and though there were old prayer books and Bibles in the house, I never saw her reading one.

Essentially, I pretended to believe, and kept up that pretence into my early twenties before finally admitting that I was not a Christian at all. Yet, like many other former believers, I took with me into my adult life a secular Methodism – (simple living, Community Aid Abroad and the peace movement) as well as, in my case, connecting meaningfully with other human beings. Like Wesley, I would show people things that really mattered and never hide behind the mask of self-righteous goodness (like the Pharisees) or mystifying expert language (like the Scribes). That was what I had absorbed from my father's yearly sermons, from my parents' lives as good teachers.

The Bible had never spoken to me in the way that secular literature did. I found the Old Testament world alien, and its jealous God harsh and punitive. Something in me turned away even from the New Testament vision of Grace, from a love that extended to those who felt they did not deserve it. Perhaps I had a dim consciousness, even then, of the hate and destructiveness within me.

There was an attempt, many years later, to bring me over to the Lord, by my Aunt Beth, the most passionately Christian of my father's siblings. She sent me an edition of Paul's Letter to the Corinthians, and a small book called *God's Smuggler*, about a quiet Dutchman who made it his life's work to smuggle copies of the Bible into Soviet Russia and Soviet-dominated Eastern Europe. I read it, admired the man's courage and determination – but I could not thereby accept the God whose will he believed he had followed in doing what he did. Beth, I suspect, saw herself as God's smuggler. She had, early in her marriage, spent a period of time in Fiji, and was greatly impressed with the enthusiastic faith of the people there. Thereafter she regularly gave money to the Church's overseas mission work, and (to my eyes, at least) seemed to find it much easier to express love and care for distant 'black and brown' (her words) Christians than for her own adopted children.

Beth became increasingly disenchanted as, in 1977, the Methodist Church merged with the Presbyterian and Congregationalist denominations to form the Uniting Church in Australia. To her, it seemed that the faith in which she had been raised was being watered down, the old ways abandoned, and that Methodism had lost its identity – which to a fair extent was true. She joined the Wesleyan Methodists who continued to meet and observe the old forms of service. In matters of faith, at least, Beth was a radical conservative – as radical in her own way as I had been in secular matters.

Beth's position on faith was always clear. The same cannot be said for the rest of her brothers and sisters. Dick, Ted, Gwyn, Ian and Cherie were all lifelong churchgoers, but being a churchgoer does not necessarily imply a deep faith. At the time, attending the Sunday service was what you did – a badge of belonging and of respectability. Ted and his wife Beryl were dedicated members of their local church community, but my sense is that Ted probably embraced the notion that one displayed one's faith through active work for social justice. He had always had leftward leanings, the only member of my father's family of whom that could be said, and Gwyn's husband Harold Armstrong had once referred to him as a 'comm' – conservatives at the time saw no difference between socialism and communism. To Harold, as to many others, communist sympathisers were dangerous, subversive criminals – as terrifying as Islamic militants seem to some people today.

Yet many of these same 'dangerous' communists, who seemed to threaten the very fabric of Australian society, were true believers in a kind of earthly paradise, a secular heaven where all people would live in equality and harmony, ruled over by a benevolent socialist state. They were every bit as idealistic as the Christian Cragos who feared and despised them, every bit as sensitive to the suffering of mankind and every bit as hopeful of a brighter, better future – albeit one on earth rather than in heaven. Loyal communists refused to believe in the growing evidence that Soviet Russia was a cruel autocracy which sent its own citizens to Siberia, or shot them on the whim of a grandiose, paranoid dictator. They clung to their faith until the evidence of the gulags and the Stalinist purges became overwhelming. We see in others the shadow side of ourselves, and hate and fear it rather than recognising what we share.

What We Need to Know

A true act of contrition

Psychotherapy – indeed, counselling of any kind – was not an option for the members of my extended family between the 1920s and the 1980s. The vast majority of them would have been deeply suspicious of it. The faith in which they had all been raised told them to turn to the Lord in their times of trouble. As my father's sister Beth put it, 'It's when you're at the end of your tether that you really need a God.' I don't think they all believed that as fiercely as she did. I'm not sure they were as convinced as she was that Christ was going to save them for eternal peace and joy in the light of His countenance. But regardless of whether or not their childhood faith endured through their middle years and into their old age, they most certainly would have continued to search their consciences, to find ways that they may have failed to be live up to the commandments and exhortations they had heard Sunday after Sunday throughout their lives.

> Almighty and most merciful father, we have erred and strayed from Thy ways like lost sheep. We have followed too much the devices and desires of our own hearts. We have offended against Thy holy laws. We have left undone those things which we ought to have done; and we have done those things which we ought not to have done. And there is no health in us.

Those sonorous words of self-reproach were not among the sections of the Book of Common Prayer that Methodism had taken over into its own service, and I did not hear them until I started attending Anglican services for a time, as a young adult, before giving up my own belief altogether. But when I did hear those words, they spoke to me. In psychoanalysis, Freud had created an instrument of self-examination as rigorous in its own way as the spiritual discipline of confession. Both were rituals in which people faced up to confronting truths about themselves, accepted responsibility for their own wrongdoing instead of blaming others, and sought a sense of acceptance and forgiveness:

> No condemnation now I dread:
> Jesus, and all in Him, is mine
> Alive in Him, my living Head,
> And clothed in righteousness divine
> Bold I approach the eternal throne
> And claim the crown, through Christ, my own.

Charles Wesley's ringing endorsement of personal salvation is a long way from the melancholy-tinged self-knowledge with which one emerges from psychotherapy – yet in both there is the sense of forgiving and being forgiven, being freed to live more contentedly and wisely in the future.

Of course there are big differences too. Psychotherapy is a dialogue between two human beings, a patient and a therapist. Examining the conscience is done in dialogue with a God who is above and beyond our comprehension. Christians look up to God, and trust Him. Patients come to trust their therapists, too, yet therapists are only human and, sooner or later, we are likely to feel angry with them or let down by them. Honest Christians also report feeling angry and let down, angry with God for the unfairness of life and for the inevitable suffering it includes. The true difference is that Christians hope for a life beyond this one, a life they owe entirely to God's mercy, while psychoanalysis and the therapies derived from it do not offer any such hope.

No, my father's Methodist relatives would never have 'gone to see someone' (except perhaps their minister, if they had come to trust him) and the idea of talking freely to a stranger (however qualified) about shameful thoughts and feelings would have filled many of them with horror. Yet some of them, at least, would have talked freely about such thoughts within the framework of their faith. They would have talked about their doubts and backslidings as well as about their trust in God's care for them, and their hope of redemption through His love.

Since the first half of the twentieth century, the language of evangelical Christians of all denominations has become more and more passionate, self-disclosing and urgent – as it had been in the early days of Methodism, as it had been two centuries earlier in the Protestant Reformation, and in the Catholic Counter-Reformation. Faith has needed regular renewals and has often adopted the language of romantic love in reaching for human equivalents of spiritual experience. The ecstatic feeling of being 'lifted up where we belong' is common to both. Human beings crave that feeling above almost all else, and never forget it when it happens to them. It is the feeling that something is happening to us, that we are part of something far greater, something we cannot understand, but which just might be *all there is to know*.

Faith and doubt

As we saw earlier, families transmit spaces – we might also call them templates or patterns – from one generation to the next. The key thing is that these spaces will be filled with different contents by different individuals. My gradual adoption of belief in the existence of an unconscious, in the reality of transference, and in the healing power of the 'talking cure' filled the same space in me as faith in God's grace had done for many in my father's family. At the heart of psychoanalysis was a mystery – just as there was a mystery at the heart of Christianity. That mystery could be unlocked if one was patient, persistent and courageous enough to face one's own demons, to own up to one's own hate, envy or bitterness, and accept that those feelings were real enough, but downright damaging to others as well as to oneself. I think I was drawn to the idea of psychoanalytic therapy from my twenties onwards, even though it took me another thirty years to risk finding out about it first-hand, as a patient. What I was drawn to, I know, was a journey, a quest – after all, I was a Cavalier!

When we embark on therapy, we take a risk. We may not like what we find inside ourselves; we may (at least for a time) feel worse than we do now; we may end up settling for much less than our grand dreams – including the grand dream of immortality – once promised us. We must lead more authentic lives, be truer to ourselves, have fewer illusions, do without our strongest defences. We must stop putting our little selves at the centre of the universe, we must let go of our investment in thinking that we can change the world, turn the unfair into the just. Christians talk of 'letting go and letting God [take over the burden]'. Psychoanalysis has no God – there is no one to hand the burden to – but the *shape* is similar.

Psychoanalysis says that what is inside us is neither good nor bad, it just is. It accepts that we humans are full of paradoxes, that we are fearful, internally riven, confused – lost sheep indeed. We do indeed follow the devices and desires of our own hearts, to our detriment and to the detriment of others. Yet we do not need to be forever enslaved to our own longings and cravings. We can accept ourselves (as, in Christian faith, God accepts us) and in so doing, we can become more loving and compassionate to others. Perhaps that, too, is Grace – though I doubt many Christians would see it that way. Love is central to the process of psychotherapy. Carl Rogers, the twentieth century psychologist who popularised the word counselling, called this love 'unconditional positive regard'. Buddhists call it 'loving kindness'. The New Testament called it '*agape*'. It is the valuing of every person, the suspension of judgement, the warmth and generosity of spirit that we humans are, at our best, capable of showing.

A spectrum of faith

In chapter 7, I described a spectrum from sanity to madness, a spectrum where most of my relatives were located somewhere between the two extremes. I strongly suspect that my family – and most families from a religious background – also exhibit a spectrum of faith. At one extreme is the absolute faith of the true believer (Beth, for example); at the other is the position of the convinced atheist (Eva, for example). Most family members, though, are situated somewhere in between. When my father admitted to me that he had never experienced any big conversion as (he believed) John Wesley had, I think he was letting me know that his faith was not absolute. He found churchgoing a comfort, it reaffirmed his abiding loyalty to his mother, Ethel, and he enjoyed church because it enabled him to sing in public without any fear of parading himself or seeking the limelight.

One way that we can keep alive our own conflict between faith and doubt is to marry someone who openly displays an aspect of ourselves that we keep secret. Dick married May, a freethinker. She befriended individual 'seekers' who followed their quest for spiritual enlightenment into paths that conventional believers would have considered very odd indeed. Dick must at times have been embarrassed by his wife, but he accepted her and did not try too hard to rein her in. He may well have doubted the beliefs of 'May's lame ducks' (as my mother disparagingly called them) but he felt it important to make them welcome in his home, as his mother had welcomed newcomers to Yass while he was growing up. And in his support for May's wish to offer them hospitality, he not only displayed the compassion and non-judgemental attitudes of a good Christian, he also, perhaps, indicated indirectly that he himself might at times share some of May's doubts about conventional religion.

This I believe was also the case with my father. No doubt he could have married a woman whose family had attended church every Sunday and who took the precepts of religion very seriously. Yet he chose to marry a woman who made no secret of her atheism – however shallow and unexamined that atheism might be. I suspect that this choice represented a way of acknowledging his own doubts about the faith in which he had been raised. Similarly, he chose a woman who had difficulty governing her own baser instincts – jealousy, dismissive arrogance, lack of empathy, and cruel words. At times she would shock him with her conduct, but he saw his role as to bear this cross with patience and compassion. With my father, Gwen replicated the relationship of her own mother with her father. 'Mum sometimes screamed at Dad… He never screamed at her.' Dad's younger sister Beth and her husband Roy also followed the template: she would turn on displays of histrionic emotion; from the start of their marriage, he apparently bore it with little protest. Maureen's marriage to me followed exactly the same pattern – only with the man as the histrionic partner.

The youngest of the Crago siblings, Cherie, was far from histrionic (except for her propensity for bursting into tears), and she married a man who was equally reserved. Yet she patiently accepted the restrictions her husband placed on her freedom to travel away from home (or even to stay longer enough after church to join the others for a cup of tea). Neither of them could have known it, but Bob's expectation that his wife would obey him in every respect and live her own life in the shadow of his anxieties was remarkably similar to the controlling, restrictive environment that John Wesley had imposed on the woman he married when, well into middle age, he finally decided to wed.

Mary ('Molly') Vazeille was a widow when John Wesley met her. Molly was forty-one and John forty-eight, a seven-year age difference. She had cared for him for several days when he was recovering from an injury, and John always seemed to respond powerfully to being looked after by a woman – perhaps it recalled to his mind the way his mother Susanna had cared for him in childhood. There was no doubt of his attraction to her, but she was not, like Grace Murray (who had almost become his wife earlier), a person who could have shared John's intellectual interests or his passionate involvement in the movement he had founded. Molly resented both John's work and his closeness to his brother Charles for the same reason – they diverted his attention from her. At first, she wanted to share the lengthy journeys John undertook as an itinerant preacher, but once she gave up accompanying him, she became paranoid and even accused him of adultery (a total fabrication). Conflicts between the two of them began very early, and after seven years, Molly left John in what would prove to be the first of several separations. Her anxieties were aroused by the affectionate letters he wrote to women of faith, and this led to outbursts of jealous rage which John endured quietly, refusing to shout back at her. John famously observed in his journal after Molly left him for the final time, 'I did not forsake her, I did not dismiss her, I will not recall her' (significantly, he shifted from English to Latin for these words). Molly's histrionic outbursts, and her rapid swings of mood from gracious and charming to embittered and rageful, suggest she might now have been diagnosed with borderline personality disorder. Or maybe she just felt lonely and misunderstood, like Ethel Crago, as her dream of a passionate relationship with a husband who would always put her first and empathise with her needs rapidly faded?

Significantly, John did not mention his wedding to Molly in his journal, and failed to alter his daily work schedule to accommodate the fact that he was now a married man. He was very controlling in his attitude to her, telling her to 'crowd all your life with the work of faith and the labour of love'. He required her to dress and govern her appearance in accordance with the rules he had long ago set up for Methodist women. John's 'saintly' patience and his well-meant but patronising admonitions would have struck Molly as cold and dismissive. His sense of entitlement to live as he had always lived, and as he felt his God required, was so strong that it blotted out any awareness of how destructive it might be to his partner. In marrying Molly, John Wesley had activated the stormy emotions that he had suppressed lifelong, and the doubts that he experienced in relation to his faith were acted out in the marital arena in the form of Molly's doubts of his fidelity – to her.

Narcissism, love and hate

Just as people assume that a manic-depressive individual behaves like a 'maniac' (frightening, dangerous, violent), so people equate narcissism with having a big ego. In the current catchphrase, 'It's all about you.' Yet narcissism is actually about having an *inadequate* sense of one's own worth. It originates in a craving for love. When, as a young child, the incipient narcissist fails to receive the unfeigned and unconditional love that all children need, he or she falls back on substitutes: praise, adoration and uncritical loyalty from others (who dedicate themselves to reassuring the narcissist of his own importance). Not all narcissists are flamboyant, larger-than-life individuals like Donald Trump. Some narcissists can be quiet and reserved. Both Hitler and Stalin lived simply and refused to wear impressive uniforms and decorations. But what all narcissists have in common is that their apparent confidence and self-belief are actually paper-thin – they cannot tolerate criticism. Even temperate expressions of a different opinion are likely to be greeted with an explosion of rage. The rage of the narcissist is the outward and visible sign of inward fear: when someone else fails to mirror back the narcissist's own feelings and opinions, he or she is instantly triggered into an overwhelming sense of black badness, of total worthlessness. Rather than experience these dreadful feelings for more than a second, the narcissist flies into a fury instead, attacking the person who has stirred up those feelings in preference to allowing himself to be vulnerable. Deep down, narcissists doubt that they are worthy of love and are driven to acts of conquest, grandiosity and sometimes creativity too, as artificial substitutes for being loved and for being able to love.

In my own therapy, I had spoken of my admiration for Sir Thomas More, who had refused to compromise his principles and been executed as a result ('Tell them I die the King's loyal servant – but God's first'), and John Proctor in Arthur Miller's play about the Salem witch trials, *The Crucible* ('He have his good name now!' says Proctor's wife despairingly after John meets his death). My therapist pointed out to me that maybe such rigid determination to tell the truth no matter what the consequence – the stuff of martyrdom – might actually be a kind of narcissism. Of course, it was different back in the sixteenth and seventeenth centuries, because the vast majority of Christians 'simply and sincerely' believed that they would be called to heavenly glory if they gave up their own lives for the cause (as radical Muslim terrorists do now). But my therapist had a point, nonetheless, and after an internal struggle, I eventually conceded it. More scales fell from my eyes. Now I could see some of my past behaviour in a different light, and recognised that some of my own relatives may well have been similar to me in sacrificing their chances of worldly success in order to be martyrs for their own beliefs. We are all human, and our doubts and uncertainties can contaminate even our faith.

Pull gently at a weak rope

In the café where I am writing the final words of this chapter, a hand-lettered sign above the door to the kitchen area reads,

> God has a plan for my life, but it's so far
> behind schedule I'll never die!'

That Christian joke speaks to the spirit of the family whose genes I have inherited. 'God has a plan for me' is something often voiced by evangelicals – a sense of joyful resignation to a power much greater than themselves, something that fits well for individuals who also submit to a more forceful partner or sibling. And then there is the assurance that, no matter how unworthy and insignificant we may feel, God will preserve us from death. It is a mighty promise and, though I cannot believe in it myself, I respect those who do. What they believe will steady them, as they age, in the face of change and decay – the inevitability of decline and death which we must all face. Why not face it with a peaceful heart? I think my father had a peaceful heart, in the minutes preceding the operation from which he never woke up. I don't think my mother did. But I will never know for sure.

10

Forgiving and Forgetting

In My Time

Blackheath, 2017

> Thou wouldst still be mine own,
> As this moment thou art,
> Let thy loveliness fade, as it will,
> And around the dear ruin
> Each wish of my heart
> Would entwine itself verdantly still.
>
> Lyrics by Thomas Moore, 1808, to a
traditional Irish air, first published in 1775

We 'grow' old, just as we 'grow' up – and it isn't accidental that our language uses the same verb. As children grow towards adulthood, a state that (for a child) is both expected and unknown, so we older adults grow towards death. Death, too, is expected yet unknown, simultaneously desired (sometimes) and feared (often). As we grow older, our longings may lose their intensity, but they do not vanish. In some ways, they become more important than they were when we filled our lives with work, with striving, with restless seeking. 'Ah, my friend, fortune was not kind to me in this world!' says the traveller to the poet in *Das Lied von der Erde.* He turns back, now, to the country of his youth, searching for inner peace before his imminent death.

*

When Dad would sit down at the piano in the evening and sing the songs that he'd grown up with or learned as a young adult – 'The Road to Mandalay', 'The Ash Grove', 'Early One Morning', 'Oh, No John!' – I cannot say that I enjoyed those songs. I found them sad, and they stirred emotions that were uncomfortable. They spoke to me of lovers' devotion, but also of men who betrayed and the women they left behind to grieve. Often I wanted to get away from the words, but the melodies held me against my will. Worst of all, though, was one particular song, a song about the inevitable loss of beauty, a touching pledge that the singer would still cling devotedly to the 'dear ruin' of his once-youthful beloved. I don't think my mother was often in the room when my father sang, but she would certainly have heard him singing 'Believe Me, If All those Endearing Young Charms' many times. Music did not sing in her soul, as it did in Dad's or in mine. Yet I found it hard not to believe that my father was thinking of her while he sang, and that she was aware of this.

In songs like 'Believe Me', I imagined that I glimpsed the secret life of my parents, the feelings that they never expressed openly in words or gestures. This made me profoundly uncomfortable. It was as if the song propelled me sixty years into my own future. Sex (about which I knew very little) and death (about which I knew even less) somehow belonged together. When Adam and Eve lost their innocence, they became knowingly sexual, they felt shame – and they knew that they would die. Did I perhaps form the belief that by remaining a child, and avoiding sexual intimacy, I might (like Peter Pan) cheat death and stay a playful, innocent child forever?

When Maureen and I were married, she was thirty and I was twenty-three. The age difference seemed of little importance, and back then I was unaware that it came close to duplicating the age gap between my mother and her brother Hughie, and also the interval between her mother Eva and my long-dead grandfather Victor, whose ages at marriage had been nearly seven years apart. Now that I am seventy-one and Maureen seventy-eight (the age at which both

Maureen's father and my own mother died) the years that separate us are suddenly significant, where they never seemed to be before. Maureen has suffered all her life from a variety of ailments which have caused her discomfort, exhaustion and depletion – problems with her digestive system; chronic fatigue; dry, cracked lips; periods of mental fog. In the face of these, she persisted with stoic cheerfulness, actively battling a tendency to depression that she recognised a long time ago. She worked loyally and earnestly, displaying her impressive range of professional competencies, until the age of seventy. Not long after her retirement she was finally diagnosed with Sjögren's syndrome, an auto-immune disease that has only became well known relatively recently. Sjögren's is similar to lupus in that it is degenerative and incurable, although not (like lupus) life-threatening. In Sjögren's, the glands that secrete body fluids (including sweat, tears and saliva) cease to function properly, and eventually do not function at all. Problems with eyes, skin and mouth become progressively worse. Eating becomes increasingly difficult, and a number of items impossible (bread, for example).

Maureen's genes aged her early, along with her brothers. She began greying in her late thirties, and now, at seventy-eight, she looks, well, old. The colour of her eyes, once a beautiful grey-green, has darkened. The silvery, well-modulated voice that so delighted me when I first knew her now sounds rougher and lower in pitch (the result of dry mouth), and she coughs painfully for the same reason. Her slender, shapely legs and arms are skinny now. She was never one to stand in front of the mirror admiring her face or her figure, and she has dressed, for much of her adult life, out of op shops, believing that she cannot afford the expense of new clothes (Gwyn? Eva? Auntie Elizabeth Anne?), weary of trying to find ones that will fit her properly. Around the time we were married, she gave up using the little make-up she then employed. Good ex-Methodists that we were, neither of us felt all that comfortable about 'painting one's face' in the interests of enhancing one's attractiveness. All of this was so typical of the women in my father's family – Gwyn and Cherie in particular.

When Maureen speaks, she pauses often while she searches for the word that eludes her. She is unsteady on her feet sometimes and, although she keeps active and busy around the house and in the garden, she needs to spend an appreciable portion of each day maintaining her body with rest, self-massage and elaborate routines for caring for her eyes and teeth (which can rapidly deteriorate as a result of the virtual absence of tears and saliva). She protects herself energetically against colds and flu, but when she does contract them, she typically takes weeks to recover. Her hearing, and her eyesight, have both declined, and she peers with narrowed eyes at her mending or at a page of print. Always quick, physically efficient and mentally acute, she is now much slower. Acceptance of these changes is not easy for either of us.

I, too, am much slower than I once was, and my memory also fails me at times. I am luckier with my general health, which has dealt me no major blow as yet. But I am losing my hair, and I stoop worse than I used to. I am clumsy and drop things easily, and I too am unsteady on my feet at times. I have lost much of my dexterity in small tasks, and my joints are increasingly stiff. I resent that my body can no longer do what I once took for granted. She faces her state with more equanimity, commenting that after a lifetime of having a body that does not perform as well as other people's, if she has not learned to accept ageing, then she must be a very slow learner. Sometimes I experience us as two candles that gutter fitfully as they come closer to their end, worn-down stubs of who we once were.

As we have always done, we get impatient with each other. Yet we forgive each other readily now, and start again without lasting rancour. Nowadays, as her body weakens and with it her emotional resilience, she often answers back sharply when, triggered by some baby-level sense of abandonment, I say something cutting or unfair. At least I remember now how my endless defensiveness and argumentativeness exhausted and depressed her in the past. She has put up with me for most of our life together. Now it's my turn – and what I have to put up with is very mild compared with what she has endured. There is still a strong connection between us, a shared history and shared values that make it almost impossible now to contemplate life apart.

I can understand why many men react with irritation and disappointment to the ageing of their partners – the firm flesh that has sagged, the curves blurred with fat – while failing to see their own spreading paunches or their faces, reddened from too much sun and too much alcohol. But I still feel warmth and affection for Maureen, and now a hug or a hand clutched momentarily conveys some of what we could once express more fully. The words my father sang, sentimental though they once seemed, have in a way come true:

> And around the dear ruin, each wish of my heart
> Would entwine itself verdantly still.

Attachment means that we feel deeply connected with, reliant upon and, above all, *safe with* a particular person. Attachment forms in infancy, between a baby and its mother, long before the baby feels love. It often turns into love, but it is not, in itself, love. And maybe, I think, attachment extends *beyond* love as life draws nearer to its end. That is the force that 'dear' has for me, now.

> Everywhere the dear, dear earth
> Is blossoming in Spring
> And growing green again!
> Now and forever, blue distances
> Shine bright!

Much of Gustav Mahler's inspiration, from his first symphony right through to his *Song of Earth*, came directly from his feelings about nature – the twittering bird calls of early morning, the blue mountain ranges fading into the mists of evening. It was to the dear earth that he clung in his final years, willing himself to stay alive long enough to re-create, in the language of music, the profound connection he felt with the world in which he lived. And so do many of us. We want to gaze one more time at the ocean rolling in towards the shore, at the plains stretching to the horizon, at the springtime renewal of green things in our gardens, at the magic of a snowfall. For these things not only remind us of who we have been, but will also outlast us, will continue forever and ever. For many of us, this is as close to a share of immortality as we can come.

What old age brings or, at any rate, should bring, is acceptance: not a facile kind of acceptance, but an owning of the decay and decline that is part of all life, an acceptance of the fact of our own death, and a need, before it is too late, to right the wrongs of our lives, to forgive and forget – to forgive others, and so to forgive ourselves. It is only by doing this that we can let go of life when our time comes.

In Family Time

1989–1991: Gwen and Ian

The latter days of my parents' marriage seemed anything but romantic to me as I (in my early fifties) glimpsed them from a distance and on short visits. My mother's physical health had always been uncertain, but from her late sixties onwards, it deteriorated rapidly. Her heart, her lungs and her digestive system all developed new problems. More alarmingly, her memory began to falter as her seventies progressed. She had energetically learned Italian and German in preparation for biennial excursions to Europe and beyond. On trains and buses she chatted confidently, to my father's admiration and surprise (he had always seen himself as the one with 'a gift for languages', albeit unrealised). But her attempt to gain fluency in a third language – French – ground to a halt when she found that she could not retain the new words she'd learned the day before. She gave away her hope of producing a comprehensive book for teachers on the teaching of reading, defeated by the mass of scholarly literature she'd photocopied. By her mid-seventies, she was reading the same few pages of a novel or a travel book day after day, unaware that she had read them the day before, and the day before that. She had to ask her grandchildren to explain the rules of Monopoly to her, though she'd played it with them for years. Sometimes fearful, sometimes defiantly fabricating, she continued to talk of further overseas trips.

Like most partners of dementing spouses, my father, extraordinarily patient for most of his life, became exasperated. For a long time, he found it almost impossible to accept that his life partner really did not have control over her actions any more. As Mum declined, he gained carer's confidence. He took over the cooking, the cleaning, the shopping. He steadied her while she tottered to the toilet in the night, changed the sheets when she 'had an accident', picked up from around her bed the mass of tissues or rags into which she'd coughed convulsively. Very occasionally, he would tell her off angrily, but mostly, he spoke to her gently and reassuringly. And for the first time in their lives, as far as I could see, she ceased to take him for granted. Her gaunt face would smile up at him from her pillows, and she would say with childlike candour, 'I don't know what I would've done without you, Ian.' Hearing her say those few words made everything worthwhile, he told me, even though Mum would not have remembered what she'd said. 'We've lived well together,' he said in 1990, trying to find an expression that would justify, but not wholly falsify, a relationship that had lasted nearly fifty years. He did not mention love.

It was now many years since he'd sung 'Believe me, if all those endearing young charms', but he was unlikely to have forgotten it. I certainly hadn't. I suspect that for Dad, as for me, the words of poets, the lyrics of songs and hymns, set a standard against which 'real life' must be measured. Inevitably, life falls short of the ideal, yet the words continue to sing themselves in our minds, challenging us to find a way of living up to them.

1947–1948: Albert and Ethel

As the Second World War drew to an end, my grandfather Albert Crago may have sensed that his own days might also be numbered. Now in his sixties, he felt increasingly weary after a life of hard physical work – at the mill, and at home on his ten acres. He was a man of few words when it came to private matters, and writing may well have been a labour for him. But he must have decided to put on paper his feelings of remorse for his angry outbursts, his regret at what had gone wrong between him and Ethel in the past. Ethel, who survived her husband by many years, seems not to have kept his letter – but she did keep her own answer to it. 'You've been a good, kind husband and father,' she wrote, saying nothing about the resentments and disappointments she had felt so keenly earlier in her married life. Forgive and forget: it was what women were supposed to do; it was also what their Church taught them to do.

In Ethel's case, I have no way of knowing how complete her forgiveness was, but she certainly forgot. Albert, my anxious grandfather, died in 1948 (I was not yet two years old, and already anxiously pacing the floor). Ethel survived him by fifteen years, gradually declining into dementia. By the time she died in 1963, she could not remember which of her three sons was which. Ironically, it was Ted, her second son (whom she had found 'a handful' as a preschooler, and whom she'd sent to school early as a consequence) who visited her most frequently and loyally, while Ted's older and younger brothers, who had once been her favourites, lived much further away and visited far less often. Whether she had forgiven them, too – for the pain they had caused her by their insistence on marrying selfish, worldly women (as she saw it) – I do not know. But then, had her son Ian forgiven his mother for refusing to attend his wedding? Surely, if he had, he would have braved his wife's disapproval and visited Ethel in the nursing home more often?

1993: Ian and Hugh

My father would almost certainly have said that he stayed away from Ethel in her decline because it was too painful to see the loved mother of his childhood cruelly transformed into an old woman with a wandering mind, who couldn't even remember who he was. But it wasn't only his mother Ian stayed away from – for more than thirty years, Ian had never revisited Yass, the country town where he had grown up, the place of all his most powerful childhood memories. When he finally decided to return there, it was after my mother's death. She had kept him away from his mother – and almost his whole family – throughout their married life and, as if a spell had been broken, her death released him into a sudden freedom to contemplate a trip back to the past. He even invited me along. Before that final visit to Yass, my father had maintained that his real reason for not revisiting his boyhood home had been because 'there was no one to see' – meaning that his mother would have been his only reason for returning, and she had moved to Gunnedah to live with her youngest daughter Cherie and her family. Yet once he crossed the threshold of 'Newton', the house Albert had built for his growing family, the house my father himself had grown up in, memories flooded back and he talked compulsively, re-creating for me each room as it had been in his childhood, almost unaware of the current owner, who had generously admitted us and was trying tentatively to talk of her own experiences in the house. His attachment had not only been to Mother, it had been to the house itself. To him, it was Mahler's 'dear, dear earth'. Renewed youthfulness surged into him as he walked around his childhood home, and when we finally drove off, he used a word I'd never heard him use in my entire life before: 'Well,' he said, 'that was *exhilarating*!' Later on the same trip, I showed him what I had written about his mother's life. He read the whole chapter sitting across from me at our motel table, put the pages down, and sighed, 'Well, that's a very sad story.' I did not press him to say more, knowing him well enough by now to recognise that he was unlikely to elaborate.

Gwyn and Cherie

Albert Crago's forthright eldest daughter Gwyn had always seemed well able to look after herself. By the end of the war, Gwyn was married to a successful grazier, with a growing family of her own. Even Beth was now married to Roy, a bank employee with a job for life. Albert probably believed she too was provided for, as indeed she was. But his youngest daughter, Cherie, had been a sickly child. Almost as shy as Beth, Cherie seemed for a long time unlikely to find a husband. In his will, Albert left Cherie all three of the rental properties his father Petherick had left him, presumably expecting their income would help support her. When Albert died in 1948, Gwyn and Beth were distressed at the way they had seemingly been 'left out' by that provision. As sensitive as their mother Ethel, Cherie's older sisters must have felt that their 'dear old Dad' had ill rewarded their lifelong loyalty by favouring their younger sister, that he had not valued them as highly as they had always believed.

Cherie, who never wanted to cause trouble or to be singled out as special, made sure that the money from the sale of the three properties was divided equally between herself and her sisters. Despite this generous act, it was some years before Gwyn was prepared to speak to Cherie, and even then, the two would drive out to meet each other at a 'neutral' halfway point between Gwyn's home at Cassilis and Cherie's near Gunnedah, rather than visiting one another in their respective homes. All of this speaks volumes about the way that Gwyn, like Beth (and like their father Albert himself), clung onto hurt for years after it had been caused, as if denying that the person who had wronged them – in this case their father, not Cherie – would ever deserve forgiveness. Of course they did, eventually, forgive. But it took a very, very long time. Among the A.C. Cragos, self-examination and forgiveness of others seemed to come late in life. In them, I now recognise my own slowness to face up to my shortcomings, my own responsibility for things I long preferred to blame on others.

1980: Dick and John

Dick and his wife May had endured a painful estrangement from their elder son John, who had felt judged, criticised and misunderstood by them. May and Dick had been shocked and confused when their 'brilliant' boy failed at one thing after another and wandered into the dark woods of mental illness. For years, John had no contact with them, believing (as many aggrieved children do) that he was better off if he kept his distance as much as possible. But when Dick knew he was dying, and seemed unable to find peace of mind, John came to see him in hospital and told him he loved him. Then, according to John's wife Jenny, Dick's anxious agitation finally settled and the two were able to forgive each other. And just a week after his father's death, John (who'd then been unemployed for some time) went out and got himself a job. The relief that came with this reconciliation must have been profound.

1991–1994: Cherie and Ian

In their young days, Cherie had always been my father Ian's 'favourite sister' (his own words). They had had an understanding, whereby Ian had done the washing up for Cherie, and she had taken over the yard chores that he hated but she enjoyed. But their childhood bond had been eroded by Ian's marriage to my mother. Just as my mother Gwen was jealous of her husband's closeness to his sister, so perhaps did Bob Adams, Cherie's husband, resent his wife's closeness to her older brother. On my father's (rare) visits to Cherie and Bob during my childhood years, my father found Bob 'unwelcoming' – by which he meant hostile. Dad, whose entire career had been in education, had attempted to tell Cherie and Bob that their children were bright kids who needed stimulation and encouragement rather than criticism, but he found Bob dismissive of his professional expertise and he took that very personally. Ted, too, saw Bob as 'a wet blanket or a drag' on Cherie, because Bob was uncomfortable with Cherie venturing too far from the farm, and did not even want her to stay on for an hour after the Sunday service with other members of the congregation.

Yet after my mother's death (actually, shortly before it, while she was clearly in her final months of life) my father seemed able to resume his old closeness with his sister. In life, both Ian and Cherie had felt controlled by their partners, and it took the imminent death of Ian's partner to permit brother and sister to relate again in the trusting way they had once been able to do. Once again, reconciliation had had to wait a very long time, but come it did.

The Kirkhams and the Sanders

On my mother's side of the family, it is harder to find examples of forgiveness and reconciliation in action. Mum had never known her father's father, for George Edward Holyoak Sanders had died suddenly of a heart attack one day short of his forty-fourth birthday. Her own father, Victor, had met his death at forty-four. Neither father nor son would have been prompted to soul-searching by a gradually increasing consciousness of their own mortality, because mortality had forced itself upon them prematurely. Of course Victor had faced possible death many times on the Western Front, but that was a different experience from the incremental awareness of death's inevitability felt by a middle-aged adult. Of the four families from which my grandparents came – Cragos, Stears, Kirkhams and Sanders – the Sanders family seemed the least known to me. Most of my relatives were (and still are) relatively incurious about their families of origin, though capable of responding if someone else temporarily showed an interest. Among the Cragos, Stears and Kirkhams there has been at least one, sometimes more than one, person who valued family memorabilia and passed on family lore to others. But I know of no such person among direct descendants of George Sanders, born in 1823. And I myself have contributed to my ignorance, finding it harder to contact my English cousins than any of my other relatives – my fault as much as theirs. My Sanders heritage, apart from my uncle and my grandfather, is largely unknown to me.

    On Gwen's mother's side, the Kirkhams had also had more than their share of early and unexpected deaths. Robert Kirkham (Junior), Eva's oldest brother, who went bankrupt in 1893 and moved to South Africa in 1895 to start again, succumbed to a sudden illness and died in Johannesburg just a few months after arriving, at the age of thirty-one. His family, still in Australia, were shocked. Robert's eldest son, Charlie, was not yet seven, and his newest son just a baby. Robert's younger brother Ern was killed in action in July 1917. He was forty-three (almost the same age at which Victor would later die, leaving his own son fatherless at seven). And then Robert's third son Eddie was killed too, in May 1918, aged just twenty-five. The parade of losses was typical of many a family during the Great War – including the family of Will Crago, Albert's older brother, whose son Billie was 'blown to smithereens' some time before hostilities ceased. But in the case of the

Kirkhams, I simply do not know of reconciliations, either late in life, or earlier, though some may have occurred.

My mother herself lived long enough to admit, under the influence of dementia, that she had done wrong. In her last days, as she became increasingly frail and confused, Gwen occasionally expressed remorse: for her jealousy of her younger brother, Hugh; for her disregard of her mother's feelings; for protecting me, her eldest child, and automatically blaming my brother instead. Yet I do not think she remembered any of these admissions after making them, and I doubt that she took much serenity to her grave. What was it that had made it so hard for my mother, as long as I had known her, to face painful truths, to express unfeigned affection and to forgive others?

On one of the last occasions on which I saw my mother, by then in a nursing home, she was only semi-conscious. She had always been querulous and demanding, and now she complained of being too hot under her blanket. 'Get it off me,' she muttered. So far, so normal – this sort of behaviour is not uncommon in dying people. Their hearts are failing and blood may be puddling internally, so feeling too hot may have little to do with the external temperature.

Then, clearly back in her childhood rather than in the present, she started calling out to someone called Vic. Of course her father's name was Victor, and his wife Eva had called him Vic, but Mum herself had always called her father 'Father' or 'Dad'. I knew that there had been another Vic in her childhood life – the young son of Eva's older sister Sue, with whom my mother sometimes played. 'Get it off me, Vic! I don't want it on me!' she exclaimed, writhing in her hospital bed as if to escape from a slimy frog – which may have been all it was. What might she had been reliving? I'll never know for sure. But I was left with the clear impression that as a young child, my mother had suffered more than simply being neglected in favour of her younger brother. As death approached, panic and disgust were struggling back into her mind, like wounded soldiers screaming in pain from no-man's-land. I realised that perhaps a long-buried, alarming experience might have helped to make her 'a hard woman to love', and it was because of this realisation that I felt the sudden compassion for her that I have described in the previous chapter. She had not forgotten, and what she was remembering was not something to forgive.

What We Need to Know

The old and the new

Life narrows down, as if the blood that pumps less energetically through our veins, the lungs that draw reduced breaths, demand that we hope for less in the future, hang onto less from the past and reduce our demands on ourselves. In old age, many of us try hard to maintain whatever has sustained us in the past – from the bright red lipstick that was fashionable in our youth to the words of a favourite hymn. If we have always worked, we must work, if humanly possible, till we drop. And most of the A.C. Cragos did just that.

Albert Crago seems to have said little about his father, Petherick. If he did, his children did not remember it – and why should they? The oldest of Albert's children, Dick, was just a baby when Petherick died. Petherick, who had boarded the *Castillian* en route to Australia as an energetic, recently married twenty-one-year-old, was forty-five years old when Albert was born, and sixty by the time his youngest son was fifteen. In Albert's eyes his father may have been a remote figure. Perhaps he even hated Petherick, as Dick and Ian, in their turn, would hate Albert. But Albert did have one anecdote about Petherick, a story that expressed a good deal about how he'd felt towards his father in the days after Petherick handed over the day-to-day running of the Crago Brothers mill to Albert (by now a young adult) and his older brother, Will. Petherick, Albert said, would sometimes come to inspect the mill, 'all dressed up in a collar and tie as if he were going to church!' The wording suggests practical Albert's scorn for a father who cared more about appearances than he did (Albert himself wore khaki to work, because it would not show the dust that hung constantly in the air). Yet I wonder now whether Albert failed to understand how his father might have felt in retirement, and how dressing oneself in 'proper' clothes when going out can conserve morale at a time when we are in physical decline. For Petherick, inspecting the mill that had been the centre of his own work life and his legacy to his sons was a way of maintaining his sense of purpose and meaning, just as his wearing collar and tie maintained his dignity. Similarly, Henry Lawson's daughter remembers him – then only middle-aged, but prematurely aged by drink and despair – dressing 'in a slightly old-fashioned way. He wore dignified high collars and he was never without his stick.'[1]

As I myself have aged, I have turned back to the formal dress code in which I was raised. After a period of aggressive dressing down that lasted from young adulthood well into middle age, I now wear a jacket and a tie regularly. It is true that I live in a cold climate, for which these clothes are more appropriate, but there is much more to it than that. I have returned to the days when, as nine-year-olds, my brother and I were dressed by our mother in little suits (with short pants) whenever we travelled into the city while on our yearly summer holidays at my grandmother's flat in Artarmon. Today, I 'dress up' on the days I board the train to go to Sydney. And now that I am in my early seventies, this habit has taken on a new layer of meaning. I dress in order to preserve a sense of myself as a functioning human being who can take his place alongside younger human beings who board the train to commute to work.

For many people, driving takes on a similar meaning. Learning to drive was a key achievement for them as teenagers or young adults; now it becomes the way they can hang onto the sense of competence and independence that driving once conferred. I know older adults who are still driving despite early-stage dementia, or worsening eyesight – they are not necessarily irresponsible (they know what they are capable of and they avoid what they're not) but they are determined to drive as long as they can. They know that to give up driving is to take a big step back, to fumble in a twilight of incompetence and dependency. 'As long as I'm with him, he goes like a bird!' said Ted's wife Beryl, at the time that Ted was still driving, albeit only to familiar destinations not too far off.

Forgiving and forgetting

If you don't feel good about yourself, you may turn your suffering into a way of being special, and this is what some in my family have done. Instead of feeling pride about what they have achieved, or about the love and support they have earned from others, such individuals feel a kind of pride at how much pain they have had to endure, often at the hands of their relatives. Some look forward to a heavenly reward to compensate them for their earthly suffering; others may not share that faith, but still feel somehow enhanced or distinguished by what they have been through – as medals acknowledge, however incompletely, the suffering and bravery of those who have served in wartime. Some victims of trauma feel compelled to tell and retell the story of what happened to them, a narrative which (in extreme cases) may leave little space for anything new and more positive.

Yet as we've repeatedly seen in the lives of my extended family, trauma is relative to the individual. What one individual experiences as upsetting at the time but later forgets, another finds unforgivable and remembers lifelong. Childhood slights and disappointments – as seemingly insignificant as being refused permission to own a pet, or to ride a pony – are remembered long into adulthood. Adult slights (like not being invited to a friend or relative's wedding) may be remembered to one's deathbed. Shame has a very long half-life, and for thin-skinned people like myself and many of my relatives, life presents countless opportunities for feeling shame and then recreating it for years to come. No wonder that some people deal with their shame by focusing their feelings on those who have caused it, converting shame (temporarily at least) into anger and bitterness. It is essentially the same process as occurs when narcissists lash out at those who criticise them, instead of enduring the feelings of shame and badness that the criticism triggered in them.

'Forgive and forget,' people used to say, meaning that once you had forgiven someone, you would be free of the pain they had caused you and hence could forget it. Yet often we persuade ourselves that we have forgiven when in fact we still remember, and it still hurts. And what about forgiving ourselves? Entitled people forgive themselves too easily, thereby protecting themselves against shame. For some of us, it is harder to forgive *ourselves* for a felt shame than it is to forgive others for what they have done to us. And if we cannot forgive, we cannot forget – except, perhaps, in the case of dementia. With the decay of memory, the slate is wiped clean.

Gene pools replicate themselves

Ethel Crago, my grandmother, developed dementia in her final years of life. But when Dick and Ian chose their life partners, they could not possibly have known that their brides would one day suffer the same sad fate as their mother. When Dick and Ian married, Ethel was in her prime. Yet Dick and Ian had long been Ethel's favourites – everyone was clear on that – and both of them had disappointed their mother by their choice of wives. Was there something in May as a young woman that hinted darkly to Ethel of uncomfortable similarities to herself? Was there something in Gwen that hinted similarly to Ethel, fourteen years later, when Ian announced his intention of marrying Gwen? Might that explain Ethel's instinctive dislike of both women? Of course I don't mean that Ethel saw evidence of dementia – nothing would have been further from her thoughts. But both May and Gwen were, in different ways, controlling of others and emotionally labile – and so was Ethel herself. When we see someone else who openly displays the same behaviour we dislike or deny in ourselves, we mostly recoil from them.

Ted, Ethel's middle son, seems to have met no opposition in his choice of wife – perhaps because Ethel was less emotionally invested in Ted than she was in his brothers. Beryl retained a clear mind to her last days, but instead, *Ted himself* developed dementia. Neither Gwyn nor Beth, both allied with their father rather than their mother, developed dementia. But *Beth's husband Roy did* (in his last years of life, Beth would set Roy to work tearing cardboard into little pieces for use as mulch in Beth's garden).

What is the meaning of all this? A genetic propensity to dementia within the family does not account for two of Ethel's sons and one of her daughters marrying someone who themselves would, many years later, develop dementia. Here again, I see the family replicating its gene pool in its choice of mates. Those who would, in old age, be free of dementia (Dick, Ian, Beth) 'married it'. One (Ted), who would in old age follow his mother into dementia, married a woman who would not.

Complicating this plausible theory is the fact that the age of onset of dementia can vary considerably, and it may be that those family members who appeared to have escaped dementia might, had they lived longer, have developed it anyway. My father Ian appeared to be functioning well in the final three years of his life, after my mother's death. But when he died, we found his house full of lists (so he wouldn't 'run out of things to say' in phone calls to his children) and evidence that he had 'over-bought' certain items (whole cupboards full of toilet paper, for example), perhaps because he had forgotten what he had already bought not long before. All of this is suggestive of the 'mild cognitive confusion' that sometimes precedes Alzheimer's-type dementia – suggestive, but not definitive. Similarly, to my knowledge, Cherie's husband Bob was not afflicted with dementia when he died, but I did not see him close enough to the time of his death to be sure.

As stated earlier in this book, Ethel Crago's dislike of both Dick's wife May and Ian's wife Gwen was almost certainly the result of unconscious recognition, in them, of aspects of her own nature. Dick and Ian may have been aware that certain qualities in their intended partners were similar to their mother's (their outspokenness, their comfort with taking a leadership role in the relationship) but, more likely, the person they had chosen simply seemed 'familiar' and 'safe' *because of* those unacknowledged similarities.

Science has already established that some qualities (both of personality and of physical appearance) appear to be 'bundled' together – see the examples provided in Theoretical Reflections later in this book. Sometime in the future, geneticists may well have established other 'bundles', which might even link the tendency to develop dementia with particular physical characteristics. In choosing their partners, both Dick and Ian would have been choosing physical traits they found attractive – but those same traits may have been bundled with the propensity for dementia late in life. All of which is completely speculative, of course.

La Belle Alliance

It was their father Albert who had wronged Gwyn and Beth by making special provision for Cherie in his will – but it was not their 'dear old Dad' that they blamed. This apparent irrationality makes sense at another level. Blaming Albert would have compromised the older girls' intense loyalty to their father – a loyalty that must be preserved at all costs. Of course I do not mean that Gwyn and Beth consciously planned or reasoned out their conduct: they simply acted as their feelings dictated. But in blaming the innocent living instead of the guilty dead, they were acting out the human impulse to hurt and punish *someone* in response to a hurtful or destructive action. It is the same emotional logic as had governed the ritual sacrifices of the Old Testament, and the idea of a scapegoat that could be driven out of the community, carrying with it the community's sins. Yet it is not necessary to have a faith in order to think this way. 'Someone's got to pay!' is the phrasing we often hear outside courtrooms and near fatal accident sites.

And of course, Albert himself believed he was being fair, 'tempering the wind to the shorn lamb'. His concept of fairness would undoubtedly have been influenced by the fact that his own father, Petherick, had treated him similarly to the way he was treating Cherie. Albert, too, had been a youngest child; he, too, had been considered by his parents to be weak – not subject to illness like Cherie, but lacking in 'gumption' or 'oomph', apparently in need of someone else's strong hand to help him cope with life. That strong hand would be supplied, at the mill, by his much older brother Will ('he was the real miller, Dad just worked') and within his own family by his wife Ethel. In Petherick's eyes, Albert ought to inherit some reliable extra income: his older brothers and sisters would easily be able to fend for themselves. But holding out one's hand to a 'weaker' brother or sister can result in major misunderstandings. In the eyes of other siblings, the extra little bit left to one of their number could easily seem like blatant favouritism – too much love for one, too little left over for the others.[2]

Just as Gwyn and Beth had refused to blame their father for his favouring Cherie, so Ian, long after his father's death, refused to acknowledge that in fact his family had been comfortably off. No, he told me, they had only got by because 'Dad had milk and eggs from the farm, and vegetables from the garden.' They were, he believed, 'not rich, but rich in the things that really mattered'. Even when I showed him a copy of Petherick Crago's will, with its 'special provision' for Albert (the three rental properties he'd eventually bequeathed to Cherie), Ian still refused to believe it. The level of denial was high in all of them, really, except for Ted and Cherie, the only two out of the six siblings who could acknowledge the good sides of both their father and their mother. Dad clung to his childhood perceptions of things. What he had been told by his parents was, it seemed, unchallengeable – another instance of the intense investment many of the Cragos had in their childhood, a childhood that, perhaps, they idealised as a refuge from the disappointments of adulthood.

Childhood's end?

The older I grow, the more preoccupied I become with my childhood. All my longings began there – it was a time when (like most children) I lived with vivid awareness but largely without *self*-awareness, without much sense of choice or decision. I was brimful of expectations, beliefs and fears that had, in a sense, nothing to do with me, and everything to do with my mother, my father and the families in which they had grown up – they, too, filled to overflowing with the feelings of those who had come before them, yet oblivious of that. The apple that Eve plucked confers the knowledge of good and evil, that quality of mind that makes us human, that makes us doubt our own instincts, that causes us to ask why, that whispers to us of our eventual death. Many of us only start to hear those whispers, very faintly, around the age of nine or ten. A few boys – and rather more girls – hear them earlier. Some don't seem to notice them until adolescence – childhood's end.

I have clung to my childhood all my life. Several others in my generation of the family have done the same, though in different ways. Large numbers of writers, musicians and artists (including Gustav Mahler) have done it too. I never wished to be prematurely adult, as some children do. I was happy enough as a child – protected from much of life's pain, often praised and admired, often left alone to play contentedly and obsessively at games that were entirely of my own creation. Finding adulthood inevitable, I did my best to fight it off. I didn't start paying my own bills until I was twenty, I didn't buy my own clothes until then either, and I didn't learn to cook my own meals until after I was married. I didn't really like the idea of adult responsibility. I enjoyed being driven places by others, so I never learned to drive (of course that was not the only reason), and have used public transport all my life. Even in my mid-twenties, I continued to think of key childhood experiences, to turn them over and over in my mind, and (by the age of thirty) to write about them. I had no thought of publication then – I just needed to relive my childhood somehow, and writing it down gave it a kind of permanence, like a verbal photograph.

I was extremely slow both to grow up and, later, to grow old. Physiologically, I reached puberty well behind most of my schoolmates. I inherited genes that ensured that I looked a decade younger than I actually was, and until my mid-fifties, I actually felt younger too. Not only in my therapy, but in many other ways, I continued to play in the same spirit of innocent, sheltered irresponsibility to which I had clung as a child. Most significantly of all, perhaps, I didn't have an orgasm until I'd been married for almost two years. Once I'd achieved that milestone (which for most other young men would have come easily and naturally, much earlier), I did feel more grown up – yet I also felt that something had changed irrevocably. I could remember the sense of utter safety and comfort I'd felt in childhood, where the urgencies and the disquiet of adulthood were safely distant, as if behind a tall brick wall. But I could no longer inhabit these feelings as I once could. That time was gone for ever.

Now, suddenly, I feel old. That has its advantages, as well as its many disadvantages, but in any case, I have no choice. I still look back on my childhood with longing, I still strive fruitlessly to recapture it, but now I know beyond any doubt that I have travelled beyond it, to those blue distances the traveller sings about in the final bars of *Das Lied von der Erde*. I feel freer, somehow, freer to value what I have right now, to live each day at a time instead of being bound to the wheel of a demanding future. I have experienced giving, and receiving, unconditional love. I have acknowledged the love – Maureen's – that I once failed to recognise, or diminished by judgements and criticisms. I still feel different, but the dark, unexplored spaces on the map have shrunk dramatically. I know that there are many who feel as different as I do, some of them in my own family of origin. That little red monkey is no longer alone.

Personal Reflections

> And whatsoever might be told concerning the creatures that other folk had met in Evilshaw [a wood reputed to be inhabited by evil creatures] of her it must needs be said that therein she happened on nought worser than herself.
> William Morris, *The Water of the Wondrous Isles*, 1895

Many traditional cultures (including the Maori of New Zealand) believe it is possible for the spirit of an ancestor to take over the body of someone in the present generation. Various kinds of aberrant behaviour (including mental illness and delinquency) may be explained in this way. The ancient Greeks believed that a god might take possession of a mortal and drive him or her to extraordinary heroism (or madness), and as late as the seventeenth century of the Christian era, possession by Satan was a credible phenomenon, leading to the cruel deaths of thousands of women in Europe. But the non-Western cultures, it seems to me, were closer to the truth of the matter: it is not gods or devils who somehow live again in us, but the spirits of our own ancestors – only today, we recognise these spirits as particular genetic combinations that recur again and again in families.

When someone in the present generation acts in the same way as a parent, an aunt or an uncle – or even a grandparent, great-uncle or great-aunt – we experience the same sense of the uncanny as people did in pre-industrial societies. Most often, we shy away from looking the repeating pattern squarely in the face. It has taken me much of my adult life (from the dawning of self-awareness in my late thirties to now, in my early seventies) to amass convincing evidence for the pattern to which my own life has conformed, and to accept that I am a product of a family gene pool, not just a product of my individual upbringing in the relatively protected, stable world of 1950s white middle-class Australia.

I have found it hard to face up to what I found, and I can well understand why others would find it hard too. In fact, there exists a story about a member of the Crago family some generations back who, like me, became obsessed with finding out the true history of his ancestors, and traced them back to the Cornwall of two or three hundred years ago. In doing so, he discovered that one of his forebears had been a highwayman (who presumably was hanged for his crimes). My distant relative never returned to his researches, and (so I was told) destroyed everything he had found, the good along with the bad. This story, which has some of the fatalism of myth or fairy tale about it, reveals the taboo associated with knowing too much about one's family past. These days it is quite fashionable to 'discover one's roots', and we even have reality TV shows in which interesting individuals (mostly celebrities) conduct such investigations (with a good deal of professional assistance, of course) and are overwhelmed with (mostly positive) emotion at what they find. But for every individual who eagerly engages in this quest, there are many others who turn away from it in holy dread (Coleridge's words in 'Kubla Khan'), fearing what they might find. In my own quest for 'what I needed to know', I think I can fairly say that I, too, have found 'nought worser than myself'.

The getting of wisdom

When, in my middle thirties, I began trying to situate my own life within the families into which I had been born, I simply knew that this was something I needed to do. Like the maps in my old school atlas, which showed the coastal fringe of Australia in white and almost the entire rest of the continent in a deep black that signalled the parts unknown to the early British settlers, my family of origin was a blank space that I needed to explore – or perhaps a space inside of me that needed, somehow, to be filled. There was also a shadowy expectation that at the end, I would find something. Something would be revealed, or discovered.

Now, as I near the end, I am aware that I have filled in that particular black space, at least to a fair degree. I know far more about my family on both sides than I did when I began, although there is much more that I will probably never know now. I recognise myself in many of my relatives and ancestors, and recognise many of them in me – not always comfortably. I have, at different times and in different ways, been Albert, Ethel, Eva, Victor, Hughie, Dick, Ted and Beth. Most obviously, I have been my mother, Gwen, and my father, Ian. I have also been my first cousin John, and my thrice-removed cousin Henry. All of this helped me to feel more sure of who I am genetically, yet simultaneously caused me to question aspects of my personality that I had always taken for granted.

Wounded healers and self-knowledge

Counsellors and therapists often report feeling like frauds (the so-called impostor syndrome). Although they have learned to sit calmly with people in considerable distress, they don't actually know the answer and may feel they have little to offer. In fact, there is no answer, and what good counsellors have to offer is simply the kind of relationship that will enable their clients to mature inwardly to the point where they cease to demand 'answers'. In the words of the Serenity Prayer, they begin to 'accept that which cannot be changed, to change that which can be changed, and [have] the wisdom to know the difference'.

I think there is another level to the meaning of the impostor syndrome, less often openly acknowledged by professional helpers. The fact is that we, like shamans and witch doctors, are wounded healers – we struggle with the same issues that our clients struggle with, and our private lives are not necessarily serene and conflict-free. Our clients may (temporarily) see us as models of maturity and goodness, but in fact we are just human beings with our own problems, our own faults and our own unmet needs. In that sense, we are indeed imposters. In my case, though, I feel far less conflicted about this than I once did.

As a still-practising therapist, albeit a part-time one, I am aware that the family research that I have engaged in (particularly my growing realisation of the role of genes in my own and my family's history) has aided me professionally too. I would term this the development of acceptance. I accept that I can help some people, despite my own problems. I also accept that I cannot help others, and this may not be all, or even partly, my fault. Self-awareness and self-acceptance is the cure for wounded healers.

Many clients in counsellor or therapy are engaged in an internal struggle: they wish to be different from who they are. Yet the harder they try to be different, the more they end up feeling the same. I followed this course too. Guilt, fear and shame played a big part in my internal world, although much of it was concealed from others by my well-functioning defences. As I began to accept that my genetic make-up was similar to the genetic make-up of so many in my family, I also began to accept that I was not 'bad' for having struggled in vain to change myself. I realised that there were some ways in which I will never change (as pioneer family therapist Sal Minuchin once put it) and this has materially assisted me to accept, as well, those aspects of my clients that were clearly genetically determined. I became more relaxed around their fear of change and more allowing of their two steps forward, one step back progress towards a greater sense of self-acceptance.

I sometimes even tell clients that there are certain aspects of our personalities that we are born with, and that we cannot blame ourselves for them, only learn to live more maturely and sensibly with them. A surprising number of my clients resist this explanation and continue to struggle fruitlessly to change themselves – I can't blame them: I did the same. I know that I can't stop them and that my power to influence them is limited. As Galadriel says to Frodo in the first volume of *The Lord of the Rings*, 'I will not give you counsel, saying "do this" or "do that", for not in doing or contriving, nor in choosing between this course and another, can I avail, but only in knowing what was and is, and in part also, what shall be.' The less anxious I become on my clients' behalf, the freer they are to advance – at their own pace – towards their own peace of mind.

Imperfect relationships

In my relationships with my parents, my partner and my children, something similar has happened, though it has been more gradual, with many slip-backs. From my mid-thirties on, I tried, on and off, to mend my relationship with both my parents. I recently found, among the papers I inherited from them, cards in which I had apologised individually to both Mum and Dad for my earlier, inept attempts to connect with them, and for the pride and ignorance which had led me to be so tactless in my communications with them. But it was only when I became genuinely interested in my father and mother as people, and enjoyed hearing them talk about the parts of their lives that had occurred before I was born, that I began to forge a better relationship. My father was more receptive to this than my mother, and I still felt painfully stuck with her when she died, but by then I had found out enough about her to realise that her distance from me had more to do with her own past, and her family's past, than it had to do with me. I had ceased to take it personally. Taking things personally is what highly sensitive individuals do – they must learn, slowly and painfully, to get over it.

I have (since at least my forties) often blamed myself for whatever problems my children have encountered in life. I still feel responsible for a good deal: I modelled for them (as my mother modelled for me) displays of poorly regulated emotion, and I offered them a template for acting impulsively in my career, informed more by fantasy than by realistic appraisal. My marriage, in the two decades during which they were growing up, was typified by frequent bickering and recurrent storms, and I can perfectly understand why both of my children would want above all to avoid such a relationship in their own adult lives. I could be warm, affirming and enthusiastic – yet I could also be critical, controlling and unempathic. *Nought worser than myself.*

Yet my growing awareness of my family's genetic legacy has enabled me to realise that there are also things in both my children that I was not responsible for, at least not directly. While I may well have *carried* some of the family genes, not all of them were directly expressed in my own personality and conduct. When some of those genes recurred in my children, taking forms that I myself had not displayed, I was gradually able to recognise that one of my parents (or some other relative) was *living again* in them. The upbringing we provide for our children can have only limited impact on the genetic legacy that we have handed on, willy-nilly, to those same children. The result of this realisation is that I no longer feel totally responsible for everything with which my children have had to struggle. I did not cause it, though my behaviour certainly reinforced it. I just have to accept what has happened, and do my best to help them with their struggles – if they are willing to accept such limited help as I can offer them. I am their father, not their therapist.

As I have come to understand myself, so I have better understood the woman I married at twenty-three, and have lived with since, 'for better, for worse, for richer, for poorer, in sickness and in health'. Death, I am relieved to say, has not yet parted us, and so (like my grandfather Albert at around the same age) I can now express to her what I was unable or unwilling to acknowledge much earlier in our relationship. Maureen has stabilised me considerably. Without her, I would have been a rocket, launching amidst excitement and acclaim, but then veering off course and crashing without ever reaching its goal. Maureen has offered me a loyalty that I simply took for granted for far too long. She was the secure base from which I felt safe to explore and experiment. Often those explorations and experiments were unfruitful, and some were damaging to her, but she did not dump me in disgust (though she must many times have wished to). She may not have offered me as much spontaneous physical affection, or as many words of praise and encouragement as I craved, but had I not been so blind to her needs and sensitivities for so long, she probably would have felt able to be more forthcoming in those regards. By being hyper-vigilant for so long to her criticisms (and imagined criticisms) of me, I trained myself not to notice the ways in which she supported me, encouraged me and cared for me.

Maureen has been a reliable, hard-working and creative partner in our various joint enterprises – an untiring data-gatherer and organiser in our joint research in the 1970s, a forthright but fair critic of my writing, an inventive, patient journal co-editor from 1997 to 2009. Her eye for detail and her refusal to accept statements that sounded good but had little basis in evidence have saved me from many scholarly blunders. Wherever we've lived, she has created gardens of great loveliness, free of artificiality and obvious display. But above all else, she stayed with me – at times resentful, at times sad and disappointed – and held onto the hope that I would one day steady down and achieve some of my youthful potential. I think I may just about have done that now. Too little, too late – but even too little is better than nothing.

When I began writing poems, in my sixties, she was visibly delighted and, more than anyone else, encouraged me to continue down this unexpected path. In the first ten years of our life together, she used often to say that she enjoyed just working together, in the garden or around the house, and that she always felt closer to me when we did. It took me a very long time to accept that I, too, felt closer to her as a result of shared activity, even if those activities in themselves seemed to me mundane or tedious. Now, I know what she meant, and it is sad that it has taken me so long to appreciate something so simple yet so profound.

What about the next generation?

The decision (as described in my preface) to leave out of this book my own generation of the family (with the single exception of my cousin John) inevitably renders my account lopsided and somewhat misleading. Where are my children? Where are my siblings and their children? Where are my cousins and theirs? I remain sure that my decision to omit all of these people was the correct one. They still have substantial portions of their lives to lead, and it is not my place to be an unwelcome intruder into those lives. Yet the same decision leaves me standing alone – as once I stood in the school playground? – the only person in my generation who is presented in the round, with all the anxieties, impulsive decisions, romantic fantasies and blind spots that I have portrayed in the earlier generations of my several lines of descent.

So perhaps this is the right time for me to say that of course, I am not alone in these things. In the next generation of the family (my own children, my siblings' children, and my cousins' children) there must surely be individuals who display the same genetic configuration of anxiety, sensitivity and reactivity that has recurred in the generations preceding my own. My hope is that at least someone in the generations of the family to which my children or grandchildren belong may recognise themselves in this book, and be motivated to find out more about the genetic combination they have inherited, and what it might mean for them. Likewise, some readers who are completely unrelated to my family may also recognise themselves, since (another theme of this book) the temperamental combination of high anxiety, high sensitivity and high reactivity affects a substantial proportion of the population.

I dedicate this book to all the people in the past who in varying degrees suffered as a result of their genetic heritage, and to those still living who to varying degrees share that suffering. If they can bear to look at the bigger picture of the family into which they have been born, some of them may also find that they are not alone, and that it is not all their fault.

'Pull gently at a weak rope'

One of the objects I recognised anew every year during our visits to my grandmother's flat in Artarmon was a small cream jug in brown, swampy green and mustard yellow. It showed, on one side, a sailing boat, bow-on to the viewer, its sail billowing out, balanced on the other by the indistinct figure of its skipper. On the reverse side of the jug were the words 'Pull gently at a weak rope'. As a child, I could never understand that injunction. It did not make sense to me, although I can now see that it is simply another way of saying 'temper the wind to the shorn lamb'. It is significant that it took me so long to realise the meaning of those words.

Why did Eva own the jug? Perhaps she inherited it from her own mother, as she inherited some of the furnishings in the Artarmon flat from the Cleveland Street home of her parents. Did she hold onto the jug out of loyalty to them, or because it meant something to her? No, the muddy colours of the jug suggest it was produced later than that, so perhaps she bought it, or was given it, as an adult. In the Kirkham family, the acknowledged 'weak ropes' were Eva's older sister Edie (who had made that disastrous early marriage to Otto Schuler) and the youngest of the siblings, Charlie (who never settled to a job, never married, refused to go to war, and drank). I never heard anything about their mother, born Eliza Allum, but from the repeated statement that 'Annie and Sue brought up those children' (Eva, May and their brother Charlie, the three youngest Kirkhams), I suspect that Eliza may have been either ill or ineffectual as a mother – perhaps a weak rope herself.

And Eva was surely a weak rope too, if not as spectacularly as Edie or Charlie. She retreated to her own family both when Victor was away in the war, and later, when his short-lived experiment with farming at Batlow was coming to an end. After Victor's shocking, premature death and Hughie's move overseas, Eva lived alone, refused to speak with her neighbours at Artarmon, eked out a restricted existence on her widow's pension, 'a proud, lonely woman' who found herself unable to call her son-in-law Ian by his given name, though she later acknowledged (not to him, though) that he had been 'a wonderful son to me'.

In my paternal grandmother Ethel Crago's birth family, the Stears, two of Ethel's brothers died early, of diabetes, and a younger sister also died young in the great flu epidemic that followed the Great War. But it was another among the Stear sisters, Gertrude (Gert), who seems to have been the true 'weak rope'. Gert, also a diabetic, continued to live with her parents until her early death, and was protected and sheltered by her parents. It was Gert who had been befriended by May Lepper, and when May later married Dick Crago, this damned May from the start in the eyes of Dick's Stear relatives. Like Charlie Kirkham, Gert never married, and (as far as I know) never held a job. 'Don't tell Gert' became a family byword – because Gert would become upset and agitated at distressing news, and nobody wanted to have to handle her in that state.

In the family of Lousia Albury and Niels Larsen, Henry's younger brother Charlie was the obvious weak rope – in and out of jails and mental asylums all his life, living with his mother for much of it – but all three brothers and their sister could qualify for the title too, if only partially (in the case of Peter and Gertrude).

Among Ethel and Albert Crago's children, Beth displayed a somewhat similar profile to Gert. Although she married and lived independently of her parents thereafter, she continued to act like a cherished, overprotected child, around whom others tiptoed lest they upset her or 'get her going'. She was the Albert Cragos' weak rope, and her relatives took exaggerated care not to pull too strongly on it. Similarly, Beth's father Albert himself required careful handling. His embarrassing shyness, his tendency to panic and his lack of social graces led his nephew Ralph to regard him as obnoxious and two of his three sons to hate him. Even Ted, who loved him, discovered that the best way to strike a deal with Father was not to oppose him outright, but to pick one's time and then get in a tactfully worded request.

In the apparently confident family of my maternal grandfather Victor, the weak rope was Victor's older sister, Ruby. Ruby, whose home I occasionally visited with my mother when I was a child, was deaf (though I do not think I realised this then). My mother summed her up in the words, 'She never worked, she never married.' There may have been much more to her life than this, but I am unlikely now ever to find out about it. I have not yet been able to locate her birth certificate. No doubt traumatised by his combat experiences, Victor himself became a weak rope after the war – moving from job to job, dreaming of writing, drinking too much – and then dying in that car accident, leaving his daughter at the same vulnerable age he himself had been when his own father died.

'Pull gently at a weak rope' encapsulates what often happens to genetically vulnerable individuals in loving families: parents and siblings protect them and avoid challenging them – but in so doing they give them (as children) little chance of gaining more confidence and building their self-esteem. Later, the 'weak ropes' may attract partners, friends and colleagues who will also support them, bail them out when they are in difficulties, find them places to live (as Henry Lawson's friends did). Yet eventually, even staunch allies lose hope that their 'weak rope' will ever improve, and some cut off contact entirely to protect themselves from further hurt and disappointment.

Today, the 'Pull gently…' cream jug stands atop the dresser shelves in my own kitchen in Blackheath – only a few kilometres from the spot where Victor Sanders met his end as suddenly and shockingly as if he had been blown to smithereens by a German shell in 1916. I keep the jug to remind me of both the grandfather I never knew and the grandmother I loved but did not know until after she was long dead. And to remind myself that I, too, have responded better to gentle pulling than to robust tugs. Accepting that with humility, rather than pushing it away in fierce denial, can be a first step towards the healing of harms – the harms done to us and the harms we may have caused to others. In the family portrait I have gradually uncovered and stripped of its patina of tactful varnish, I have, once again, found therein nought worser than myself.

Theoretical Considerations

Repeating patterns

The forty-eight preludes and fugues of J.S. Bach's *Well-Tempered Clavier* unfold in time as a single great composition that runs the gamut of human emotion – by turns serene, ebullient, melancholy, funereal, playful, stern, majestic, harsh and triumphant. As generations ebb and flow, as individual lives journey from birth to death, a family's life will often display a similar spread of emotional experiences. Bach's 'Forty-Eight' included two preludes and two fugues in each key, so that every note on the keyboard was included, enabling anyone with a good ear to test the 'tempering' (tuning). Bach's instrument was the harpsichord, which had strings less robust (and less tightly wound) than those of the later-invented pianoforte, so harpsichords notoriously needed constant retuning.

Our word 'temperament' is a metaphor taken from the tuning of this keyboard (and bowed instruments, like the violin). How tightly a string is wound will affect the sound it makes when plucked or struck. When we speak of people being 'highly strung', we mean that they feel more intensely, and react more strongly, than others. The 'tuning' of their genetic 'strings' will result in them experiencing emotions – both joyful and painful – more powerfully than most people, with the result that they often act impulsively or irrationally, and (at the extreme) may even be classed as 'mad'.

We have seen repeatedly in this book how individuals who are born thin-skinned ('sensitive'), reactive ('highly strung', 'irritable') and anxious ('shy', 'nervy'), will feel fear, sadness and anger more often and more keenly than their thicker-skinned siblings or cousins. In those whose genetic 'strings' are wound to a high pitch, these emotions may take the form of phobias, depression or rage. But no life, however genetically blessed, is free from both the lighter and the darker feelings that we all share. It is a matter of degree. We human beings are supremely vulnerable creatures. Even the most stable of us can easily enough be thrown off balance, or temporarily traumatised, by some unexpected life event, like a car accident, the sudden death of a loved one or the loss of a taken-for-granted physical capacity.

Bach – his life extended from the late seventeenth century to the mid-eighteenth – composed his music in the contrapuntal style that prevailed in his day. A 'round' (like 'Green Grow the Rushes-O') is the simplest form of such a composition, with an initial voice being echoed by a new voice taking up the same theme, only starting a bar or two later. In the complex fugues that Bach excelled at creating, three voices may be interwoven like this, the well-known theme emerging again and again within a continuously-unfurling tapestry of sound. It is an intellectual exercise to compose a fugue, and its intricacy may appeal to the intellect of the listener (if she or he knows enough about composition to appreciate what is going on), but many listeners are aware of the cumulative emotional impact of the interwoven voices, even if they cannot tease out the design.

Families are like this, too. A family theme may be 'played' in one life, and then repeated in another – perhaps in the life of a direct descendant of the first individual, often in another branch of the family. None of this is conscious or intentional. Bound up in our daily experiences, overwhelmed, perhaps, by our own pain, or preoccupied with our own dreams of success and achievement, we have difficulty in seeing how closely the pattern we are living out may resemble that of another family member, even one who is no longer living. The less we know about those relatives, the less we will possess the equipment to discern the similarities. And perhaps this protects us from knowing too much about the awful mystery of which we are an unwitting part. 'Awful' in its original sense, meant 'worthy of awe' – in 'Kubla Khan', Coleridge referred to it as 'holy dread'.

Family behaviour over time, like a Bach fugue, is multilayered. It's easy to pick out one layer and believe that it explains everything, that it is 'all there is to know'. It isn't, not ever. There are always going to be other layers, making nonsense of our attempts to oversimplify. One part of the human brain (the left hemisphere of the cerebral cortex) insists on separating out an aspect of a complex whole and 'explaining' the whole on the basis of that analysis.[1] That doesn't work when it comes to understanding family process. We need to grasp the whole as well as the parts – and that is the province of the right hemisphere, which can reintegrate the different parts, as perceived by the left hemisphere, into a whole that 'makes sense' at the deepest level.

Families are unique entities – more than the sum of the individuals who comprise them. Patterns don't just exist at the level of behaviour, or beliefs, or personality – they exist at all three levels simultaneously. Layers 'confirm' or replicate each other, rather than contradicting each other: the right hemisphere's 'both/and' encompasses the left's 'either/or'. What appears random, surprising or shocking in one generation may seem predictable and familiar once we look at the generations that came before. When we look beyond an individual to the social system into which he or she was born, what appears to be a 'flaw' or deficit unique to that person seems more like a 'family trait' – handed down both by nature and by nurture.[2]

Opposites attract, yet gene pools replace themselves

As it is usually defined, assortative mating means the tendency of individuals (from birds and animals to humans) to select mates who are somewhat similar to themselves. That happens much more often than we would expect if mating choices were simply random. Among human beings, the 'similarities' can range all the way from physical appearance (as when we select partners of comparable attractiveness) to features like education level, socio-economic status or sense of humour. Partners are usually consciously aware of these similarities ('We come from similar backgrounds'; 'We both laugh at the same things').

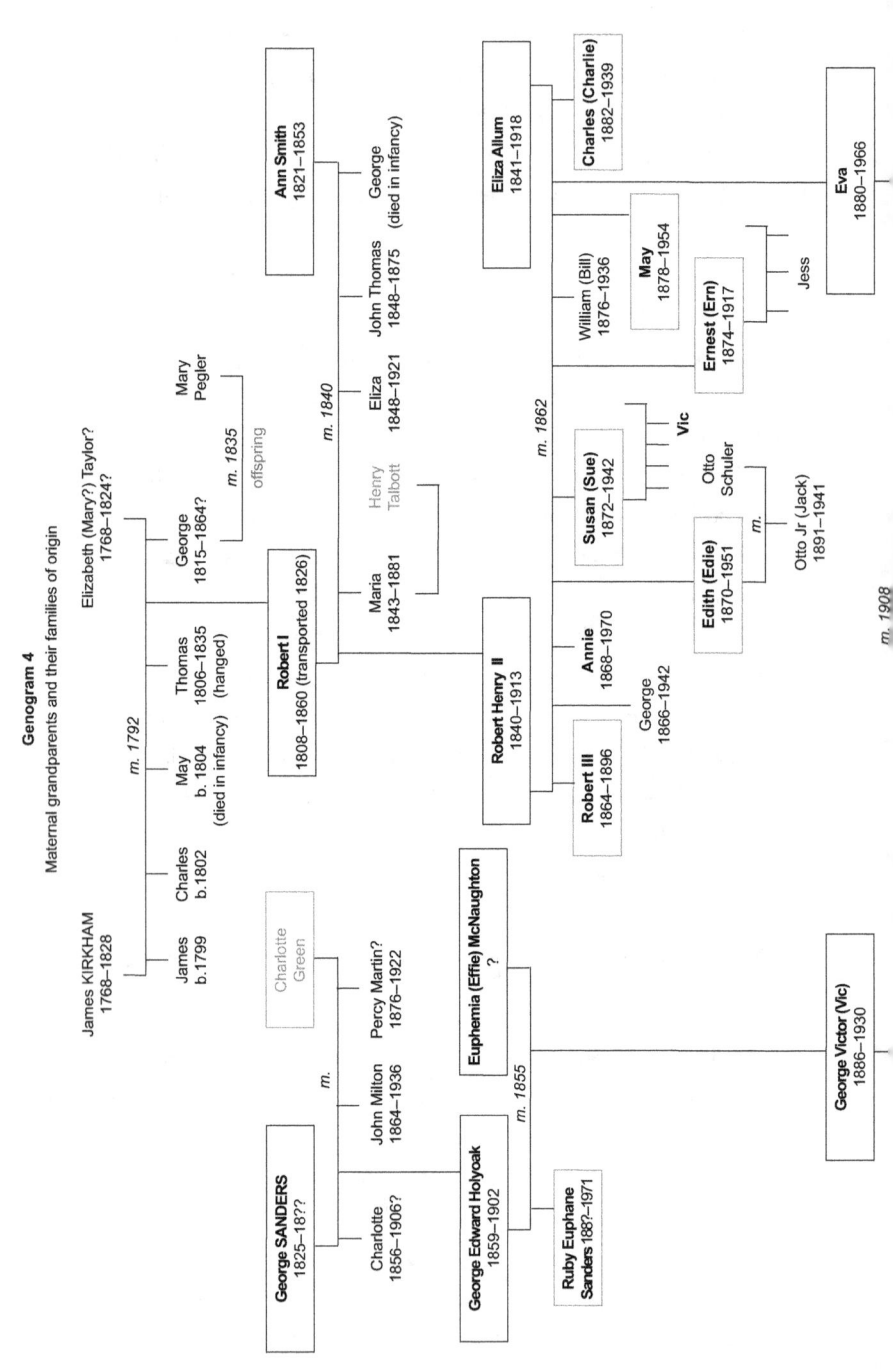

Needless to say, individuals are also drawn to partners who differ from themselves in key ways. 'Opposites attract' may seem like a contradiction of assortative mating, but I don't think it is. We may well see the advantage in teaming up with someone whose strengths and weaknesses complement our own (and vice versa), but we are not drawn to just anyone who seems to 'complete us' in this way. Rather, I think we are drawn to a particular combination of difference and similarity, only the differences are usually easier for us to 'see' than the similarities. The first differences we perceive in our chosen mates are desirable differences. We want to be with that person because we admire the ways in which she or he can do what we ourselves cannot, can be the person we are not. Further into the relationship, of course, those same differences often become irritants. Now we may find ourselves wishing that our mate could be more like us.

The *similarities* that initially draw us to our chosen mates may be less conscious. They are the qualities that make us feel 'safe' with him or her, that seem comfortable and reassuring. Why? Because the comfortably 'familiar' qualities are *literally* 'familiar' – that is, they tend to be those that our mate shares with key members of our family of origin – most likely, with one or both of our parents, sometimes with a sibling or other family member (like a grandparent). These similarities are not necessarily pleasant ones – as when our chosen partner has a bad temper, or is cripplingly shy. But they are still 'familiar' in the sense that we already know people who are like this. We 'know what they are like'.

Freud's narrower version of this was that we tend to be attracted to an individual who reminds us of one of our parents. I would hypothesise a strong genetic basis for such attractions. Individual family members select partners who may look and sound very different from their parents, but who later prove to share key characteristics of those same parents, because they share many of the same genes. If we shift from the level of conscious individual 'choice' to unconscious 'family process', my hypothesis is that families replicate (copy, replace) their own gene pools. Hence the paradox: we select a partner (usually, to have children with) who is desirably different from ourselves, yet who is simultaneously similar to someone else in the family whose genes we do not carry, or carry them without expressing them (they are not 'switched on' in us).

Thus, in the case of my family, emotionally inhibited 'Roundheads' were drawn to mate with more extroverted and expressive 'Cavaliers' – so far, 'desirable difference' prevailed. But at a deeper level, both these pairings reproduced similarities at the genetic level. Both Albert and Ethel were highly sensitive and easily overwhelmed by stimulus – they just expressed it differently. Albert 'roared' in panic, Ethel retired to bed with 'a headache'. My mother, like Ethel, ran from the room in tears, or retreated into illness, real or imagined. Dad panicked like his hated father Albert, though he did not 'roar'. After the birth of my younger brother, Dad 'nearly had a breakdown' when my mother developed mastitis and could not breastfeed the new baby.

Pioneer family therapist Murray Bowen[3] proposed that individuals pair with partners at the same level of self-differentiation as themselves. Broadly 'self-differentiation' means being able to balance our own needs and wishes fairly with the needs and wishes of others. A well-differentiated person can follow his own path in life without undue anxiety about what others may think or feel; yet this same person is sufficiently sensitive to others' needs to treat them with consideration and respect. A well-differentiated person can maintain a relationship with other family members even in the face of real differences of opinion or feeling, and does not distance herself or 'cut off' emotionally as her only means of preserving selfhood.

In my father's family of origin, only Dad's older brother Ted and (despite her shyness and tearfulness) his youngest sister Cherie, seemed to possess this capacity. Both my father and my mother dealt with painful differences by what Bowen called 'emotional cut-off' – refusing to communicate with the person who had offended them – and I was raised within an extended family where 'cut-offs' were common ('Oh, we don't see much of them'; 'Oh, we don't talk about that'). Bowen's observation was that families preserve a baseline level of anxiety across the generations, and that individuals tend to partner with those whose level of self-differentiation (and hence, their level of basic anxiety) is close to their own – though not identical. One is usually a little less anxious than the other.

I believe that Bowen's observation can be explained in terms of family gene pools replicating themselves. Families (like mine) with a substantial level of genetic anxiety transmit it anew in each generation because anxious individuals are predictably drawn to partners who are somewhat less anxious ('opposites attract') yet their partners' own families embody a level of genetic anxiety that matches that of the spouse's family. By contrast, confident, 'thick-skinned' individuals (from families where there is less anxiety) will tend to replicate their family's genetic endowment in their choice of partners – choosing someone who may be a little more anxious than they are, but still far less anxious than would be the norm in families like mine.

Thus families unconsciously acquire affines whose genes will bring back into the family (via their children) the same genetic 'bundles' that are already present within it. We ourselves may not manifest some of those genetic combinations. But we will be drawn to partners who exhibit the outward signs (physical appearance, characteristic behaviours) that signal the presence of those genes. Researcher Jerome Kagan has assembled evidence that blue-eyed women often exhibit a genetic temperament that includes proneness to anxiety and panic. Kagan's evidence also suggests that Sheldon's long-discredited theory about body types may not have been so wide of the mark: the 'ectomorph' body (tall, thin, with a narrow head) is significantly associated with a high level of genetic reactivity. There are probably many more such links between physical appearance and emotional temperament that have yet to be identified. When we choose a partner, we are aware of the physical indicators, but not of the genetic traits that those physical indicators carry with them.

Worrying similarities and desirable differences

When I married Maureen I was reassured to find that she, like me, often had difficulty sleeping. I did not know that this was a sign of an anxious, sensitive temperament, I simply knew that it felt comfortable. Here was someone who would understand me, because she was similar to me. A thicker-skinned person might have felt less comfortable at the thought of a partner who slept poorly and might wake him or her by tossing restlessly in the night. I also felt comfortable with Maureen's slim body – it did not resemble the bodies of my parents (who were tall, like me, but were mesomorphs – sturdily built and well-covered). Others had laughed at me for my thin, lanky body, but she would not be likely to do so. I was consciously aware that I was choosing someone whose personality and behaviour reminded me of my father (patient, quiet, emotionally restrained, willing to be led). I was unaware (at that time) that with her I would reprise my mother's role in relation to my father – apparently confident and controlling, actually easily wounded, anxious and irritable. My mother's body was not ectomorphic like mine, but her brother Hugh's was. So was the body of my grandfather Albert and (so far as I can gather) the body of my grandmother Ethel's cousin, Henry Lawson. All three of them had narrowish heads and prominent ears. The body type to which I belonged had come to me from both my father's and my mother's family lines, and it seemed to be accompanied by similar emotional traits as well. As I gradually became acquainted with the various families that had contributed to my family gene pool, I realised that again and again, family members had married into families that in key respects resembled their own. The 'desirable differences' that were visible to both partners concealed deeper 'worrying similarities' (more obvious, perhaps, to their relatives than to themselves), which may explain why those relatives often disliked the new entrants to the family.

My father Ian married Gwen, an apparently confident but emotional, reactive woman whose mother was not unlike his own father Albert and his younger sister Beth. My grandfather Albert married Ethel Stear, an apparently confident but emotional, reactive woman, whose maternal grandmother, Harriet Albury, had herself been shy, anxious and critical – and less than happily married to the over-confident, entitled, combative Harry Albury. Louisa Albury, Ethel's aunt (apparently confident but emotional and critical) married Peter Larsen ('Lawson'): quiet, passive and prone to depression. And so on.

On my mother's side, my maternal grandmother Eva Kirkham (shy, anxious and critical) had married over-confident but easily wounded and impulsive Victor Sanders, who (like Henry Lawson on my father's side) was restless and dissatisfied, and relied increasingly on alcohol as his dreams slipped away from him. He left Eva an early widow when he died in an accident in his mid-forties. Eva's older sister Edie had also been drawn to a partner (Otto Schuler) who was full of big schemes but who proved unreliable, alcoholic and abusive. Edie filed (unsuccessfully) for divorce on the grounds of desertion, publicly resumed her maiden name and never remarried.

Edie and Eva's father, Robert Kirkham II, my great-grandfather, was a successful building contractor – successful enough to retire in his forties – but he concealed the shameful fact that his own father (my great-great-grandfather, who I shall refer to for clarity as Robert Kirkham I) had started life in London as a poor boy from the East End who gave in to the temptation to steal and ended up transported for life. Robert cannot be blamed for an impulsive act in youth at a time of grinding poverty for the working class, but impulsiveness was clearly in his genes. Impulsiveness comes out again in Robert I's older brother Thomas (also transported for theft and hanged ten years later for repeated offences), in his younger brother George (who arrived in Australia as an assisted migrant but was fined and imprisoned for drunkenness, and died young), and finally (though less dramatically) in Robert Kirkham II's eldest son Robert III (Edie and Eva's much older brother) who overreached himself as a building contractor and had to file for bankruptcy before also dying young.[4]

Parental responses potentiate genes

Had my grandfather Robert Kirkham not concealed the truth about his father's past, would his son Robert have been so likely to act unwisely in his own business career? Would his daughters Edie and Eva have been attracted to men who promised much but did not deliver, and who were not above massaging the truth in their own interests? How families respond to their own genetic legacies can make a difference to whether the genes they pass on inadvertently are fully, or only partially, expressed in the next generation.

All babies look tiny, vulnerable and cute. Their very appearance invites us to pick them up, cuddle them, cherish them – thus ensuring their survival. But individual babies' particular gene-combinations also invite responses from their parents, responses that are likely to differ depending on what genes the baby's behaviour expresses. We know that 'easy babies' (confident, smiling, readily comforted if upset) elicit mainly positive reactions from their caregivers. It is easy to like easy babies, to praise them and to give them lots of love and attention. It is less easy to like 'slow to warm up' babies, whose mood seems more 'serious', who hang back warily instead of enthusiastically enjoying their food, or their bath, and who take longer to settle after becoming upset. But hardest of all to respond to with unconditional love is the 'difficult' baby – the one that experts have identified as having exactly that combination of genes (shy, anxious, reactive) that runs through my family of origin. 'Difficult' babies try our patience sorely.[5] It is hard not to lose our tempers with them. They are easily upset. They react badly to changes and surprises. They resist our attempts to soothe them and settle them. And so parents feel helpless and incompetent around them. It is so easy for parents to blame the child, to assume that it is 'trying to get its own way' or 'attention-seeking'. Difficult babies (now tactfully referred to as 'feisty'!) scream loudly when physically uncomfortable or emotionally distressed, and refuse to be comforted for long periods – something that would try the patience of the most loving parent. And so a child may grow up feeling 'bad', not just because its genes make it anxious and self-doubting, but also because its parents have treated it as bad, and even called it bad. That, in a bald, oversimplified summary, is how particular sets of genes get 'cemented in place' by parental behaviour, right from the beginning of a child's life.

There are, of course, alternative responses. Some 'difficult' children elicit from one or both parents an anxious over-protectiveness ('helicopter parent' is the current phrase) which can keep the child from trying new things and reinforce its doubts. I suspect that Beth, in my father's family, was parented in this way, and that in my mother's family, Eva may have been also. Some parents find within themselves the capacity to be patient with their vexing, frustrating child, to read its signals correctly and to continue to offer it love and non-judgemental acceptance. Reading the difficult child's signals might involve realising that loud, angry screams might in fact signal the child's panic in the face of something it feels as frightening or overwhelming. My grandfather Albert's 'roaring' (as an adult) almost certainly meant that he was afraid – but it seemed that only Ted (quietly confident to be himself) perceived that fear lay beneath his father's loud shouts of 'We'll all be up King Street!' (That is, 'ruined' or 'declared bankrupt'.) Difficult children need to be coaxed to face their fears in small, incremental steps, so that they build confidence – the opposite of anxious 'overprotective' parenting.

At the other extreme, some 'difficult' children are simply neglected or even abandoned by parents whose own capacity to function adequately as adults is impaired, and who find their child too taxing to cope with. They shake it, beat it, dump it for someone else to find or even murder it – sometimes in the irrational belief that they are somehow 'helping' or 'protecting' their child by so doing.[6] Those children who survive such treatment will most likely be severely compromised in their ability to believe in themselves, realise their potential, form stable relationships and parent their children. Fortunately, the family lines that have contributed to my own are in the anxiously overprotective category.

Parents modelling trumps parental teaching

Parents attempt to raise their offspring within whatever system of values they consider appropriate. It was not acceptable for my father or his siblings to lie – ('Tell the truth and shame the devil' was the phrase that my wife's family used for this compulsive honesty). But to my mother's father Victor Sanders and his family, a more relaxed attitude to the truth was favoured. Telling a 'white lie' was nothing to be ashamed of, and concealing certain things from one's children (or one's intended bride) could be a smart thing to do, a way of avoiding 'a spot of bother'.

While parents may tell their children what they consider good behaviour, and punish or discourage bad behaviour, they influence them far more powerfully by the behaviour they themselves demonstrate. Albert's outbursts legitimated loud shouting when everything else in the family's conscious value system forbade it. The fact that it scared most of his young children made it even more influential. As we have seen earlier, traumatic events that are not talked about or not properly understood can create opportunities for repetition. Albert's yelling traumatised my father, Ian, leading him to refuse to speak about his father to me or my siblings. Ian rigidly inhibited such 'uncouth' behaviour in himself – but he married a woman whose own mother had modelled 'screaming' at her spouse, and who therefore saw nothing wrong with it.

In turn, I learned from my mother that there was nothing wrong with raising my voice in dramatic anger, and (from the quiet, passive way my father received it) that there was no danger in doing so, because your partner would not abandon you just because you yelled at her. When my father saw in me, around the age of twelve, worrying signs that, both physically and emotionally, I might be growing into someone rather like his father, he expressed his distaste at my lanky appearance ('Long streak of misery', he called me once – a slip into disgust that I was unable to forget), but he never disclosed to me the fear and hate he had felt in his growing up years, when his father 'roared' at him. The taboos of childhood constrain us well into adult life, sometimes all the way through it.

As a child, I do not remember being told that my grandmother Eva had never learned to drive. I simply saw her walking back from the Chatswood shops with her string bag, wearing her black felt hat. I saw her walk to Artarmon railway station and take the train to see one of her relatives. I wonder whether this modelling of non-driving by the one grandmother I felt attached to might have influenced me too – in part because it took me away from the modelling provided by my parents (who both drove and in later years had a car each), and back to a time before cars were widely available. As an adult, many of my lifestyle choices did look to my relatives like 'living in the past'. No wonder I was so drawn to the character Hathaway in Diana Wynne Jones's fantasy *Archer's Goon*: Hathaway, one of a family of wizards, chooses to live in the 16th century to avoid the modern world, and can only be reached by magic. The choice not to drive necessarily restricted me and Maureen, as adults, to living close to shops and public transport – exactly as my grandmother was. Eerily, I had adopted Eva's way of life. And in her latter years, Maureen often wore a black felt hat not unlike Eva's – though she was unaware of the similarity until I pointed it out to her.

Family values reinforce genetic propensities

It is perfectly possible for children with troublesome genetic combinations to develop into relatively normal, stable adults – albeit adults who will still have trouble coping with their own intense feelings. In this transformation, consciously-transmitted family values play a major role. Here there is an observable difference between my father's and my mother's families. For Dad's family, a strong religious faith supplied a stability that my mother's family seemed to find harder to achieve. The inner sureness that my father's people lacked came to them in what they knew as God's grace. It strengthened them in the face of life's troubles and challenges, and held them to the 'strait path' in the face of temptations to stray. They knew they should forgive, as God had forgiven them. They knew they should not break the law. They knew that if they'd made their bed, they had to lie in it – most especially their bridal bed. Wesley's ideology reinforced individual Crago children's experiences of 'social defeat'. If they had already experienced themselves as 'helpless' and 'worthless', their Church told them that this was the natural condition of humanity and that only by embracing God's love could they transcend their despair. My own youthful preoccupation with defeated armies and navies (the French under Napoleon in 1805 and 1815, the Germans in 1914–18; the Japanese in 1939–45) shows how, unconsciously, I already felt myself 'defeated' on the battlefield of social acceptance and worldly success.

Yet 'social defeat' and 'spiritually sanctioned retreat' are only one aspect of an upbringing that also yielded much that was positive. The Cragos created a family culture that kept its anxious offspring safe from external dangers. Law-abiding people drive safely and do not break the speed limit (though no doubt grumbling at those who do). People who 'turn the other cheek' do not get into brawls and 'king-hit' those who have slighted them. Lifelong non-drinkers do not compound their existing impulsivity and sensitivity with intoxication – thus avoiding most of the 'risky' behaviour that reactive, impulsive youths engage in when they come from families where alcohol is an accepted part of daily life. Those who took 'Thou shalt not kill' literally were less likely to volunteer for military service if a war came, and instead to opt for a role such as that of ambulance driver. Overall, the Albert Cragos were raised in a solid framework of customs and beliefs that would make it less likely they would die early, shocking deaths in road accidents, in street brawls and in combat.

To a generation raised in a very different moral climate, some of the precepts that I and other family members absorbed as children will now seem harsh and unnecessary. But has the freedom to divorce and choose again really made people happier or more content? Sometimes yes; often (I fear) no. And we learned values that today's young people sorely lack. In my own lifetime, society has come to place a higher value on 'freedom to choose' and 'entitlement' than on obligation and loyalty. In the days of my grandparents, what was valued was a dedication to 'doing one's best' no matter how tedious or unrewarding the task; and people paid more than lip service to 'family ties'. Keeping in contact with relatives was seen as inherently good. My father's people frequently fell short of these informal 'commandments', but at least they *knew* that they were falling short. Today, too many of us are 'laws unto ourselves' and fail to see the injustice and hurtfulness of some of our own behaviour – 'careless' behaviour, as Paul Kelly memorably expressed it in his song of the same name.

Despite the more secular nature of their provenance, some of the same precepts that had governed my father's family also influenced my mother's. When Victor Sanders turned his back on his new love in 1919 to return to his wife Eva, he did not do it because he felt God required it of him, yet he did it anyway – placing obligation and loyalty before impulsive, romantic dreams. Half a century later, I did much the same. Neither of us were believers but we followed the same imperative as any sincere Christian would have followed.

The two different family cultures that contributed to forming me balanced each other out, offering me the possibility of choice and change. Methodists could find it hard to enjoy themselves, even in comparatively innocent ways, and many of them may have turned to hard, unrelenting work as a way of suppressing their own appetites. Guilty because he had not completed a stack of inspectorial reports by the time we were due to go on our annual beachside holiday, my father would take the paperwork with him to the Gold Coast, and sit scribbling while the rest of us played happily in the sand and in the water. He could not relax and enjoy the holiday wholeheartedly while there was still work to be done (to be fair, though, he did not enjoy the beach all that much anyway). In my own adult life I have often enough been guilty of similar 'workaholic' behaviour.

In my father's choice of my mother, he was exposed to a different set of values, values in which 'having a good time' was prized. To be sure, the 'good time' might centre on drinking, having a flutter on the horses, playing cards and other things that Methodists viewed with suspicion. But my father also came to feel more pride in his appearance (the Kirkham and Sanders families spent money on studio photographs and on dressing well) and learned much more in the way of social skills – 'knowing how to behave'. My father eventually acknowledged that he had been 'a pretty rough diamond before I met your mother', and that he had become 'a lot more broad-minded' than he had been as a young man.

As we saw in chapter 1, the Albert Cragos felt 'different', in part because of their religious heritage and its associated values, in part because of their genetic heritage. By contrast, the Kirkhams and the Sanders families would not have felt nearly so different. Those who attended church regularly (as most people then did) attended the Anglican church – the religious mainstream. They lived in the city, a more sophisticated environment with many more choices to offer than were available to my father's people in the country town of Yass. They embraced the secular culture of their time – patriotic devotion to 'King and Country'; the idea that it was their duty to fight for the Empire (failure to sign up was 'cowardice'); admiration for 'progress'; shopping for fashionable clothes and household items, a strong interest in sports (Victor Sanders excelled at boxing and unarmed combat).

On our summer visits to Evie in Artarmon, my mother took us shopping, and we were left in no doubt about what the 'right' shops were (the large department stores like David Jones and Farmer's, where quality shoes, clothes and other items could be bought). Evie's flat was full of the detritus of two world wars in which her husband and, subsequently, her son, had fought – and faded 'DON'T WASTE WATER' signs from wartime had never been removed from the bathroom walls. The framed photographs of Eva's Kirkham relatives were displayed prominently. The books in the shelves were best-sellers like *Gone with the Wind* and *The Sun is My Undoing*, official war histories, and thrillers dealing with war and adventure. The entire place, and what we did there, told me eloquently who my mother's people had been and offered me an alternative to the ethos of my father's family, despite the fact that we spent only five weeks in Artarmon each year.

In all of these ways, the values of my mother's family offered me an alternative to a lifetime of feeling 'different' – though significantly, I mostly continued to take 'the road less travelled'. I believe it was my genetically based sense of 'difference' that contributed to that.

Attempts to be different lead to 'more of the same'

Young adult choices – the very choices in which we assert our difference from our families – may have their origins in templates already present within those families. In my early adult discomfort with women wearing make-up, I was explicitly adopting an ethos of 'naturalness' which formed part of 1960s 'flower power'. Yet I was also (without realising it) following the template of my father's Methodism. In making this choice, I was siding with my father against my mother, who wore make-up and enjoyed choosing new clothes. I chose to marry a woman who belonged to the same Methodist tradition as myself and who was already uncomfortable with bodily self-display. Later, I sometimes wished that she would make more of an effort with her appearance – because it made *me* feel better – and in so doing, I had begun to swing back towards my mother's example. But of course, I had already made it harder for her to buy quality clothes that suited her by my impulsive choice to retrain as a counsellor, which for years condemned her and our daughters to genteel poverty.

In embracing vegetarianism and eschewing car ownership, we had also, unwittingly, chosen a course entirely consistent with the 'giving up' typical of an ascetic religious tradition. I had been brought up, like the vast majority of people at that time, to eat meat – my mother often served it three times a day – and to turn my back on that most fundamental 'badge of belonging' to the human race at one stroke returned me to the level of 'undesirable difference' that my father's family had experienced, as Methodists, in Yass a generation before. In my own life, I have replicated my paternal family's sense of being different, choosing my own ways of being different, but in so doing, repeated a value that was already part of my family heritage – that is, to follow the route dictated by one's conscience.

Once more, with genotyping

Throughout this book I have referred to the genetic 'bundle' of fearfulness, sensitivity and reactivity, which (depending on the intensity with which the genes are expressed) gives rise to either the 'slow to warm up' or the 'difficult' baby that Thomas and Chess described. Yet it may be that these three traits, which we conventionally see as separate and different, are actually different manifestations of the same gene, or even the same genetic mutation. For example, the two most-studied mutations of the MTHFR gene (which governs the body's ability to absorb folate and folic acid) seems to me to produce individuals who display much the same combination of intense fearfulness, acute sensitivity and high reactivity that we have encountered again and again in particular members of my family.[7] In all, there are thirty-four possible mutations of this particular gene, and other genes may be involved as well, or instead, so all of this must remain tentative for now. I carry one of the most studied MFTHFR mutations, the 'worse' one; my wife carries the other (the 'milder' one, whose effects are less far-reaching and dramatic), which greatly increases the chances of one or both of our children carrying one of the mutations, or even both. My hypothesis, as suggested earlier, would indicate that those who carry the more severe mutation would tend to marry those who carry the less severe variant (or no mutation of that gene at all) but whose families of origin do carry the more severe C6773 allele.

Although I carry the C6773 mutation, I do not have the elevated level of homocysteine to which it often leads. And some of the effects of the mutation are masked in me by a temperamental optimism that was also evident in at least three of my close male relatives: my father, my grandfather Victor and my uncle Hughie. This optimism has enabled me to conduct myself, in many circumstances, as confident, cheerful and encouraging, while shielding me (in other circumstances) from full awareness of my capacity to dismiss or devalue the needs of people close to me, to be 'careless' in fact.

It has been estimated that thirty to fifty per cent of the population carry one of the two MTHFR mutations, and some fourteen to twenty per cent carry the more severe C6773 mutation. C6773 has been linked with a wide range of physical and mental health problems, though at this stage, only a minority of them have been proven to be directly caused by the mutation. The list of problems includes depression, ADHD, both vascular and Alzheimer's-type dementia, autism, addictions, bipolar disorder, chronic fatigue, irritable bowel syndrome (and comparable disturbances of the eliminatory system), proneness to blood clots, and Type 1 diabetes. The majority of these conditions can be found somewhere in my extended family on one side or the other. Though that in itself does not prove that MTHFR mutations are present, it has to be a strong possibility.

The MTHFR mutations exemplify the far-reaching physiological and emotional consequences of an apparently innocuous disturbance to a one particular biological function (folate absorption). But this is just a single example of what can happen to human beings when genetic mutations pass down from one generation to the next. There must be many more, equally profound in their effects – for example, a mutation of another gene, APOE4, seems also to be implicated in the development of Alzheimer's-type dementia along with MTHFR-C6773. I hope that in *All We Need to Know* I have been able to provide at least some examples of how such genetically determined effects on both physical and emotional health might continue within one family and the family lines that have contributed to its gene pool through assortative mating.

All we need to know?

When the romantic poet John Keats wrote his famous lines ('Beauty is truth; truth, beauty / Tis all ye know, and all ye need to know') he was still a young man. At that stage of life, most of us do not question the knowledge that has been handed down to us – by our families or by our formal education. As I have tried to show in this book, there is always more to know than we know now. We cling to the 'truths' we have absorbed as children or discovered for ourselves in youth but, if we are honest, we are bound to find many of these truths only partial, and even misleading. Roger Gould[8] proposed years ago that adult emotional development could fruitfully be charted in terms of the sequential questioning of beliefs formed earlier – beliefs like 'I will always belong to my parents and believe in their world' or 'There is no real death or evil in the world.'

Yet as my life curves back towards its end, I begin to think that maybe there is less and less truly 'new' to learn – rather, I am simply re-learning, or elaborating on, things I already know. Maybe this is another of those things that distinguishes right hemisphere wisdom from left hemisphere cleverness. Cleverness can go on for ever, multiplying examples, observations and theories, inventing new rhetoric to give the impression of novelty to old perceptions. But wisdom is content to say, 'Well, Plato said it fourteen hundred years ago' or 'Shakespeare was on the money when he said…' The Mann-Weill duet 'Don't know much (but I know I love you)', so touchingly sung by Linda Ronstadt and Aaron Neville towards the end of Ronstadt's career, shifts from 'all I *need* to know' in the earlier stanzas to 'all *there is* to know' in its final line. Personal knowledge (as in love between two individuals) ultimately gives way to universal knowledge. We glimpse the universal through the particular. In the individual life we see the wider pattern of the family, and in the family, we see the entire human race: its compassion and its bitterness, its striving and its pathos, its victims and its heroes.

Notes

Chapter 1

1. Of course I cannot be sure of this, but I do know that 'Albert' was not a name handed down in the families of either of Albert's parents or grandparents.

Chapter 2

1. Hugh Sanders added a full two years. He was only sixteen when he enlisted (his father's age when his father, George Edward Holyoak Sanders, died suddenly). Significantly, in the light of other material in this chapter, Hugh claimed to have been born in Birmingham, UK! On the Kirkham side, my great-great-grandfather Robert Kirkham used the alias 'Jackson' when he went on trial for theft in London, presumably to protect his family from shame, and after being transported to Australia as a convict continued to use that alias from time to time – it even appears on one copy of his wedding certificate. Robert Ralph Kirkham, son of my grandmother's older brother George, added eight months to his age at enlistment despite being legally over eighteen in the first place! John Kirkham, son of Eva's older sister Edie and her then-husband Otto Schuler, used aliases on several occasions, following in the footsteps of his 'ne'er do well' father, Otto, who had deserted his mother.

2. C.V. Wedgwood, *The King's Peace, 1637–1641*, London, Collins, 1955, p. 55: 'The overwhelming majority of the King's subjects, whatever their doctrines, their education or their interests, were simply and sincerely religious. They did not doubt that their souls were immortal, or that Christ had died to redeem them.' Wedgwood's is a classic account of a man – Charles I – who, like Wesley a century later, suffered the consequences of his own indecision.

Chapter 3

1. The term was originally coined by Edward Gibbon Wakefield, 'who recognised their suitability as colonists'. 'The anxious class had reason to be so. In good

times their regular earnings gave them stability and order, and they appeared far removed from the condition of the 'rough', casual poor, who lived from day to day, even from hour to hour. But one bad winter could change everything. If a clerk or a tradesman missed weeks or months of work, his savings or his Friendly Society could not keep him out of debt for long, and once his clothes became shabby, he was immediately under suspicion: was he drinking? Was he gambling? Was he losing his self-respect?... It was an unforgiving society, and they could not afford to make mistakes either at work or in leisure.' (Janet McCalman, *Journeyings*, p. 30)

Chapter 4

1. The lost tomato savoury: there are several parallel stories. Beth's elder sister Gwyn remembered how as a child she had lost a prized doll on a train journey, and it was never recovered. Her younger sister Cherie lost her train ticket while working in Sydney at the age of twenty, and innocently asked the man who'd just sold her a newspaper if he would take the paper back in return for what she had paid for it, so that she could get back to her lodgings. And Beth herself had as a child wanted to keep a stray kitten as a pet, and been refused. All these memories were remembered and retold much later. The prevalence of 'loss' stories in the family discourse suggests more profound losses and lacks that were harder to acknowledge.

2. In the generation of my great-grandmother Phoebe née Albury, no less than four of Harry and Harriet Albury's twelve children divorced, or had a complicated marital history (Phoebe's eldest sister Emma Albury had four children all out of wedlock), and the pattern continued into the next generation, with two of Emma's children, one of Louisa's and two of Susanna's experiencing divorce, separation or annulment. This, it should be remembered, was at a time when marital conflicts were as common as they are now, but divorce extremely rare. In the generation of my great-grandfather (Robert Kirkham Sr), his sister Maria Kirkham (1843–1881) was deserted by her husband and they were subsequently divorced. In the next generation of Kirkhams, the generation to which my grandmother Eva belonged, the marriage of Edie Kirkham (1870–1951) followed a very similar pattern to her aunt Maria's. Edie sued for divorce but was not granted it, and so changed her

name by deed poll, announcing this by a public announcement in the *Sydney Morning Herald*.

Chapter 6
1. See Kerrie Davies, *A Wife's Heart*, pp. 68–69. One of Bertha's letters claimed that Henry was abusing her, and had attempted to kill her with a carving knife. She may have been deluded – there is no evidence that Henry had ever been violent before his marriage, or that he was violent after it – but plenty of men become violent only in the context of an intimate relationship. What is clearer is that Henry alternated between being loving and supportive, and periods when he found Bertha impossible to tolerate, and almost certainly raged at her (whether or not he was actually violent as well).
2. See Averil Earnshaw's *Time Bombs in Families: And How To Survive Them* (Sydney, Spencer Publications, 1998) and Ann Ancelin Schutzenberger, *The Ancestor Syndrome: Transgenerational Psychotherapy and the Hidden Links in the Family Tree*, London, Routledge, 1998; first published in French in 1993.

Chapter 7
1. For the Larsen family's history of manic-depressive illness, see Colin Roderick, especially pp. 1–4.

2. A.N. Wilson, *Victoria: A Life*, London, Atlantic, 2014, p. 473.
4. See John-Paul Selten, Elsje van der Ven, Bart P.F. Rutten and Elizabeth Cantor-Graae, 'The Social Defeat Hypothesis of Schizophrenia: An Update' in *Schizophrenia Bulletin*, 39, 6 (2013): 1180–1186. Sixty years previously, Gregory Bateson and R.D. Laing had proposed a somewhat similar theory of the origins of schizophrenia – a theory which family therapy has since repudiated. The 'nature/nurture debate' swings backwards and forwards over time, and the only firm conclusion that emerges is that, ultimately, both genetic propensities and failures of nurturing are involved in the development of emotional disorders.

Chapter 8
1. See Frank Sulloway's highly original study, *Born to Rebel: Birth Order, Family Dynamics and Creative Lives* Little, Brown, 1996.

Chapter 9
1. See Janet MacCalman, pp. 144, 294–295.

Chapter 10
1. Quoted in Kerrie Davies, op. cit., 147.
2. A comparable situation can be found in the Kirkham family,

where May, the second-youngest of my great-grandfather's family, remained a spinster until forty-three. Along with her sister Edie, who had been deserted by her husband Otto, May was left an additional three hundred pounds from Robert Kirkham's estate because she was not expected to marry.

Theoretical Reflections

1. My understanding of the different perspectives and emphases of the two hemispheres of the human cerebral cortex is largely derived from Iain McGilchrist's interpretation of fifty years of research evidence in his 2009 book *The Master and his Emissary: The Divided Brain and the Making of the Western World*, London/New Haven, Yale University Press). See especially pp. 32–93.

2. For more on general systems theory, see Lynn Hoffman, *Foundations of Family Therapy: A Conceptual Framework for Systems Change*, NY, Basic Books, 1981.

3. The best introduction to the important work of Murray Bowen can be found in Ker and Bowen's *Family Assessment: An Approach Based on Bowen Theory*, NY, Norton, 1988). Jerome Kagan's evidence: see his *Galen's Prophecy: Temperament in Human Nature*, NY, Basic Books, 1994, pp. 161–165. This curious association may help to explain the fact that (in Western Europe) blonde, blue-eyed women have for many centuries been seen by men as more 'desirable' mates than brunettes or redheads. Could this be because the physical type suggests an underlying vulnerability and timidity with which men feel comfortable, and which enables them to feel like 'confident protectors' of the 'weaker sex'?) Relationship between ectomorphic build and 'inhibited' (reactive) temperament: Kagan, op. cit. 162–163.

4. See Donald Kirkham's *Eastenders: The Kirkhams from Poplar*.

5. Easy, slow-to-warm up and difficult babies: see the ground-breaking research of Alexander Thomas, Stella Chess and Herbert Birch: *Behavioural Individuality in Early Childhood*, NY University Press, 1963; *The Dynamics of Psychological Development*, NY, Brunner-Mazel, 1980.

6. Abusive, neglectful parents' belief that they are 'protecting' their children. See Patricia McKinsey Crittenden's controversial but thought-provoking *Raising Parents:*

Attachment, Parenting and Child Safety, Routledge, 2012 (first published 2008).

7. On the MTHFR gene and its mutations, see 'Beginner's Guide to MTHFR Symptoms and Diet', updated March, 2018 (www.dietvsdisease.org/mthfr-mutation-symptoms-symptoms); Traci Stein, Psychology Today, 'A Genetic Mutation That Can Affect Mental and Physical Health' (https://www.psychologytoday.com (posted September, 2014); 'MTHFR Gene Variant', Genetic and Rare Diseases Information Centre, US Department of Health and Human Services (https://rarediseases.info.nih.gov/diseases/10953/mthfr-gene-mutation). Arguments for the significance of the MTHFR mutations and the importance of testing for them have also been challenged. See for example, Sara Long and Jack Goldblatt, 'MTHFR genetic testing: Controversy and clinical implications', *Australian Family Physician*, 45, 4 (2016): 237–240.

8. See Roger L. Gould, *Transformations: Growth and Change in Adult Life*, NY, Simon & Schuster, 1978.

Sources

Unpublished and privately published genealogical materials

Brooks, Alison, *A Shepherd from Kent: The Story of John Albury and his Family, 1838–1988*. Privately printed for the Albury Family Reunion, 1988.

A.L. Brown (compiler), 'Cragoe/Crago of Broadoak, St Pinnock, Liskeard, Cornwall', incorporating 'Petherick Crago: from Liskeard to New South Wales'. (Courtesy of Lesley Evans).

Kirkham, Donald, *Eastenders: The Kirkhams from Poplar*, KirkGen Publishing, 2017.

I have also made use of a family tree of the descendants of Thomas Sanders (b. 1720) which was in my mother's possession. I am afraid I have no idea who compiled it.

On Middle-class Australians 1860–1960

MacCalman, Janet, *Journeyings: The Biography of a Middle Class Generation, 1920–1990*, Melbourne University Press, 1993. An oral history of middle-class Melbournians, covering the same period as the Cragos of my father's generation, and offering much of relevance to both Methodism and the 'anxious class' generally.

Brett, Judith, *Robert Menzies' Forgotten People*, Melbourne University Press, 2007. Psychologically acute and balanced account of the relationship between Menzies and the Australian middle class, particularly its lower echelons.

Kingston, Beverley, *The Oxford History of Australia, Vol. 3: 1860–1900: Glad, Confident Morning*, Melbourne, Oxford University Press, 1988. Though it covers only the earliest part of the century relevant to this book, Kingston's well-written, thematically organised account illuminates many aspects of what came later.

On the Lawsons

Matthews, Brian, *Louisa*, Melbourne, McPhee-Gribble, 1987. Eccentric and at times tiresomely clever, Matthews's biography still casts valuable light on Henry Lawson's mother, the highest-achieving Albury of her generation.

Roderick, Colin, *Henry Lawson: A Life*, Sydney, Angus & Robertson, 1991. Roderick's obsession with detail often dominates to the detriment of the narrative, but this remains the authoritative biography.

Davies, Kerry, *A Wife's Heart: The Untold Story of Bertha and Henry Lawson,* St Lucia, UQP, 2017. Slight, but offers some intriguing new perspectives on Lawson's relationship with the mother of his children.

On John Wesley and Methodism:

Ayling, Stanley, *John Wesley,* Abingdon, Collins, 1979. Sympathetic and warm, but realistic about Wesley's faults.

Byard, Trevor, *Grandpa was a Methodist: The Life of John Wesley*. Melbourne, Joint Board of Christian Education, 1993.

Hattersley, Roy, *A Brand from the Burning: The Life of John Wesley*, London, Little, Brown, 2002. More acerbic and also more up-to-date than Ayling's, Hattersley's biography, with its focus on Wesley the founder and organiser of early Methodism, somehow fails to capture the appeal of the 'best-loved man in England'.

E.P. Thompson: *The Making of the English Working Class*, London, Gollancz, 1980. Thompson's classic study contains two highly influential chapters on the way that Methodism functioned to keep the working class in its place.

Oral sources

From the early 1980s to the early 1990s, I visited and interviewed Gordon and Heather Crago; Jan Martin; Ralph Crago, Tony Crago, Ted and Beryl Crago, Alison Hattersley, Cherie Adams, John and Jenny Crago, Alison Crago, Richard and Roslyn Crago, Bronwyn and Meredith Crago, Edwina Southern, Peter and Wendy Armstrong, Murray Armstrong, David and Jennifer Spinks, and Graham Plumb.

I had several telephone conversations with Jane Neyland, and corresponded with her mother, Beth Plumb.

Through the courtesy of Bronwyn Crago, I was able to listen to a recording of her grandmother May Crago (née Lepper) speaking about her life.

On my mother's side, I interviewed Jess Lewis (née Kirkham, my mother's older cousin and childhood confidante), and made the acquaintance of my own cousin Richard Sanders, Hughie's middle son, and spoke briefly by telephone with his older brother Charles Sanders.

Many of the gaps in my knowledge of my grandmother Eva's family, the Kirkhams, have been filled by family historian Donald Kirkham (see details of his book above), who himself interviewed some of the older generation of Kirkhams, including my mother.

In my father's generation, my best informants were his brother Ted Crago (with his wife, Beryl) and his youngest sister, Cherie Adams. I visited them on a number of occasions, and also had several phone conversations. Not only were they forthcoming with information, they were also open to being known by me – I think partly because of their affection for my father.

My father's cousin Ralph, youngest son of his Uncle Will Crago, also became well known to me in the last few years of his life and I was able to audiotape him talking about his aunts on the Crago side (Petherick and Ann's daughters).

In my own generation, I became close to Richard and Roslyn Crago, and they filled in many details concerning my father's oldest brother, Dick (who had died before I embarked on my family researches).

Later, Peter and Wendy Armstrong helped me in the same way in relation to Peter's mother Gwyn, whom I had not met since I was a child, and whom I had still not met as an adult when she died in 1988 (see chapter 7).

Jane Neyland was wonderfully frank about her troubled relationship with her adoptive mother, Beth.

I did not tape record the interviews, but scribbled brief notes while listening to my informants, and wrote them up immediately afterwards, quoting exact words that I had written down. Words and phrases in this book taken directly from these interviews have been placed in inverted commas, and supplemented by quotations taken verbatim from correspondence with one of the interviewees or other family members.

www.ingramcontent.com/pod-product-compliance
Lightning Source LLC
Chambersburg PA
CBHW071811080526
44589CB00012B/751